Economics

MW00425714

Economics

FROM THE OUTSIDE IN

"Better than Plowing"
and Beyond

James M. Buchanan

Texas A&M University Press
College Station

Economics from the Outside In is a revised and expanded edition of *Better than Plowing:*
And Other Personal Essays, published by the University of Chicago Press, 1992.

The paper used in this book meets the minimum requirements
of the American National Standard for Permanence
of Paper for Printed Library Materials, Z39.48-1984.
Binding materials have been chosen for durability.

Library of Congress Cataloging-in-Publication Data

Buchanan, James M.
 Economics from the outside in : "better than plowing" and beyond / James M.
Buchanan.
   p. cm. — (Texas A&M University economics series ; no. 17)
 Expanded edition of: Better than plowing, and other personal essays, published by
University of Chicago Press, 1992.
 Includes index.
 ISBN-13: 978-1-58544-603-2 (pbk. : alk. paper)
 ISBN-10: 1-58544-603-3 (pbk. : alk. paper)
 1. Buchanan, James M.   2. Economists—United States—Biography.
I. Buchanan, James M. Better than plowing, and other personal essays.   II. Title.
HB119.B67A3 2007
330.092—dc22

                                                            2007003208

CONTENTS

PREFACE TO THE EXPANDED EDITION

Autobiographical narratives, almost by definition, can never be "finished," and even selected autobiographical essays may be interpreted differently as one passes threescore and ten, with more than "labour and sorrow." Despite felt deterioration along some dimensions, octogenarians are not sans everything. Opportunities open up; gaps in earlier assessments are recognized. Most important, one comes to a greater appreciation of the spectator's, as opposed to the participant's, perspective.

Is the spectator impartial? Almost by necessity, identification with particularized interests apparently in current conflict becomes less noticeable as one passes certain age thresholds. It is surely easier, at well beyond fourscore, to shed partisan commitment and emotional involvement, although, with me, these elements have never been important, either personally or professionally.

At another, and arguably "higher" level of evaluation, however, this enforced spectator, for one, remains fiercely partial to the ethical, institutional, political, and economic parameters that define the civil order of "the West." Here, the neutrality stance of the putative positive social scientist–economist offers no succor, and its emptiness reveals that which so many would deny—the ultimate *raison d'être* of political economy, unchanged since first articulated by Adam Smith. For who would find value in explaining and understanding the complex processes of social interaction from some imaginary, completely detached vantage point—that, say, of alien Martians who observe, yet remain aloof? Surely, some normative purpose must offer the motivation for engagement with the economic, political, and social discussion, even if this purpose remains beneath our level of conscious awareness. We seek to understand in order that we may offer suggestions for improvement.

But improvement by whose standards? Responses to this question plague us yet. Must we accede to God's dictates, as revealed in holy books, and/or as interpreted by popes, mullahs, and philosophers? Or must we, each alone, confront the options with no awareness of the inclusive exchange in which we variously participate? If the answer to either of these questions is positive, what is on offer as an alternative?

The presumptive arrogance of those who simply "know best" what is good for the rest of us denies our dignity as members of the human species. But the temptation to resort to hierarchical classification of our fellows is omnipresent throughout time and place. Resist indeed we must, even as we acknowledge that others adhere to attitudinal and behavior patterns that seem incomprehensible to us—patterns that we, as participants in the social order must accord equal value with our own. Can we do other than define improvement in terms of the equally weighted values of all those who claim rights of participation in the interaction? There can be no masters or slaves, no differential winners and losers in the reckoning of things that affect us all.

The social order that is "the West" may, indeed, in part be seen as an historical miracle, one that emerged mysteriously, as if from nowhere. This much may be acknowledged without denial of the value of scientific effort to understand its working, and to suggest ways through which results may be bettered, again as measured by gains for all who share membership in the club described as "the free society."

All such matters are clarified, at least a bit, as the partial spectator meditates on human progress. Man did, in fact, escape from the Hobbesian jungle. He is threatened again, as always, by the jungle's tentacles, always grasping to recapture once-protected ground. But there can be, must be, and will be a rebirth of Western spirit.

ACKNOWLEDGMENT

The motivation and implementation of this book through several stages was due, almost exclusively, to Jo Ann Burgess, who served variously as archivist, business manager, editor, entrepreneur, and research associate. I am grateful to Jo Ann for her efforts along these and other dimensions.

James M. Buchanan

PREFACE

In 1985 I was asked by the editor of the *Banca Nazionale del Lavoro Quarterly Review* to contribute an autobiographical essay to an established series which had already featured many well-known economists. "Better than Plowing" was the result of my efforts, and I include this essay here as the first and title chapter of this book. I should emphasize that this chapter was initially written as an independent, self-contained autobiographical essay, prepared at a time when I did not expect to write anything else that might be considered autobiographical at all.

The events of 1986 changed my life, in this as in other respects. With the award of the Nobel Memorial Prize in Economic Sciences in late 1986, both my work and the evolution of ideas that went into that work aroused more interest. And I found that "Better than Plowing" did indeed save me many hours of unnecessary effort. This essay, itself published in late 1986, proved to be a godsend, since I could simply hand out copies or reprints to all and sundry who asked the oft-raised question: Who is James Buchanan?

The Nobel award also served to prompt autobiographical reflection on my own part, and I became especially responsive to invitations to prepare papers or lectures that attempted to identify particular influences on my intellectual career or that assessed specific periods of my life. I was pleased to accept William Breit's invitation to participate in the extension of his series, *Lives of the Laureates*.[1] My essay, included here as chapter 5 and entitled "Born-again Economist," was the second item written. In similar fashion I accepted the invitation of the Virginia Association of Economists to present a lecture on "Virginia Political Economy," which becomes chapter 7 in this book. A special celebration in my honor at Middle Tennessee State University in February 1988 gave me the occasion

---

1. *Lives of the Laureates: Seven Nobel Economists*, ed. William Breit and Roger W. Spencer (Cambridge, Mass.: MIT Press, 1986). This initial edition contained essays by seven Nobel Laureates in economics. A second edition includes three additional essays, mine among them, *Lives of the Laureates: Ten Nobel Economists*, 2d ed., ed. William Breit and Roger W. Spencer (Cambridge, Mass.: MIT Press, 1990).

to write down the material contained in chapter 3. The invitation to write an introduction to an Italian translation of one of my books prompted me to write the initial version of what is now chapter 6, and a visit to the United States Naval Academy in 1989 gave me the excuse for chapter 4. The *American Economist* invited the introspective essay that becomes chapter 10, and a George Mason University student group, as well as the Eastern Economic Association, invited the lecture on the Nobel Prize experience that is included as chapter 11. Finally, a festschrift conference in late 1989 offered the occasion for chapter 12.

I cannot recall precisely at what point in this sequence the notion emerged to put the separately written essays together into a single volume. My best estimate is that this idea occurred somewhere after three or four of the essays had been done. To complete the set so that the finished product would have any claim to completeness, I wrote chapters 2, 8, and 9 specifically for this book.

For those who might want to read only the capsule summary, chapter 1 remains sufficient. The remaining essays, separately, reflect a differing time perspective along with much material not treated at all in the summary essay.

As the author, I am perhaps the least qualified person to classify just what this book is. I do not present it as an autobiography in the familiar sense of a personal narrative account of my life. On the other hand, it is not purely an intellectual autobiography either; there is more here than the mere tracing out of the sources and the history of the ideas that I have been credited with developing, in whole or in part. Indeed, some of these ideas are not mentioned at all here. There remain chapters that I might have written that would add material of some interest. But the possible dating of some of the essays already written prompts me to close the book and to present it for what it is or may be.

I am grateful for permission to reprint versions of those chapters that have separately appeared. Chapter 1 was first published in the *Banca Nazionale del Lavoro Quarterly Review*, 159 (December 1986): 359–75; chapter 5, in *Lives of the Laureates: Ten Nobel Economists*, 2d ed., ed. William Breit and Roger W. Spencer (Cambridge, Mass.: MIT Press, 1990); chapter 6, in translation, in "Ricordo di un anno in Italia," *Libertà nel contratto costituzionale*, ed. di Paolo Martelli

(Milan: Arnoldo Mondadori Editore, 1990); chapter 10, in *Eminent Economists: Their Life Philosophies*, ed. Michael Szenberg (New York: Cambridge University Press, 1991), 98–106; chapter 11, in the *Eastern Economic Journal*, 15, no. 4 (October-December 1989): 339–48.

The essays are autobiographical, but they do not include reference specifically to what might be called my "production function," and especially they neglect the aid and assistance I have received over the years from students, colleagues, and staff. I do not, of course, need to write down my indebtedness to Betty Tillman, who has, for three decades, been more or less directly involved in getting me and my work organized sufficiently to pass muster. Her help has been critically important in the post-Nobel years, during which the simple chores of keeping afloat seem to have become much more difficult. Finally, let me add that Jo Ann Burgess came along at just the right time to prove of much help in putting this book into final shape.

Fairfax, Virginia

Economics from the Outside In

CHAPTER

1

Better than Plowing

I. *Family Origins*

MY TITLE'S DESCRIPTION of an academic career is taken
directly from Frank H. Knight, from whom I take so
much. Nonetheless, my origins in the rural agricultural
poverty of the Upper South (Tennessee) in the United States, along
with the sometimes pretentious efforts of the middle-class poor to
impose social distinctions, are surely explanatory elements in any
narrative account of my own history.

My family was poor, but, in the county, it was important. My
grandfather, John P. Buchanan, was the county's only governor of
the state of Tennessee. He was a one-term phenomenon, having
been elected as the nominee of the Farmers' Alliance party, one of
the several successful Populist electoral triumphs in 1891. By 1893,
the Democratic party had put its house in order, and the Populists
had seen their best days. But Buchanan's governorship established
the family in the community. The local public school which I attended for ten years was named "Buchanan School."

My father was the youngest of a large family, to whose lot fell the
operation of the family farm after his siblings had departed. I grew
up in a huge house on a hill, in varying states of disrepair, on a farm
that had no owner. It was owned by "the Buchanan estate," which
was not divided until the farm was sold in 1944, and long after I had

1

entered military service. My father had no incentive for effective maintenance. He was a jack-of-all-trades—farmer, sometime carpenter, veterinarian, insulator, and equipment operator. He was locally political, a community justice of the peace during all of my childhood. A handsome man, he had been a fine athlete (two years of varsity football at the University of Oklahoma); and, with a fine sense of humor, he was a favorite with the ladies. He was possessed by intense personal courage; he made no pretense to intellectual interests.

My mother was the best and the brightest of a family of deputy sheriffs and Presbyterian preachers which had roughly the same class standing as my father's. As was general in rural Tennessee in the early years of this century, both families were pure Scotch-Irish. My mother, Lila Scott, finished high school, took teacher training, and taught for a decade before meeting my father. Hers was the most curious mind I have known; she devoured anything she could find to read, and she was not discriminating, with interests ranging at least from Latin grammar through calculus through Zane Gray westerns. She, too, assumed easily a leadership role in the local community, organizing the parents' association for the school, rising rapidly to county and regional offices. But, for this narrative, she was my teacher, and beyond the teacher that is in all mothers. She advanced me two grades by home instruction, and helped me in assignments through college years.

II. *Early Education*

From my early years I was assigned the role as family successor to my grandfather. I was to be the lawyer-politician, and Vanderbilt University (prelaw, then law) was understood as the final rung on my educational ladder. There were early family misgivings about my personality; I did not exhibit the behavior of the exaggerated extrovert required for any budding politician. But law remained my career focus, and I was trained in public speaking. Economic reality destroyed this dream; Vanderbilt moved beyond the possible as the Great Depression moved in. College was what I could afford, Middle Tennessee State Teachers College in Murfreesboro, which allowed me to live at home and to earn enough for fees and books by milking dairy cows morning and night for four years.

My college education was nonsystematic and stochastic. There was waste in the requirements in formal education, and poor instruction in biology, history, psychology, economics, and other subjects. But there was much of value in my exposure to Shakespeare, modern poetry, mathematics, and physics. When I finished, I had accumulated majors in three areas—mathematics, English literature, and social science, including economics. These college years were important as confidence builders; by the end of my second year my academic standing was the best in the college; the country boy more than held his own against the boys and girls from the towns.

Upon graduation in 1940, I faced three options—school teaching at $65 per month; employment in a Nashville bank at $75 per month; or a $50-per-month fellowship in economics at the University of Tennessee. My career as an economist was settled by the dominance of the third opportunity, not by any desire to save the world. The 1940–41 graduate year in Knoxville, Tennessee, helped me meet the world beyond. I learned no economics during that year, but I did learn about women and whiskey, which, after all, are important parts of an education. There were few good economists on the faculty; I was, however, exposed to a genuine scholar, a man whose work habits were important in shaping my own. Charles P. White became my example of the research economist who took his position seriously, and he conveyed to me the notion that there is, after all, a moral element in academic employment. It was White also who, despite his own self-acknowledged limits in these respects, strongly advised me to stick with economic theory as the basis for all applications. Plans were open beyond the one year until I secured a fellowship in statistics at Columbia University for the 1941–42 academic year. But before I could take up this appointment I was drafted into military service, and found myself in the United States Navy by August 1941.

I had an easy war. After officer training in New York, and a special stint at the Naval War College, I was assigned to the operations staff of Admiral C. W. Nimitz, commander-in-chief of the Pacific Fleet. Aside from a six-week experience-gathering tour at sea during one of the island invasions, I worked throughout the war at Pearl Harbor and at Guam, at fleet headquarters control deep in the bowels of the earth. I enjoyed the military, the colleagues, the work, and the setting; and I was good at the job. For the first and only time in my life, I worked closely with men who were important in shaping the lives and destinies of many others. I saw these military leaders as ordinary mortals, trying to do their job within the constraints they faced, and burdened with their own prejudices like everyone else. This experience has helped me throughout my academic career; I have been able to relegate to the third order of smalls the sometime petty quarrels that seem to motivate professors everywhere, in their roles both as instructors and as research scholars.

In one sense my only career choice involved the decision to leave the navy and to return to civilian life. This decision was not easy: I knew the important persons who urged me to stay; I had enjoyed the four years. But I made the correct choice, and was discharged in late 1945. With the GI subsidy for further schooling available, and with a new wife for partial support, I considered alternative graduate schools. Columbia University no longer beckoned because New York City had not made me want to return. I knew nothing about the competence or the ideological makeup of the University of Chicago economics faculty. But a teacher from my undergraduate days at Middle Tennessee, with a Chicago Ph.D. in political science, conveyed to me the intellectual excitement of the place. Off to Chicago I went in late 1945, along with the many others who were just returning from military service.

III. *Chicago, Frank Knight, and Knut Wicksell*

Had I known about the ideological character of the Chicago faculty I might have chosen to go elsewhere. I was not overtly political or ideological in my salad days; emerging from the family populist tradition, I grew up in a solidly Democratic setting, with Roosevelt emerging as the popular leader in the 1930s. I was basically populist and pacifist. But officer training school in New York radicalized me. Along with many others, I was subjected to overt discrimination based on favoritism for products of the eastern establishment universities. This sobering experience made me forever sympathetic to those who suffer discriminatory treatment, and it forestalled any desire to be a part of any eastern establishment institution.

When I reached the University of Chicago, I was what I now can best describe as a libertarian socialist. I had always been antistate, antigovernment, antiestablishment. But this included the establishment that controlled the United States economy. I had grown up on a reading diet from my grandfather's attic piled high with the radical pamphlets of the 1890s. The robber barons were very real to me.

At Chicago, I found myself no different from my graduate student colleagues, almost all of whom were socialists of one or another stripe. But within six weeks after enrollment in Frank Knight's course in price theory, I had been converted into a zealous advocate of the market order. Frank Knight was not an ideologue, and he made no attempt to convert anybody. But I was, somehow, ready for the understanding of economic process that his teaching offered. I was converted by the power of ideas, by an understanding of the model of the market. This experience shaped my attitude toward the use and purpose of economic instruction; if I could be converted, so could others.

Frank Knight was the intellectual influence during my years at the University of Chicago, and his influence increased over subsequent years, enhanced by the development of a close personal relationship. Knight became my role model, without which I wonder what turns I might have taken. The qualities of mind that Knight exhibited were, and remain, those that I seek to emulate: the willingness to question anything, and anybody, on any subject anytime; the categorical refusal to accept anything as sacred; the genuine openness to all ideas; and, finally, the basic conviction that most ideas peddled about are nonsense or worse when examined critically.

A second Chicago event profoundly affected my career. Having finished my work, including the German language examination, I had the leisure of a scholar without assignments in the Harper Library stacks during three months of the summer of 1948. By sheer chance, I pulled Knut Wicksell's 1896 dissertation on taxation from the shelves, a book that was untranslated and unknown.[1] The effect on me was dramatic. Wicksell laid out before me a set of ideas that seemed to correspond precisely with those that I had already in my head, ideas that I could not have expressed and would not have

1. Knut Wicksell, *Finanztheoretische Untersuchungen* (Jena: Gustav Fischer, 1896).

dared to express in the public-finance mindset of the time. Wicksell told us that if economists really want to apply the test of efficiency to the public sector, only the rule of unanimity for collective choice offers the procedural guarantee. If we seek reform in economic policy, we should change the rules under which political agents or representatives act. Economists should, once and for all, cease and desist proffering advice to nonexistent benevolent despots. Wicksell's were heady words, and from that day I was determined to translate Wicksell's contribution into English.[2]

Visitors to my office know that photographs of only two economists grace the walls, Frank Knight and Knut Wicksell. I consider them coequals, Knight in his influence on my attitudes toward the world of ideas generally, and Wicksell in his influence on the specific ideas that have come to be associated with my work in public choice and constitutional economics. Both of these influences were embedded in my psyche when I left Chicago in mid-1948.

I entered the highly competitive world of American academia with no conscious sense of intellectual direction. In one of my first articles, based in part on the Wicksell exposure and, in part, by reading a translation of De Viti De Marco, I called for a tie-in between the theory of the state and the norms for taxation.[3] The point seemed so simple, indeed obvious, yet so locked in was the utilitarian mindset of orthodox public finance that the article was widely cited as seminal. In 1951, Kenneth Arrow published his widely heralded book on the general impossibility theorem.[4] For three years I was bemused by the failure of reviewers and critics to make the obvious point that the whole Arrow construction was inappropriate for a democratic society. Why should the social ordering satisfy consistency norms if individual values and preferences generated inconsistencies? I published a review article in 1954 that few economists understood then, or understand now. Almost as a footnote, I published a second short article comparing individual choice in voting and in the market.

2. My translation of the centrally important part of the book was published in *Classics in the Theory of Public Finance*. James M. Buchanan, translation of Knut Wicksell, "A New Principle of Just Taxation," in *Classics in the Theory of Public Finance*, ed. R. A. Musgrave and A. T. Peacock (London: Macmillan, 1958), 72–118.

3. Antonio De Viti De Marco, *First Principles of Public Finance*, trans. E. P. Marget (London: Jonathan Cape, 1936).

4. Kenneth Arrow, *Social Choice and Individual Values* (New York: Wiley, 1951).

Again, the points made seemed simple, but surprisingly no one had made such a basic comparison. In those two papers there were elements of much that was later to be developed in my contributions to public choice.

The two 1954 papers were published in the *Journal of Political Economy*, under the editorship of Earl J. Hamilton, who deserves special mention in this narrative. I had not taken his courses at the University of Chicago, and only in my last few months there did I get to know him personally. But we did establish a friendship, and from him I got the advice that one major key to academic success was to "keep the ass to the chair," a rule that I have followed and that I have passed along to several generations of students. But Hamilton's influence was not primarily in this piece of advice. Through his editorship of the journal, he encouraged rather than discouraged me as a potential author. He was a tough editor, but his comments-reactions were never wholly negative, and it was only after several submissions that the two 1954 pieces were hammered into acceptable shape. Negation at that stage of my career might have been fatal.

IV. *The Italian Year*

Hamilton was also influential in encouraging me to keep up with the languages, and I commenced to learn to read Italian. I wanted to go to Italy for a year's reading in the classical works in public finance theory. I got a Fulbright grant for the 1955–56 academic year, which I spent in Perugia and Rome. This Italian year was critical in the development of my ideas on the importance of the relation between the political structure and the positive and normative theory of economic policy. The Italians had escaped the delusions of state omniscience and benevolence that had clouded the minds of English and German language social philosophers and scientists. The Italians had long since cut through the absurdities of Benthamite utilitarianism and Hegelian idealism. Real rather than idealized politics, with real persons as actors—these were the building blocks in the Italian constructions, whether those of the cooperative-democratic state or the ruling class-monopoly state. Exposure to this Italian conceptualization of the state was necessary to enable me to break out of the idealistic-utilitarian mindset that still imposes its intellectual straitjacket on many of my peers in social science. The Italian year was also important in the more general sense of offering insights into the distinctly non-American historical-cultural environment.

V. *Public Debt and Opportunity Cost*

The Italian research year was indirectly responsible for one strand of my work that may seem to represent a side alley, namely, my work in the theory of public debt, which was less convincing to my economist peers than other work in public choice and public finance. At the very end of the Italian year, I suddenly "saw the light." I realized that the whole conventional wisdom on public debt was simply wrong, and that the time had come for a restoration of the classical theory, which was correct in all its essentials. I was as excited by this personal discovery as I had been by the discovery of the Wicksell book almost a decade earlier. Immediately on my return to America in 1956, I commenced my first singly authored book, *Public Principles of Public Debt.*[5]

In my overall assessment the work on public debt was not a digression. This work was simply another extension or application of what can be discerned as a central theme in my efforts from the very first papers written. I have been consistently reductionist in that I have insisted that analysis be factored down to the level of choices faced by individual actors. The orthodox theory of public debt that I challenged embodied a failure to treat relevant choice alternatives. My reasoning, once again, was simple. National economies, as such, cannot enjoy gains or suffer losses. The fact that making guns "uses up" resources in years of war tells us nothing at all about who must pay for those guns, and when. The whole macroaggregation exercise that had captured the attention of post-Keynesian economists was called into question.

My work on public debt stirred up considerable controversy in the early 1960s, and I realized that the ambiguity stemmed, in part, from an absence of clarity in my initial challenge. Confusion cen-

5. James M. Buchanan, *Public Principles of Public Debt* (Homewood, Ill.: Richard D. Irwin, 1958).

tered around the conception of opportunity cost, and I laid my plans to write a short book, which I consider my best work in economic theory, narrowly defined. This book, *Cost and Choice*, again emphasizes my central theme, the reduction of analysis to individual choice settings which, in this extension, implies the necessity of defining cost in utility rather than commodity dimensions.[6]

VI. *Gordon Tullock,* The Calculus of Consent, *and Public Choice*

I first encountered Gordon Tullock in 1958, when he came to the University of Virginia as a postdoctoral research fellow. I was impressed by his imagination and originality, and by his ability to recognize easily the elements of my own criticism of public debt orthodoxy. Tullock insisted not only that analysis be reduced to individual choice but also that individuals be modeled always as maximizers of self-interest, a step that I had sometimes been unwilling to take, despite my exposure to the Italians. Tullock wrote his seminal paper on the working of simple majority rule, and we decided to collaborate on a book that would examine the individual's choice among alternative political rules. We more or less explicitly considered our exercise to be an implicit defense of the Madisonian structure embodied in the United States Constitution.

The Calculus of Consent was the first work in what we now call "constitutional economics," and it achieved the status of a "classic" in public choice theory.[7] In retrospect, it is interesting, to me, that there was no sense of "discovery" at any point in that book's construction, no moment of excitement akin to those accompanying either the discovery of the Wicksell book or the insight into public debt theory. Tullock and I considered ourselves to be applying relatively simple economic analysis to the choice among alternative political decision rules, with more or less predictable results. We realized that no one had attempted to do precisely what we were doing, but the exercise was essentially one of "writing out the obvious" rather than opening up wholly new areas for inquiry.

6. James M. Buchanan, *Cost and Choice: An Inquiry in Economic Theory* (Chicago: Markham, 1969; reprint Chicago: University of Chicago Press, 1978).
7. James M. Buchanan and Gordon Tullock, *The Calculus of Consent: Logical Foundations of Constitutional Democracy* (Ann Arbor: University of Michigan Press, 1962).

We were wrong. Public choice, as a subdiscipline in its own right, emerged in the early 1960s, in part from the reception of our book, in part from our own organizational-entrepreneurial efforts which later emerged in the Public Choice Society, in part from others' works. Once the whole complex web of political decision rules and procedures was opened up for economic analysis, the range of application seemed open-ended. Public choice, in the 1960s, was both exciting and easy; it is not surprising that graduate students in our program at Virginia were highly successful and that budding economists and political scientists quickly latched onto the new subdiscipline.[8]

My own work does not exhibit a dramatic switching to public choice economics from standard public finance. As I have noted above, from my earliest papers I had emphasized the importance of political structure, a conviction that was strengthened by my exposure to the Italians. Immediately after my excursion into the theory of public debt and before collaboration with Tullock on *The Calculus of Consent*, I wrote a long survey essay on the Italian tradition in public finance and published this essay, along with other pieces, in *Fiscal Theory and Political Economy*.[9] Considered as a package, my work over the decade 1956–66 involved filling in gaps in the taxonomy of public goods theory along with various attempts to factor down familiar propositions in theoretical welfare economics into individualized choice settings. The paper "Externality," written jointly with W. C. Stubblebine, was an amalgamation of strands of argument from Wicksell, Coase, and Pigou.[10] The paper "An Economic Theory of Clubs" was a filling in of an obvious gap in the theory of public goods.[11]

During the early 1960s, my work specifically shifted toward an attempt to tie two quasi-independent strands of inquiry together,

8. For two volumes devoted largely to applications, see *Theory of Public Choice: Political Applications of Economics*, ed. James M. Buchanan and Robert Tollison (Ann Arbor: University of Michigan Press, 1972), and *Theory of Public Choice, II*, ed. James M. Buchanan and Robert Tollison (Ann Arbor: University of Michigan Press, 1984).

9. James M. Buchanan, *Fiscal Theory and Political Economy* (Chapel Hill: University of North Carolina Press, 1960).

10. James M. Buchanan and W. C. Stubblebine, "Externality," *Economica*, 29 (November 1962): 371–84.

11. James M. Buchanan, "An Economic Theory of Clubs," *Economica*, 32 (February 1965): 1–14.

those of orthodox public finance and the theory of political decision structure. The result was a relatively neglected book, *Public Finance in Democratic Process*, which contained implications for normative theory that remain unrecognized by modern research scholars.[12]

The research program embodied in elementary public choice theory developed almost naturally in a sequence of applications to the theory of economic policy. The whole of the Keynesian and post-Keynesian theory of macroeconomic management (including monetarism) depends critically on the presumption that political agents respond to considerations of "public interest" rather than to the incentives imposed upon them by constituents. Once these agents are modeled as ordinary persons, the whole policy structure crumbles. This basic public choice critique of the Keynesian theory of policy was presented in *Democracy in Deficit*, written jointly with Richard E. Wagner.[13] I have often used the central argument of this book as the clearest example of the applicability of elementary public choice theory, the implications of which have been corroborated in the accumulating evidence provided by the regime of quasi-permanent budget deficits.

VII. *Between Anarchy and Leviathan*

Through the middle 1960s, my analysis and interpretation of the workings of democratic politics were grounded in a relatively secure belief that, despite the many political failures that public choice theory allows us to identify, ultimately the governing authorities, as constrained by constitutional structure, respond to and implement the values and preferences of individual citizens. This belief in the final efficacy of democratic process surely affected my analysis, even if unconsciously, and allowed me to defend the essential "logic" of political institutions in being against the sometime naïve proposals made by social reformers.

This foundational belief was changed by the events of the late 1960s. I lost my "faith" in the effectiveness of government as I ob-

12. James M. Buchanan, *Public Finance in Democratic Process* (Chapel Hill: University of North Carolina Press, 1966).

13. James M. Buchanan and Richard Wagner, *Democracy in Deficit: The Political Legacy of Lord Keynes* (New York: Academic Press, 1977).

served the explosive take-off in spending rates and new programs
engineered by self-interested political agents and seemingly divorced from the interests of citizens. At the same time I observed
what seemed to me to be a failure of the institutional structure, at all
levels, to respond effectively to mounting behavioral disorder. The
United States government seemed to take on aspects of an agent
driven Leviathan simultaneously with the emergence of anarchy in
civil society.

What was happening, and how could my explanatory model be
applied to the modified reality of the late 1960s and early 1970s? I
sensed the necessity of plunging much deeper into basic political
philosophy than heretofore, and I found it useful to examine more
closely the predicted operating properties of both anarchy and
Leviathan. I was fortunate in that I located colleagues who assisted
and greatly complemented my efforts in each case. Winston C. Bush
formalized the anarchy of the Hobbesian jungle in terms of modern
economic theory. Bush's independent and foundational analysis
provided me with the starting point for the book that remains the
most coherent single statement of my research program, *The Limits
of Liberty*.[14]

Although chapters in that book raised the threat of the Leviathan
state, I had not worked out the formal analysis. Again I was lucky to
be able to work with Geoffrey Brennan in pushing along this frontier of inquiry. We commenced the exciting project that emerged as
The Power to Tax.[15] That book explored the implications of the hypothesis that government maximizes revenues from any taxing authority constitutionally granted to it. Such analysis seems required
for any informed constitutional calculus involving a grant of taxing
power to government. As reviewers noted, the result of our analysis
here was to stand much of the conventional wisdom in normative
tax theory on its head.

VIII. *Constitutionalism and the Social Contract*

As I noted earlier, *The Calculus of Consent* was the first explicit contribution in the research program that we now call "constitutional

14. James M. Buchanan, *The Limits of Liberty: Between Anarchy and Leviathan*
(Chicago: University of Chicago Press, 1975).
15. James M. Buchanan and Geoffrey Brennan, *The Power to Tax: Analytical Foundations of a Fiscal Constitution* (Cambridge: Cambridge University Press, 1980).

economics" or "constitutional political economy." Gordon Tullock and I were analyzing the individual's choice among alternative rules for reaching political decisions, rules to which he, along with others, would be subject in subsequent periods of operation. Such a choice setting is necessarily different in kind from that normally treated by economists, which is the choice among end objects within well-defined constraints. In a very real sense, the choice among rules becomes a choice among constraints, and, hence, involves a higher stage calculus of decision than that which most economists examine.

We were initially influenced to analyze the choice among political rules by at least two factors that I can now identify. First, we were dissatisfied by the apparent near universal and unquestioned acceptance of majority rule as the ideal for collective decision processes. Second, we were influenced by our then colleague, Rutledge Vining, himself an early student of Frank Knight, who hammered home to all who would listen that economic policy choices are made not among allocations or distributions, but, necessarily, among rules or institutions that generate patterns of allocations and distributions. Vining's emphasis was on the stochastic nature of these patterns of outcomes and on the necessity for an appreciation for and understanding of the elementary theory of probability.

How does a person choose among the rules to which he will be subject? Vining took from Knight, and passed along to me, a fully sympathetic listener, the analogy with the choice of rules in ordinary games, from poker to basketball. The chooser, at the rule choosing or constitutional stage of deliberation, cannot identify how any particular rule will precisely affect his own position in subsequent rounds of play. Who can know how the cards will fall? The choice among rules is, therefore, necessarily made under what we should now call a "veil of uncertainty." *The Calculus of Consent* was our straightforward extension of this nascent research program to the game of politics.

In constitutional choice there is no well-defined maximand analogous to that which describes garden-variety economic choice. The individual may still be modeled as a utility maximizer, but there is no readily available means of arraying alternatives. The formal properties of choice under uncertainty, properties that have been exhaustively explored during the middle decades of this century, did not concern us. But we did sense the positive value of the uncertainty setting in opening up the potential for agreement on rules. If an individual cannot know how specific rules will affect his own position, he will be led to choose among rules in accordance with some criterion of generality rather than particularity. And if all persons reason similarly, the prospects for some Wicksellian-like agreement on rules are much more favorable than prospects for agreement on political choices to be made within a defined rules structure. In my own interpretation, in *The Calculus of Consent*, Tullock and I were shifting the Wicksellian unanimity norm for efficiency in collective choice from the inperiod level, where its limits are severe, to the constitutional level where no comparable limits are present.

This construction in *The Calculus of Consent* was essentially worked out independently of the comparable construction of John Rawls. But discovery of his early paper on "Justice as Fairness" during the course of writing our book served to give us confidence that we were on a reasonable track. As early as the late 1950s, Rawls had spelled out his justice-as-fairness criterion and had introduced early versions of his veil of ignorance, which was to become universally familiar after the publication of his acclaimed treatise, *A Theory of Justice*.[16] The coincidence in both the timing of our initial work and the basic similarity in analytical constructions has made me share an affinity with Rawls that has seemed mysterious to critics of both of us.

The subject matter of economics has always seemed to me to be the institution of exchange, embodying agreement between or among choosing parties. The Wicksellian extension of the exchange paradigm to the many person collective has its most direct application in the theory of public finance, but when applied to the choices among political rules the analysis moves into areas of inquiry that are foreign to economists. At this research juncture, the disciplinary base merges into political philosophy, and the exchange paradigm becomes a natural component of a general contractarian theory of political interaction. Almost by definition, the economist who shifts

---

16. John Rawls, *A Theory of Justice* (Cambridge, Mass.: Harvard University Press, 1971).

his attention to political process while retaining his methodological individualism must be contractarian.

As noted earlier, my emphasis has been on factoring down complex interactions into individual choice components and, where possible, explaining and interpreting such interactions in terms of cooperation rather than conflict models. Interpersonal, intergroup, and interparty conflict can scarcely be left out of consideration when we examine ordinary politics within defined constitutional structures. The contractarian or exchange program must shift, almost by necessity, to the stage of choices among rules. The contractarian becomes a constitutionalist, and I have often classified my own position with both these terms.

I have continued to be surprised at the reluctance of my colleagues in the social sciences, and especially in economics, to share the contractarian-constitutionalist research program and to understand the relevance of looking at politics and governance in terms of the two-stage decision process. A substantial share of my work over the decade 1975–85 involved varying attempts to persuade my peers to adopt the constitutional attitude. In two volumes of collected essays, *Freedom in Constitutional Contract*, and *Liberty, Market, and State*, as well as in a book jointly with Geoffrey Brennan, *The Reason of Rules*, I sought to defend the contractarian-constitutionalist methodology in many applications.[17]

IX. *Academic Exit and Virginia Political Economy*

In this summary chapter I have, aside from the first two background sections, concentrated on the intellectual record, on the development of the ideas that have characterized my work, and on the persons and events that seem to have affected these ideas. I have deliberately left out of account the details of my personal, private experiences over the course of a long career. My effort would, how-

17. James M. Buchanan, *Freedom in Constitutional Contract: Perspectives of a Political Economist* (College Station: Texas A & M University Press, 1978). James M. Buchanan, *Liberty, Market, and State: Political Economy in the 1980s* (Brighton, Eng.: Wheatsheaf Books, 1985; New York: New York University Press, 1985). James M. Buchanan and Geoffrey Brennan, *The Reason of Rules—Constitutional Political Economy* (Cambridge: Cambridge University Press, 1985).

ever, be seriously incomplete if I should neglect totally the influences of the academic-intellectual environments within which I
have been able to pursue my work, including the stimulation I have
secured from colleagues, staff, and students, whose names are not
entered in these accounts.

I cannot, of course, test what "might have been" had I chosen
academic settings other than those I did select. I feel no acute sense
of highly valued opportunities missed, nor do I classify any choices
made as having been grossly mistaken. I have exercised the academic exit option that the competitive structure of the United States
academy offers. In so doing, I have reduced the ability of those who
might have sought to modify the direction of my research and teaching efforts, while, at the same time, I have secured the benefits from
the unintended consequences that shifts in location always guarantee.

This much said, I would be remiss if I did not include some form
of tribute to the three academic settings within Virginia that have
provided me with professional breathing space for almost all of my
career. Mr. Jefferson's "academical village," the University of Virginia, where I spent twelve years, 1956–68, allowed Warren Nutter
and me full rein in establishing the Thomas Jefferson Center for
Studies in Political Economy. This center, as an institution, encouraged me, and others, to counter the increasing technical specialization of economics and allowed me to keep the subject matter
interesting when the discipline, in more orthodox hands, threatened to become boring in the extreme. Virginia Polytechnic Institute, or VPI, where I spent fourteen years, 1969–83, allowed
Charles Goetz, Gordon Tullock, and me to organize the Center for
Study of Public Choice, a center that became, for a period in the
1970s and early 1980s, an international haven for research scholars
who sought some exposure to the blossoming new subdiscipline of
public choice. Finally, George Mason University, to which the
whole center shifted in 1983, insured a continuity in my research
emphasis and tradition, even beyond that of my active career.

X. *Retrospective*

Other contributors to the Banca Nazionale del Lavoro series have
discussed the influences on their developments as economists. I am

not at all sure that I qualify for inclusion in terms of this professional or disciplinary classification. I am not, and have never been, an economist in any narrowly defined meaning. My interests in understanding how the economic interaction process works have always been instrumental to the more inclusive purpose of understanding how we can learn to live one with another without engaging in Hobbesian war and without subjecting ourselves to the dictates of the state. The "wealth of nations," as such, has never commanded my attention save as a valued by-product of an effectively free society. The ways and means through which the social order might be made more "efficient" in the standard meaning—these orthodox guidelines have carried relatively little weight for me.

Neither have I considered myself a "pure scientist" and my work as "pure science." I have not been engaged in some exciting quest for discovery of a reality that exists independently of our own making. I have sensed acutely the exhilaration in ideas that is shared by all scientists in the broader meaning, but the ideas that capture my attention are those that, directly or indirectly, explain how freely choosing individuals can secure jointly desired goals. The simple exchange of apples and oranges between two traders—this institutional model is the starting point for all that I have done. Contrast this with the choice between apples and oranges in the utility-maximizing calculus of Robinson Crusoe. The second model is the starting point for most of what most economists do.

If this difference between my foundational model and that of other economists is recognized, my work takes on an internal coherence and consistency that may not be apparent absent such recognition. The coherence was not, of course, a deliberately chosen element of a research program. I have written largely in response to ideas that beckoned, ideas that offered some intellectual challenge and that had not, to my knowledge, been developed by others. I have rarely been teased by either the currency of policy topics or the fads of academic fashion, and when I have been so tempted my work has suffered. The coherence that the work does possess stems from the simple fact that I have worked from a single methodological perspective during the four decades that span my career to date, along with the fact that I have accepted the normative implications of this perspective. The methodological perspective and the normative stance are shared by few of my peers in modern social science. This location of my position outside the mainstream has the inestimable value of providing me with the continuing challenge to seek out still other ideas and applications that may, ultimately, shift the frontier of effective agreement outward.

2

Early Times

I. *Introduction*

I T IS DIFFICULT for me to think of my "early times" as anything
but ordinary. It is only when I force myself to think of the displacement in time, technology, location, and social distance between the boy, Jim Buchanan, and the seventy-year-old man, James
Buchanan, who writes this narrative, that I realize how extraordi-
nary indeed my early times may seem to many of those who find the
other autobiographical essays in this volume interesting. My motivation for writing this particular essay is, then, somewhat different
from that which applies to others. Here there is perhaps some purpose in setting down my own "remembrances of things past" not so
much to describe the stages in my personal and private life as to offer
a partial description of the "way things were." Therefore, this essay
becomes social history in a way that is quite different from the
others.

As I write this, my span of remembered consciousness extends
almost precisely over two-thirds of the century, a period during
which so many of what were, to us, technological miracles have become commonplace items of everyday usage. My early times were
times without indoor plumbing, electricity, radio, television, or air
travel. And think of what electricity made possible: lighting, refrigeration, and all the rest. These things were all wonderful to me,

as to others who grew up without their services. And there was an excitement about these things that can scarcely be described; surely it was an excitement beyond that sensed by any modern child who grows with the expansion of computer technology.

I did not quite experience the miracle of the automobile; that fortuity was granted to those of my father's generation. I recall the "buggy house," with two buggies parked inside, but I recall them as seldom used and gradually falling into states of disrepair. From my earliest remembered years, there was the Model T Ford, reliable in relation to its own time but totally unreliable by modern standards. For me, the automobile was there; it did not replace the buggy; it was never the horseless carriage.

Books there were and magazines and politics and baseball. And, perhaps most importantly, there was work: plowing, manuring, harrowing, planting, cultivating, hoeing, haying, threshing, picking, milking, herding, feeding—work for long hours on days during growing seasons and in weather foul and fair throughout the year. To this day, I enjoy summer rain for the quite simple reason that rain, to me, meant two good things—the crops would grow and the plowing would stop for a few days. And there was school, both at home and at the place called by the name. I was the exception in the community; my mother insisted that I should never miss a day because of farm work needs. And miss a day I did not, while all of my schoolmates did, an experience that provided me with a very early realization of the relative importance of learning and sharply distinguished it from ordinary work. Indeed, to me then and forever after, learning has never seemed onerous or chorelike, no matter what the subject.

I shall resist the temptation to present a chronological account of my early times. Such a narrative would interest few beyond members of my family and close friends. I shall, instead, treat selective features in somewhat more detail, with the selection itself indicating my own priorities at this time of looking back, not necessarily identical to those experienced during the events.

II. *Hard Times*

Early times were hard times, but they seem more so when viewed retrospectively. But my family was never prosperous, even by the limited standards of its own peer group in rural Middle Tennessee. My father, the youngest of six adult siblings, was residually left with the operation-management of a farm that had been neglected by his own father, a man who had been psychologically tarnished by his too-early successes in state politics. The farm had produced abundance in the agricultural boom of World War I. And my father, newly married in 1918 and with a son in 1919, was beginning to expand his own horizons just as the postwar agricultural recession emerged. He had already purchased, on mortgage to the bank, an adjacent farm; he had also invested heavily in a herd of registered Jersey dairy cows. These two investments were but marginally productive at best, and his financial straits became more binding after my mother's protracted serious illness in 1922.

My father was, however, a perennial optimist, and especially in choices involving the potential productivity of new technology. Despite what must have been the precarious state of his balance sheet, I recall the installation of a gasoline-powered milking machine, the first and only one in the community. I recall also an early (too early) purchase and use of a Fordson tractor, which I actually was allowed to drive when I was six. I recall the construction and use of a standing wooden silo. These innovations were all premature in the Tennessee of the middle 1920s.

They were all gone by the time I reached the age of active sharing in the farm work itself. By 1928 or 1929, when I was nine or ten, the plowing was done by mule and horse power, not by tractor; the milking was done by hand; the silo, which was blown down in a windstorm, was not replaced. And, more seriously, the adjacent farm that my father had purchased as his own, was lost by default on the bank-held mortgage. The technology of farming, for us, reverted to that descriptive of a prior decade; the scope of the farming enterprise was narrowed to cultivation of the "Buchanan farm," owned first by my grandfather and then, after his death in 1930, by the siblings jointly through the "estate" until final disposition in 1944.

I lived through an example of the inefficiency of common ownership arrangements. I can now understand that it was entirely rational for my father to allow the paint to peel on the old house in which we lived; to watch the barns and outbuildings fall into varying states of dysfunctionality; indeed to "mine" the property that he was expected to operate and maintain without promise of ultimate personal ownership, and all of this through a period of a depressed agricultural economy. But perhaps a modified ownership would have made only minimal difference; there were simply no sources of funds for even limited investment. But, of course, I did not personally sense deprivation. To me, the boy growing up, the family was well-ordered; there was no alcoholic abuse; there were no domestic squabbles; there was no consciousness of lost opportunities.

The Great Depression of the 1930s was perhaps less damaging to my family than the sequence of events in the 1920s previously noted. By the 1930s, the family enterprise has already been scaled down, both expectationally and actually; the operation was bare bones. The direct impact of the Great Depression arrived from quite a different source. My mother's younger sister, whose husband had been industrially employed, arrived suddenly with her two sons in tow. These three, along with my grandmother, came to live with us for the quite simple reason that they had nowhere else to go. The unemployed prior breadwinner returned to his mother's household, accompanied, however, by a refusal to take in the family. Our farm offered subsistence living which was better than the alternative—the welfare rolls in an alien, northern city.

This year-long expansion in family size was, for me, a boon rather than a burden. I found myself with two smaller boys as "peons," whom I could "boss around" as I carried out my entrepreneurial ventures, which included using farm animals to pull small wagons of varying designs.

The external state of the national economy took on an observed form in the wandering "tramps" who hitchhiked the highways and rode the railroad boxcars, with the occasional stopover at or near our house or school. At one such time, a wonderful musician appeared at our school and gave us a marvelous concert on his accordion in exchange for his lunch. Another encounter with a "hobo" was more intimate. My father's cousin, the son of a distinguished academician, joined the ranks of the wanderers and came by our place for visits on two or three separate occasions. In each case my father would exploit local contacts to secure employment for his cousin, only to have the drifter, each time, walk away after not more than two weeks of steady work.

There was also "Brother Stevens," an ancient, wizened sage,

who claimed to be a preacher of sorts, but who held no position, had no permanent abode, and spent his years moving from family to family over roughly a three-county area in Middle Tennessee. He was a person I enjoyed immensely; he could talk for hours an any and all subjects, and he was learned in matters well beyond the biblical. He would arrive unannounced, by foot, and we could expect him to stay roughly from a week to ten days. He always departed after my mother had done all his laundry, but just before his welcome turned sour. But after the required number of months had passed each year, we found ourselves asking, "When is Brother Stevens coming back?" He provided value-for-money by his presence and his talk, and he somehow filled a niche in the institutional arrangements for those times. Where have such persons gone today? I wonder.

III. *Hard Work*

I do not envy the youngsters in modern suburbia, who lack a sense of scarcity along any dimension, but notably that of time itself. I cannot escape a renewed shock at each observation of children walking at a pace that would have seemed impossibly slow to me. How, then, can anyone for whom even time is superabundant begin to understand a childhood in which work was as natural as play?

Many hours in my early years were occupied in physical labor. But work on the farm or around the house was so much a part of my ordinary existence that I do not recall any particular resentment. Work was, quite simply, there to be done, and there was no social norm that suggested the exemption of children from family responsibilities. Hence, I was never ordered by my father or mother to "go to work"; in a remembered image I was always a volunteer and, as noted, my mother insisted that school time never be sacrificed. Play was never considered to be a serious alternative when work was to be done. (Saturday and Sunday afternoons were accepted to be baseball times during which work was inappropriate.)

Work is not exclusively measured by time; putting in the hours is only part of the story. In this respect I was never lazy; indeed, quite the opposite. From my very earliest efforts, when I followed the turning plow after school on spring days and chopped corn in summer, I acquired an in-family repute for speed. Patience was not, then or later, one of my characteristic qualities. From the outset I was driven to finish any job commenced in the shortest time possible.

This feature of my labor served to "promote" me to a leadership role very early. Two brothers from a nearby farm, hired as field workers, were both mentally retarded, but they could carry out simple farm chores such as chopping the Johnson grass from corn. They could not, however, be trusted to work on their own. Their rate of input was strictly determined by the leader who worked alongside. I was placed in this role, as a ten year old, setting the pace for two physically strong young adults with the full understanding that I was, in fact, the "foreman."

Throughout his life my father boasted to his friends about my work rate. When I was fourteen, or thereabouts, I was left to "split the middles" of a twelve-acre field of corn, the last act of cultivation after which the corn would be "laid by" until fall harvesting. This work involved a plow pulled by a single mule down the middle between each row of corn. We had a high-strung but strong mule, Rhoda, whose inner tensions matched with my own. The day was mild for Middle Tennessee in late July, and our pace was such that we finished the whole field in one-half the predicted number of hours. My father was amazed that the mule survived; he seemed less concerned about my prospects for self-destruction.

Hard cash was nonexistent for me as a child or teenager; allowances were unheard of in the rural culture of that time and place. My first "income" was earned by working on neighboring farms during periods of peak labor demand, such as threshing or haying. The going rate in the early 1930s was 75 cents for a full working day. I was, therefore, excited when I landed a job as waterboy, at a dollar per day, on a bridge construction project. This employment lasted sixteen days; my earnings were sixteen dollars, which my father supplemented to purchase (for $40.00) a "pony" all my own. But with a difference. He purchased a small mare, named her Pony, gave me full ownership rights, but also insured that she could pull a full workload alongside the other horses and mules in the barn.

As I grew stronger through my teenage years, I commenced to contract for special work. One summer I cut and sold firewood; another summer I deconstructed (or tore down) old barns; another summer I dug footings for an extension of a school building. These small jobs supplied some needed cash. Finally, when I entered college, I contracted with my father to take on all the milking chores, as my full responsibility, in explicit exchange for one-half of each month's check received for milk sent each morning to the local Carnation plant.

Work is perhaps a part of my genetic makeup; or, at the least, it is a product of cultural evolution that lies well below the level of my consciousness. I am possessed of a work ethic that others find hard to appreciate and understand. My early times did nothing to exorcise this feature of my psyche. The dominant family member in my life was my mother who, herself, was a role model in this as in other respects. Habits, acquired early, influenced my work patterns through my career. I have always been a very early riser, and my best hours are those spent before my colleagues arrive. And what seem long days to others seem quite ordinary to me. On balance, I have enjoyed work—from the hard physical labor of my early times to the mental agony/ecstacy of developing and writing out ideas in later years.

IV. *Water, Heat, and Light*

From the perspective of the 1990s, the way we lived in the 1920s and 1930s seems primitive indeed. But a more balanced assessment would emphasize the differences between that era and this rather than any shift in measurable well-being. Nature was more niggardly in releasing the energies demanded in everyday use. Water was not available at a tap to be turned on or in a toilet tank to be flushed. Central heat did not diffuse itself throughout a house as controlled by a thermostat. Lights did not emerge from the ends of wires embedded in ceilings or attached to lamps. Food did not get cooked on stoves that contained no fires.

Water was drawn from a well in a covered wellhouse near the back porch of the big house. A slender bucket was attached to a rope that was lowered a hundred feet into the ground, then, after being allowed to fill up, pulled up again by a windlass. This source supplied water for all uses. There was no "bathroom." A bath involved a large basin of heated water in front of the stove in the kitchen at the allotted time on Sunday morning. Drinking water was available from a commonly used dipper and a cedar bucket on the back-porch shelf. Water was heated on the kitchen wood-burning stove, upon which meals were cooked.

Bodily functions were carried out, expeditiously in winter months, in a privy removed some fifty yards from the house and located on the edge of a creek, just upbank enough to insure against flooding in normal times, but downbank enough to guarantee that, when the rains came, flooding would carry away the accumulated wastes. On balance, not a bad sanitary system for that time and place.

Heat was supplied by open fireplaces. There were as many as ten fireplaces in the huge, old, fourteen-room house. All but one of these fireplaces were small—designed for coal rather than wood. Needless to say, only one was actively used during ordinary times. Others were actuated as needed; in the parlor on Sundays and evenings when company arrived; in the upstairs bedrooms when overnight relatives or guests came. Coal was purchased; wood for the kitchen stove was locally cut, and one of my boyhood chores was to keep full the woodbox near the stove.

I slept in a nonheated bedroom far removed from any fireplace. And winters in Tennessee can be very cold; I recall mornings where there was ice formed by my breath on the blankets. And the warmth of the burning fire to a boy who had just jumped out of bed in a freezing room is a sensation not soon forgotten.

Light was supplied by kerosene lamps, moved from place to place as needed. Candlepower was limited, but, somehow, reading by the light of a visible flame seems more adventurous than reading in a setting where all uncertainty has been eliminated.

To me, in those early times, water, heat, and light were necessary parts of ordinary existence, and improvements in the technology of supply were just that, improvements which, even if miraculous, were not really life-expanding opportunities. Indoor plumbing, central heat, and incandescent lighting—these features that emerged as characteristics of town and city living in the 1920s and '1930s did not seem to me to mark the dawn of a new age.

Radio was dramatically different. To pick out voices and music wirelessly from the air promised to open up worlds yet unknown.

My father, always a sucker for untested technology, had installed a radio as early as 1928, a decade before electricity. Perhaps the radio was purchased only on approval, for I recall a huge panel of batteries which were very soon exhausted and proved too expensive to replace. In any case the early radio was in place only a few weeks, just sufficient to give me a sense of its mysteries and to motivate a genuine sense of deprivation—a sense that was not there for the other services electricity made possible.

My desires had been whetted, and sometime later, perhaps in 1931, I put together my crystal set. I did not construct this primitive radio from scratch. I ordered a partially finished set, to be assembled by parts, which included a coil, a cat's whisker, a piece of "crystal" mounted in a piece of lead, a connection for earphones, the earphones themselves, and a long aerial which was mounted high on the house and extended for some fifty yards to an outbuilding connection. The main parts were placed in a wooden cigar box, and, when everything was ready, radio signals could be picked up by placing the cat's whisker (a very small wire) gently and strategically on the crystal—provided that there was a single broadcast station in the area sufficiently dominant to drown out frequency interferences. I was lucky; WSM-Nashville, one of the early strong stations, met the requirement. And, for some six years, the miracle of WSM radio became an important part of my early times.

Electricity arrived, as a part of the TVA (Tennessee Valley Authority) program sometime during my college years, probably in 1937 or 1938. For me, the availability of a loudspeaker and selective radio was much more significant than the lighting, refrigeration, and other advantageous services made newly possible.

V. *Books, Schools, and Speech*

I do not know when I learned to read; I know only that by the time I started school I could more than match the talents of second-grade peers. With my birthdate in early October, my mother chose not to send me to school two months before my sixth birthday. She assumed the role as my private tutor, on a more formal basis than earlier, and when I did enroll I was put in the second grade. Hence, I was placed, throughout my school years, in a peer group of somewhat older classmates. But, despite an age gap, my superior early instruction was sufficient to keep me at the head of the class and allowed me to accumulate at least as many "headmarks" as anyone else. By the time I reached seventh grade, perhaps because the teacher was not competent, my mother again took on a formal role as private tutor and put me through all eighth grade requirements in a summer. High school, grades nine through twelve, found me two grades in advance of my peers.

Reading was not confined to school assignments; reading was from the start important at home. My house did have books around the place, and this fact was influential in my life. And, even before I could myself read, I recall my mother, and occasionally my father, reading stories to me that were not childlike. From my very early years, and well before school times, I was given books for Christmas, and I remember that each year my first look under the tree was at the books, not the toys. I must have conveyed the differential excitement that books generated, because the number increased year by year.

One room in the big old house was called "the library," but there were only two bookcases there and only a few of the classics in English literature. But there were several Zane Grey westerns, which I devoured very early. And my "rich aunt," who lived in Nashville, arrived two times each year with several mystery novels and stacks of the *Saturday Evening Post, Collier's,* and *Liberty,* which published serials as well as short stories. In the unused "back hall" upstairs in the house, there was, literally, a pile of books and pamphlets, perhaps six cubic yards. These were the residues of my grandfather's political career; they included books and pamphlets sent to him before, during, and after his tenure as governor of the state of Tennessee (1891–93). Since he was a populist leader (Farmers' Alliance party), the material received was clearly biased ideologically. But I found this source of early reading fascinating and instructive.

Western popular novels, murder mysteries, and radical political pamphlets—these were not inputs into a well-balanced and carefully selected reading program. But this motley assortment accomplished a purpose that a forced diet of the classics might have thwarted. I learned to enjoy reading, as such, and I became "bookish" early. Regardless of subject matter, books have always been, for me, objects that attract, excite, and challenge me. From these beginnings there must have emerged the sources of my fascination with bookshops, especially those that sell old books, and of my eclectic tastes in reading matter.

Lower school years were, for me, pleasant but unchallenging. I enjoyed going to school; I had a near-perfect attendance record, and I sailed through the requirements. I was acknowledged to be the leader or coleader of my classes. This intellectual status was such as to generate some measure of respect from others who were leaders in other capacities. My lower school teachers ran the scale from excellent to poor. One high school teacher, Mary Frances Snell, deserves mention here, since she taught me English for four years and French for two. From her, and my mother, I learned to write within an understood and remembered grammatical structure of rules, no small achievement when I examine the prose style of my peers in the professional social sciences.

In retrospect, in application to both my lower and my higher schooling, my main regret is the now-felt opportunity loss that stemmed from a failure to push me to my learning limits. No child, and precious few families, can sense at the time that which is sacrificed in a failure to learn, or can even begin to appreciate the permanent loss involved in a choice made to neglect the creation of human capital that acquired knowledge represents. I could have learned so much more than I did learn, and at so little cost.

My mother vaguely sensed this failure, but she could not correct it alone. She expressed regret at the absence of a Latin offering in high school, and she insisted, over my objection, that I take the two years of French. She also forced me, again against my will, to take private tutoring in "public speaking," as offered by my aunt, who had retired from a college position as drama instructor. I now consider those few weeks of public speaking to be among the most valuable of my whole educational experience. Quite literally, I learned to speak, and this skill has been helpful all the way from countywide declamation contests in elementary school; through practice teaching in college; classroom teaching over a long academic career; presentations of seminars to professional colleagues throughout the world; lectures to large audiences on many subjects, including the Nobel and many post-Nobel performances. I have generalized from my own experience to suggest that all academicians should be required to take courses in public speaking at some stage of their education.

VI. *And There Was Politics*

In a directly practical-participatory sense, I have never been political, but politics has always been important, even if it took quite different forms in my early and my later times. Politics "framed" my early years in the sense that my family lived in the shadow of my grandfather's electoral success—and failure—events that occurred a full quarter century before my birth. There was always talk of politics, and, as I grew up, there were remarks about my own prospective talents "as a politician." I was urged by my mother to be more outgoing with persons whom I did not know; to learn how to initiate conversations; to shake hands; to smile as if I shared genuine concern for the stranger. I did not succeed in acquiring this set of talents, and by the time I was a teenager, any early hopes for a true politician in the family had vanished.

Uncles had enjoyed minimal political success, and my father occupied local political office as a justice of the peace and member of the county's legislative body throughout my early years. Elections were talked about and celebrated, and "politicking" over the backyard fence, on the front porch, or at the country store took up much of my father's time in preelection weeks, often providing him with an excuse to leave the plowing, chopping, or milking to me.

The politics that engaged attention was, however, local and state rather than national. I can scarcely recall the 1928 contest between Smith and Hoover or even the 1932 contest between Hoover and Roosevelt. The politics that really mattered to me, as a boy of nine or thirteen in those years, was that involving statewide contests for governor, and, less importantly, countywide elections for sheriff, trustee, county clerk, etc. The governor's race each biennium took center stage.

Tennessee at that time was, of course, a part of the "Solid South"; hence, the real struggle for the power in state government took place within the Democratic party, and the single important election was the Democratic party primary in August of alternate years. There was a "two-party" contest during my formative years of intense interest. On one side, there was Boss Crump of Memphis and his candidate chosen from among his political cronies scattered throughout the state. On the other side, there was some fine, public-spirited citizen who was selected to fight off Crump's attempted dominance. I saw politics through the lenses captured by this simplistic description, and there was no difficulty in identifying the villain and the hero. Crump, the arch villain, usually won, and his minion was placed in the governor's chair. The hero, who usually lost, was someone named Lewis S. Pope, who made several hopeless efforts.

I collected election posters, made some of my own, and plastered these around the stairways in the old house. I imagined the house to be the electoral precinct. And, although I neither mastered nor understood the glad-handing part of being a politician, I relished in the speechmaking. I made hundreds of imaginary speeches as a spellbinding candidate talking to a huge crowd in the courthouse square on a sweltering summer's day. It mattered little that only the mules could listen.

Even in my early times, I recognized that Middle Tennessee could boast of one politician of national stature, and, in one of his easy races for the Senate, I listened to Cordell Hull speak on the courthouse square in Murfreesboro. I was, of course, many years away from any real understanding of economics, but, somehow, I took in Cordell Hull's free trade message, and I sensed that the free trade principle was indeed central to the traditional democratic-southern-populist set of values. And further, I understood that this principle had been subverted throughout much of the nation's history by the protectionist-monopolist interests of the East and North. A socialist of sorts I might later become, but I could never have become a protectionist.

As I suggested, however, Cordell Hull and national issues seemed remote from the reality of the state politics that mattered. My efforts at recall of these early times suggest the extent of the change wrought by Roosevelt's New Deal. Before Roosevelt and the Great Depression, we did not, as ordinary folk, adult or child, think much about Washington and national government solutions to problems. After the New Deal, this focus shifted, and someone who grew up in the 1940s or 1950s or thereafter would think of politics almost exclusively in national terms.

VII. *My Field of Dreams*

In early December 1989, on a flight from New Zealand to San Francisco, I watched a film, *Field of Dreams*. I looked with wonder as, in its first minutes, the film seemed to be made for me, privately and personally. Surely no one could quite appreciate what came across the screen, no one who had not ridden alongside me on the cultivator in the cornfield in Tennessee in 1930. And yet here it was, presented as someone else's imagined utopia. The experience was uncanny, so much so that shivers ran through my spine.

There was some very productive bottomland on the farm—land that lay at the intersection of two streams, which insured silting in floods and hence renewed fertility of the soil. Here we grew corn year after year, and its rate of growth in late June and July must have matched that of Iowa's best. And there is no single remembered sight quite equal to that of dark green corn, three to four feet high, literally crackling as it grows. At this stage of its growth, corn required cultivation for weed control, and for this purpose there was the disc cultivator, upon which I would ride behind a well-trained team of fat mules. It was indeed a time for dreaming, and my dream was precisely that of Kevin Costner in the film. I imagined that, through some miracle, the flat bottomland along the river was transformed into a baseball park in the city, with crowded grandstand, a well-manicured diamond, and an outfield of green grass. This imagined setting was indeed my own private utopia. I do not recall an accompanying vision of myself as hero, as the "natural," who hit game-winning home runs or pitched shutouts. I recall only that the baseball park was there, at home, on my place, where I could watch professional games every day.

This image of my field of dreams was presumably fixed forever during some summer when baseball dominated my everyday existence, perhaps a few days before a promised trip to Nashville to see the Vols—a good Class AA Southern League team that commanded all local attention. Each year, over my ages from eight to eighteen, my father organized one or two trips to Nashville, some forty miles away, to see the Vols—a team that was either a New York Giants or

Cincinnati Reds farm. Usually, a group of some ten or twelve men and boys from the local community made the trip on a farm truck. We would arrive early at Sulphur Dell, the sunken ballpark north of the State Capitol, and sit in the bleachers—paradise enow!

My father was a fine athlete, and he had played varsity football, baseball, and track for two years at the University of Oklahoma. In the years immediately after World War I, he had organized, managed, and played on a good community baseball team. This team fell apart in the mid-1920s as players grew older and some moved away. The village of Gum had no team at all during the critical middle years of my boyhood. But my father kept what had remained of the old team's equipment—catcher's mitt, mask, and breast protector; infielder's glove; a few bats; parts of his old uniform. These scarce items were to serve me in good stead as I grew older. Games were organized in our rock-strewn front lot, because I had the equipment, and, even if I was the youngest of the group, I was allowed to play. These Sunday afternoon games evolved over the course of several years into the formation of a new community team with a better field and some additional and better equipment, and I was still allowed to play, even if my talents were limited. Perhaps I knew the rules better than anyone else, but such knowledge did not help me hit the curve ball.

From early August through October during each of my four years, my high school organized a baseball team in competition with other high schools in the county. I was always on the team, in part because there were just enough minimally qualified candidates. My good qualities were diligence in practice, enthusiasm, and knowledge of the rules. There was, however, one thrilling moment, one that my father remembered until his death at ninety-one. In the late innings of a close game against Rockvale, a cross-county rival, I hit a home run that won the day. The event was so unexpected that I could not imagine that the ball actually sailed over the fence into the adjoining hayfield. For the one and only time in my life, I was, for a day, the full-fledged sports hero.

Baseball remains efficient by my standard of values; I do not for a moment sense opportunities lost during the many hours that I played, thought about, or imagined this game, which remains a thing of wonder. I shall never regret my field of dreams. High school basketball, viewed in retrospect, seems so different. The hundreds of hours spent in practice, only to sit on the bench for three years as a rarely used substitute—these were hours that could have been used far more productively in work, other play, or learning. But to have behaved differently, either voluntarily or as coerced by my mother, would have surely involved psychologically damaging costs of yet another sort.

VIII. *Endnotes*

There is no extended discussion of religion or race in this account of my early times. These subjects are left out, because they did not loom large in my childhood consciousness. An attempt to reconstruct my narrative around these subjects would be false from the start. Institutionally, religion was important. As noted in my summary essay in this volume, there were Presbyterian preachers on both sides of my family—uncles and cousins. And my family was churchgoing; rarely did we miss a Sunday at the rural Mt. Tabor Cumberland Presbyterian Church: Sunday school every week and a sermon once each month. But church was, for me, a required Sunday morning event before Sunday afternoon baseball. My priorities were very clear. I also "joined" the church at the appropriate age when one got "converted"; but I did so for the satisfaction of conventional family-community expectations, not from any remembered inner convictions. I have never, then or later, felt a need to wrestle with God or to spend much time worrying about its existence. Perhaps I remain deficient in this sense.

The socio-economic-political structure was one of caste. Blacks made up some twenty percent of the population with separated schools, churches, holidays, drinking fountains. Some were independent landowners, small farmers; some were day laborers; most were sharecroppers. But the terms of trade with black sharecroppers were identical to those with white sharecroppers, and, generally, in that place and time, the blacks were considered "better hands." But there was little or no racial tension, at least as it spilled over to affect my remembered consciousness. The Upper South that was Middle Tennessee in the first half of this century was not the Lower South; the homogenization imposed by abstracted external images counters the reality of experience.

3

At the Turn of a Half-Century
Middle Tennessee and Murfreesboro,
1936–40

I. *Introduction*

I WAS BORN in Rutherford County, on a farm near Murfreesboro in Middle Tennessee. But to say I am from Murfreesboro
itself is misleading; I am from the country village of Gum. And I
went to public school not in the town of Murfreesboro, but in the
country, to Buchanan School, so named because the original site
was on a few acres of worthless land cut off from a corner of the old
Buchanan farm. Only after high school did I come into town, and
on a day-student basis attended what was then Middle Tennessee
State Teachers College for the years 1936–40. I left Tennessee for
good in 1940, for many points beyond.

These are all familiar facts. But I do repeat them for a purpose.
One theme of this chapter is to suggest that if Jim Buchanan can get
a Nobel Prize, anyone can. Recognition and acceptance of this simple truth are very important. And many persons, from all over the
world and from many professions, have indeed sensed this truth as
they have conveyed their understanding to me in their varied responses to my receipt of the Nobel Prize. It is, I think, safe to say that
my selection in 1986 gave hope and encouragement to more people
than most other awards, and certainly more than any other previous award in economics. Here was Jim Buchanan, a country boy
from Middle Tennessee, educated in rural public schools and a local

public teachers college, who is not associated with an establishment
university, who has never shared the academically fashionable soft
left ideology, who has worked in totally unorthodox subject matter
with very old-fashioned tools of analysis, chosen by a distinguished
and respected Swedish committee. It was not at all surprising that
the sycophants for the orthodoxies, in both ideas and institutions,
were shocked and dismayed. And it is indeed gratifying to me that
members of the "great unwashed," the unorthodox in many dimensions, looked on me as the representative embodiment of that
which might be.

     What I propose to do in this chapter is to isolate and to identify
influences of my four years' academic experience in Murfreesboro,
influences that contributed, directly or indirectly, in placing me
where I am today. In order to do this, it will first be necessary to dispel any romantic notion of singularity or uniqueness that attaches
to me personally. There exist a subinfinity of "might have beens"
arrayed along many dimensions. It will also be useful to lay out, in
retrospect, a brief description of the socioacademic environment of
the Middle Tennessee of the 1930s. Within the limits imposed by
those two sets of constraints, I can then reconsider my college years
more carefully.

II. *Many Forks in the Road*

I shall not, nor am I even tempted to, engage in fanciful autobiographical reconstruction. I did not move along a childhood-
education-academic-research-publication career path that was
foreordained by some single decisive event in childhood, adoles-
cence, or even young adulthood. There was no early act of will or
determination to achieve a specific life goal, ambition, or objective.
Perhaps even more than most, my career path was shaped by a continuing series of personal choices which were themselves constrained by exogenous events, many of which were themselves
stochastically determined. The choices that were made emerged
only in the settings in which they were made; it would be folly to
model the series of choices as dynamic utility maximization.

     I once wrote the lyrics for a country song, but I could not write any accompanying music. (My mother discouraged me from even listening to country music, but it was so much a part of Middle Tennessee that all of us variously imagined ourselves to be songwriters.) The theme of my song was, of course, tragic, and the chorus was as follows:

> There are too many forks in the road,
> There are too many forks in the road,
> And I never could learn,
> Not to take the wrong turn,
> There are too many forks in the road.

The analytics of this chorus remain relevant even if the element of tragic lament is wholly eliminated, and even if I interpret my career, or my life, as a series of successfully seized opportunities presented within a series of fortuitous settings. The principle to be emphasized is that each of us, described in terms of who we are and where we are today, depends on a long series of choices we have made within a series of externally imposed constraints, and with chance or stochastic elements entering at almost every cut in time.

You may illustrate my argument here on the back of an envelope. Draw a simple tree diagram. From a beginning node draw in several branches, each one of which terminates at a different node. From each one of this set of nodes, draw in a series of branches, each one of which, again, terminates in a node at some "higher" level of the tree. Continue this process for only a few steps, and it becomes easy to see that you are soon well off the envelope, and that you have already generated a subinfinity of possible end points, any one of which might have been reached by a unique path from the beginning node.

As of today, in the here and the now, today in this place, each one of us can describe our life in this abstract way. And we can identify many nodes at which differing choices, differing external circumstances, or differing falls of the dice might have produced differing locations on the tree, or along the road, or whatever other metaphor you want to use.

This rather abstract way of looking at a life or a career is helpful in several respects, It suggests, first of all, that a person is only partially responsible for where he or she finds himself or herself today. Both

exogenous events and chance may be far more relevant than personal choices. We are familiar with this argument in defense of the
criminal, but we should recall that the argument applies to the other
side of the tree. If external events shape the path for the criminal, the
same thing must apply to the successful, whether success be measured in business, politics, or science. But note that the construction
here does not attribute everything to external events and to chance.
The construction does leave room for personal choices; there are
many steps along the way where any person might have chosen differently from the way that he did, in fact, choose. There is no escap-
ing personal responsibility.

The construction is also useful in indicating that, tracing backward or downward from a single point, there is a unique path that
was traversed. The implication is dramatic. Each and every choice
made becomes necessary in the progression to the end point from
which you start the backward or downward tracing. Each and every
set of constraints imposed that allowed or generated each choice
was also necessary. A change at any node would have guaranteed a
final location somewhere else among the thousands of branches of
the tree.

I illustrate this point with only a few autobiographical details.
Had I not been reared on a farm in Rutherford County, had I not
attended the county public schools, had I not attended Middle Tennessee State Teachers College (and none of these were choices that I
made; these steps were laid out for me by others and by events), had
I not chosen to enter graduate school in economics, had I not joined
the navy, had I not chosen to enroll at the University of Chicago for
my doctorate, had I not returned to the South for my career, had I
not chosen to write this or that paper or this or that book, had I not
organized this or that group—and, obviously, the list could be extended almost indefinitely—I would be someone different from the
man I am today, and I would not have been selected for the Nobel
award in 1986.

I think it is in a poem of Robert Browning that there is the statement, "I am a part of all that I have met." This statement can be
turned around to say also that "all that I have met is also a part of
me," and, indeed, a necessary part.

III. *Choice and Circumstance in the 1930s*

Many of my age cohorts in academic economics say that they chose economics as a disciplinary specialization because they were driven by an urge to make a personal contribution toward the solution of the nation's economic woes, which were the center of public attention in the 1930s. These economists among my peers acknowledge that they were reformers first, economists second. In entering undergraduate major programs or in enrolling in graduate schools, they imagined themselves to be either in ultimate positions of political power or advising others who did possess such power.

It is perhaps not surprising that I did not enter economics by this route. For one thing, a student from Middle Tennessee in the late 1930s was unlikely to dream that he might attain a position of authority, either directly or at some stages removed. For another, such a student viewed the "choice" of a career path as totally unreal. Positions, jobs, employment—these were scarce items, and one simply did not choose from a long menu of options. External opportunities dominated personal choices in these respects, as in others, and we sought to place ourselves in settings where we might seize any opportunity that came up. The projected scarcity of options reduced the profitability of investment in time worrying about career alternatives, and it also, presumably, influenced us toward keeping our options open by remaining nonspecialized. I do not consciously recall choosing among courses on the basis of any criterion of relative contributions toward postcollege careers. I simply selected courses that were, first, required, second, offered in the time periods I could attend, and third, prospectively interesting.

The courses I did take on this basis were not an inferior mix, all things considered. It is not surprising that I graduated in 1940 with three separate majors, mathematics, social sciences, and English literature. This mix, along with other courses, some of which I shall mention later, provided me with a broad introduction to many areas of inquiry, and it was this mix that convinced me, from the outset, that almost any subject matter can be interesting. I could have been as excited about a career as a mathematician or a literary critic as I have been about my work as an economist. In this sense I am not, and have never been, a "natural economist," a description that I attributed to one of my coauthors and my longtime colleague, Gordon Tullock.[1]

I became an economist because this "choice" was dictated by the set of options that I faced in June 1940. C. C. Sims, who had taught me political science, was instrumental in getting me an offer for a fellowship in economics at the University of Tennessee, with a stipend of $50 per month. When I could get $50 monthly for continuing in school, regardless of subject, I could scarcely consider seriously my other options, teaching in Rutherford County high schools at $65 monthly, or working in the Commerce Union Bank in Nashville at $75 per month. And $50 in Knoxville in 1940–41 was fully sufficient, especially when board was obtained at $26.

IV. *Confidence, Community, and Culture*

I want, now, to concentrate more closely on the years, 1936- 40, and on the nodes and branches on my decision tree that can be dated to fall within those years.

As I indicated, I attended MTSTC as a day student, not as a full-time participant in the college community. I paid for my fees and books by milking cows night and morning, and I rode into town at eight and rode out of town at four, usually with a Methodist preacher who was trying to finish college while riding the circuit. This item in my narrative is important, not because I missed much of college life, but because I gained so much by staying at home. The temptations of college-away-from-home were not available to me until graduate school in 1940, and I succumbed then to too many of these temptations not to know now that I would have been much less successful in Murfreesboro had I had the greater opportunity of full live-in participation in the college community. In this sense, the restrictions imposed by economic circumstance on my set of available options were, in the net, surely beneficial to me rather than harmful.

During these years, while at home and both working and attending college, I experienced no now familiar frustrations of growing up, of in-family tensions and conflict, or psychological hang-ups of

---

1. See James M. Buchanan, "The Qualities of a Natural Economist," in *Democracy and Public Choice*, ed. Charles Rowley (New York: Blackwell, 1987), 9–19.

any variety. I was, quite simply, kept too busy to worry about such matters. And I have always thrived when I am busy. I suppose that a work ethic is imbedded in my genes, and was also environmentally transmitted by my mother as an example. But from early childhood I gained a localized family reputation for hard work, and my father often boasted to his friends about how much I could plow in a day. And throughout my career I have, indeed, worked longer hours than most of my academic peers, one factor that has surely contributed mightily to my relative success.

I remained in this home work culture while a student in college. I was required, therefore, to undergo much less of a culture shock than many of my peers in the student community. I was not "picked up," literally, and placed in an alien culture. In this sense, I was, I think, fortunate indeed. I can imagine what might have happened had a good fairy come to me and provided me with the financial wherewithal to attend Vanderbilt, to find myself transported into a culture inhabited by boys and girls from the Nashville social set, with both experiences and funds so foreign to my own environment. I doubt seriously whether I could have made the grade. I was, of course, relatively poor even by the standards of my student peers in Murfreesboro. But the distances were not so great, and the participation was limited. I could, with legitimacy, remain outside the student social world without being treated as an outcast. I could concentrate on college work, as such, and such as it was.

Such as it was. In retrospect, I am sure that I was not challenged sufficiently; I could have done more with my talents than I was forced to do. But let me also acknowledge that I could have exploited the academic resources available more than I did. I could have taken Dr. Cheek's courses in Latin and Greek, and, looking back, I wish that I had done so. Instead, I spent too much time playing pickup basketball and gambling with the locker room set of country day students, who were my closest friends in Murfreesboro, and among whom was Grover Maxwell, later to become a distinguished philosopher of science, who spent most of his academic career at the University of Minnesota.

I was bored only in the required courses in education, which, even then, seemed to involve an almost total waste of my time, along with that of others, faculty members and students alike. The remaining courses contained sufficient substantive material to stir my interest, and, somehow, I got started on an intellectual quest that has never stopped. I shall discuss some of these courses further, but, before doing so, I want to evaluate one aspect of the whole academic environment, as it impacted on my psyche in 1938.

I found the ideas at MTSTC sufficiently challenging, the faculty sufficiently stimulating, and my student peers sufficiently competitive to provide me with a meaningful criterion for achievement. Up until the end of my second year, I was not really sure about my own competence or ability. At the end of that year, however, the academic rankings were published, and, with all A's that year, my name led all the rest. I recall, even now, the upsurge of self-confidence that this result generated in me. This result made me forget all about the first year C that Nooby Freeman had given me in mechanical drawing, the only C that I got during the whole of my academic career.

After that second year, I was indeed a different person. I knew that, at least among my Middle Tennessee peers, I could more than hold my own. This confidence did not extend into the great world beyond Middle Tennessee, but I felt, at least, ready to face the new challenges.

V. *Exposition, Ideas, and Analysis*

From my earliest recollection, books were more important than toys. And I recall, each Christmas morning, the stack of books under the tree got my very first attention. Encouraged directly by my mother, I devoured all reading matter that was available, from Zane Grey to the political pamphlets of the 1890s that I found upstairs in the old house. As with most voracious readers, I, too, had early ambitions to write, and I must have commenced hundreds of stories only to finish none. I know now what the barrier was; my imagination was not of the sort that allowed me to leap into fanciful, fictional worlds of my own making.

I now know that, thanks to my mother and to Mary Frances Snell, who taught me English (and French) in high school, I could, even then, write well. But it was Anne Ordway (Miss Ordway to us) who showed me that my relative strength was in expository writing not in fiction. I recall, almost as if today, her praise of a freshman paper I had written, a character sketch of someone I knew well. From that time I knew that my own comparative advantage lay in being able to take a single central idea or theme that was grounded in ultimate reality and to write around and about this theme in a systematic argument. Through many papers and books written over more than four decades, this structure served me well. From Anne Ordway I also learned to appreciate the genius of Shakespeare, and her two courses on the comedies and tragedies were, I think, the most pleasant of my college days. I can still hear the rustle of Miss Ordway's taffeta petticoats as she walked in front of the class.

Eva May Burkett taught me poetry and drama, and she helped me to bridge the gap between the reader-observer-critic and the person whose words we see on the printed page. By bringing literature closer in time, she "thawed it out" for me, so to speak, and I began to sense how language combines emotions and ideas as writers spoke directly to me, and offered an invitation for me to speak back. In particular, Miss Burkett's course introduced me to the poetry of Thomas Hardy, whose emphasis on chance and circumstance I found congenial. Perhaps by natural temperament I could never have been a true romantic, but the philosophical stance I acquired surely influenced me in my subsequent enthusiastic response to the ideas of the philosophers of the eighteenth-century Scottish Enlightenment, ideas from which classical political economy emerged. And, even more importantly, the philosophical stance that emerged in Murfreesboro, in part from Burkett's tutelage, became the basis of the intellectual bonding to Frank Knight, my great professor at the University of Chicago in the late 1940s, with whom I discussed our commonly shared admiration of the poetry of Hardy.

The ideas rather than the imagery contained in literature were the sources of my interest, then and now. I have always found ideas central to my interest, even when totally shorn of imagery. I appreciate the aesthetics of logical structure. And I found mathematics to be fascinating, challenging, and exciting. Courses in mathematics in Murfreesboro were fun, despite my now remembered recognition that neither Horace Jones nor Tommie Reynolds conveyed the ideas with the enthusiasm intrinsically deserved. But instruction, good or bad, could not have made this material dull for me, and especially when my student peers in mathematics were fewer and brighter than anywhere else in the college.

I shall mention only one more course favorably, the year-long sequence in physics that I took only in my senior year. Here was material and instruction ideally suited to my intellectual inclinations; analysis rooted in reality and taught by a man who conveyed something of the excitement of science. William Mebane was a wonderful liar, as everyone acknowledged, but this feature was only one part of his fine instructorship. Had I been exposed to physics three years earlier, I am certain I should have chosen to major in the subject. Again, in this respect, chance, circumstance, and choice caused me to take one fork in the road, and I can only speculate on what "might have been" had events been different.

As I noted earlier, the mixed curriculum, both self-selected and imposed, served me well. Economics, the discipline that was to become my scientific home, requires expository writing skills, logical structures of analysis, and a grounding in ultimate reality. And political economy, the branch of moral philosophy from which economics springs, requires philosophical coherence. I came away from Middle Tennessee with all of these, even if there were many forks in the road to be chosen by me or imposed upon me.

VI. *The Sense of Authority*

I shall note, only briefly, two other aspects of my four years' experience at Middle Tennessee, aspects that were not locally academic in the strict sense of those discussed. First, I can state, and categorically, that the easiest of all requirements for me during the whole four years was practice teaching. I taught algebra, under Roy Simpson's general supervision, at what was then called the Training or Demonstration School.

This was the easiest of all chores because it was clear, from the first day, that I should have no difficulty at all with students. From that day to this, instructional problems have been absent from any listing of my own. This experience told me, for the first time, that I carry with me a natural aura or sense of authority. And my self-confidence was thereby extended along quite a different dimension from that already discussed.

This embodiment of authority is, I suspect, genetically determined, and involves no choice of my own. It has allowed me to assume positions of leadership in several capacities throughout a long career, and without the apparent difficulties so often encountered by others. This trait also has its costs in that students, employees, and peers hold me in such awe sometimes that personal relationships are difficult for me to establish. Elaboration on this personality characteristic is not called for here; suffice it to say that from that algebra class onward I knew that I would face none of the standard problems of instruction.

VII. *The Image of Chicago*

I have, as yet, scarcely mentioned the most important single figure in my Middle Tennessee experience. I did note earlier that C. C. Sims had been instrumental in getting me a post-Murfreesboro graduate fellowship in economics at the University of Tennessee. But Sims filled a far more important role for me; it was on his advice and counsel that I chose (and here the choice was my own) to enter the University of Chicago for my doctorate after I spent almost five years in the United States Navy.

I took courses from Sims in political science, public administration, and related subjects. These have not been exciting subjects for me, then or now, because the material is too devoid of theme, of ideas, of theory, of analysis. But Sims had, only in the mid-1930s, completed his Ph.D. at the University of Chicago, and he was able, for the most part in private conversation, to pass along to me his sense of the intellectual excitement of Chicago. When, in 1945, I had the GI Bill for financial security, and I could, indeed, choose my own fork in that road, I headed for Chicago. I knew next to nothing about the faculty in economics, where I was to enroll. I knew only that Sims had stressed for me the general life of the mind that characterized that place.

Sims was totally correct, and I made one of the most critical, and best, decisions I have ever made by choosing to go to the University of Chicago. I have detailed my experience there in chapter 5, and I shall not repeat that discussion here. But my acknowledgment of debt to Carleton C. Sims deserves a place in this account. While I owe him next to nothing for what he taught me in his courses, I owe everything to him for his guidance in what was for me a critical step.

VIII. *Half-Century Retrospective*

It is difficult for me to realize that the Middle Tennessee college, the faculty, and the student whose experiences I have discussed here are a part of a history that is a half-century past. History, as such, has never interested me, and the remarks here are drawn exclusively from retained images of people, places, and things rather than from any research record. This procedure has seemed appropriate for my limited purpose, but apologies are in order for errors, biases, and omissions.

In this final section I shall develop further the two themes mentioned at the outset. First, if Jim Buchanan could win a Nobel Prize, anyone can. Second, anyone is, in the now and here, a product of literally thousands of choices made by and for him or her over a whole series of sequential and many-dimensional forks in the road, each and every one of which was necessary in getting from where one started to where one is, now and here. Superficially considered, these two themes may seem contradictory. The second suggests that each person is a uniquely determined unit of present consciousness, whereas the first suggests that there is little or nothing singular about anyone. But the contradiction is indeed only superficial.

By saying that if Jim Buchanan can be awarded a Nobel Prize, then anyone can, I am suggesting only that there is no single recipe, or even an inclusive large set of recipes, from or among which a successful career can be "constructed"—whether this career be scientific, literary, professional, financial, political, or otherwise. There are, literally, no starting points, no early nodes for choice, no branches of the tree, that automatically *preclude* ultimate success. A preppy-Ivy League establishment education is *not* a prerequisite for scientific achievement. Who a person is, where a person starts, where or how he or she acquires what passes for educational skills—none of these things determines or even constrains the destination or end point.

And what is critically important for all those who may enter the game at some apparent disadvantage in one or another of several dimensions is the attainment of an ability to resist discouragement and despair. This ability, in turn, depends on the achievement, early on, of a constrained and realistic, but finally unshakable, self-confidence.

The implication of my second theme is that Middle Tennessee and Murfreesboro "mattered" in getting me the success I may have attained. I have tried, in the main part of this chapter, to identify what seem, from a half-century's retrospective view, to be the influences that mattered most. An omniscient and more objective biographer might, of course, stress quite different persons and events. But my purpose here has been to give you an accounting of what the Middle Tennessee of 1938, and the years before and after, seem to have offered. I could not, and should not want to, do more than this.

4

An Easy War

I. *Before Pearl Harbor*

ON BIOGRAPHICAL FORMS, under *Education*, I have often listed the United States Navy in addition to the schools, colleges, and universities I have attended. I commenced active duty a few weeks (September 1941) before my twenty-second birthday and was released a few weeks (November 1945) after my twenty-sixth. These years were times of maximum "educability," and I did, indeed, learn much that has, on balance, served me well.

With an early number in the 1941 draft lottery, continuation of graduate school seemed impossible, and the Naval Reserve Officers' Training Program seemed much preferable to service in the army. At summer's end off I went to New York, a world unknown, since I had never been far from Tennessee and surely not north of the Mason-Dixon Line. Even before I reported for duty, New York, as such,

My own recollections of events discussed in this chapter are supported, and in part stimulated, by an autobiographical monograph by Carl Soden, Great Bend, Kansas, who shared much of the same experience. See Carl Soden, "Some Funny Things Happened to Me on the Way and During World War II" (duplicated, Great Bend, Kan., 1987).

This is a personal autobiographical narrative; it is not presented as history. Upon completion of the first draft, I did verify the major events discussed by reference to two sources: E. B. Potter, *Nimitz* (Annapolis: Naval Institute Press, 1976), and Edwin F. Hoyt, *How They Won the War in the Pacific: Nimitz and His Admirals* (New York: Weybright and Talley, 1970).

failed to attract me. I recall the initial disappointment at Times Square which was so much smaller and filthier (even then) than I had imagined. New Yorkers were (and are) strange beings; already I felt I was in enemy territory.

There were several hundred officer candidates enrolled in New York's midshipmen's school. Each of us faced a period of almost four months' training which, if successfully completed, would produce an ensign, USNR. We were housed and trained on the Spanish-American War battleship, the USS *Illinois* (better known as the *Prairie State*), sitting in the mud of the Hudson River just below the George Washington Bridge. Although gutted for training purposes, the quarters were still cramped and rat-infested. But the old ship did offer a feel for navy life that I am sure was missing for later midshipmen when the facilities were all moved ashore. Our instructors were retired regulars, scarcely competent, brought back to active duty by the threatening war clouds.

Initially, and before being qualified even as midshipmen, we were put through an accelerated boot camp with rifle, close order, and boat drills. But some organization was required early on, and, well before there could be any testing, midshipmen officers were appointed, as the group was divided into companies, platoons, and sections.

This initial appointment of cadet officers "radicalized" me to such an extent that emotional scars remain, even a half-century later. I can now, of course, understand the rational basis for statistical discrimination, and, probabilistically, graduates from Ivy League universities were predictably superior to those of us from the academies west of the Hudson. But the disproportionate favoritism for the establishment types was extreme and extended even to the importation of Bill Rockefeller to head up our platoon of A's and B's, because there were too few A's and B's (last name orderings) with an Ivy League background whereas there was an apparent surplus down among the R's and S's. This on-hand experience with blatant discrimination, no matter how rational, against southerners, midwesterners, and westerners served to reinforce in concrete my populist preconceptions. And, for the first time a class basis for conflict moved from abstraction to reality. From that day forward, I have shared in the emotional damage imposed by discrimination, in any form, and "fairness" assumed for me a central normative position decades before I came to discuss principles of justice professionally and philosophically.

The standards of the midshipmen's school were not high, and I and the other members of my platoon ranked highly, reconfirming my initial hunch that we did not really need to import our leaders. I ranked seventh in the class of more than five hundred, not sufficiently high to get one of the prized swords which went only to the top five but high enough to tell me that I could hold my own with peers—regardless of university and class.

We were into the final month of New York training when the Japanese attacked Pearl Harbor on December 7, 1941. This event caused little change for us, except for the amusing accident to a disliked junior instructor who shot his own foot immediately after receiving live ammunition. But Pearl Harbor did generate other changes that opened up new roads for me. Initial orders directed that I proceed to communications school at New Groton, Connecticut, upon completion of New York training. These orders were rescinded, post–Pearl Harbor, and a small group of us, eight in all, were ordered to the Naval War College, Newport, Rhode Island, for six weeks of special training. But this training was specifically temporary, and we knew precisely the next step in our careers. Four of us were already assigned to the Operations Staff, CINCPAC (Commander-in-Chief, Pacific), to which we were to proceed upon completion of the training in Newport.

The few weeks in Newport at the Naval War College evoke some of my most pleasant memories. We arrived as fresh ensigns (all reserve officers), but distinguished by the fact that we were the very first junior officers ever to have been assigned to the college. Socially, as well as professionally, the whole institution was organized to accommodate senior officers as its students; we were unwitting beneficiaries of war's occasional small fortunes. We were invited to teas at the admiral's quarters; we were allowed to participate in the war games; we were given private offices. For our studies, we were assigned problems in navigation and in fleet maneuvers; we learned types and characteristics of ships; we mastered the mooring board as an instrument. We read histories of naval warfare.

At the war college we were, indeed, exposed to postgraduate education. We were also especially fortunate in having as our instructor (and almost as role model and father figure) a fine man who will reenter this narrative at a later point. James (Jimmy) Carter (no relation to the namesake who later achieved some prominence and who, also, served in the navy) was a professorial type who took us under his wing and made us appreciate what the navy was all about. Carter had, himself, taken what was for his career a "wrong turn" in the 1930s when he chose to specialize in lighter-than-air ships, thereby missing the stages of surface ship experience that might have moved him up faster and further given developments in technology and the events of history. But Carter was not a bitter man; instead he was relaxed, serious, and dedicated to his task.

Lest I forget (as if I could do so), I remind you that being a young naval officer in the spring of 1942, whether in Newport or San Francisco, where we awaited transportation to Pearl Harbor, carried with it some of the war's spillover benefits. The girls were also patriotic.

II. *CINCPAC Operations*

We arrived in Honolulu in late March 1942 aboard the SS *Lurline*, a Matson passenger liner that had already been converted for troop-carrying operations. We reported for duty at CINCPAC headquarters, officially onboard a battleship, but in fact temporarily established at the submarine base, Pearl Harbor, which had sustained little or no damage. Despite the time lapse of almost four months, Pearl Harbor, both physically and organizationally, appeared still to be in shock. Facilities seemed chaotic and affairs sometimes confused. Personnel from destroyed and damaged ships waited around for new assignments. Admiral Chester W. Nimitz had assumed command, but the word "order" could not be used to describe CINCPAC fleet headquarters.

Pearl Harbor was "at war." Blackout was total after dark; there was concern for subversion by ethnic Japanese in Oahu; there was widespread fear of follow-up raids by land, sea, and air. The confidence that was exhibited seemed quiet and seemed based on an assessment of long-term prospects rather than on any immediate or short-range plans for victory. The mood was strictly conducive to work not play.

Our assigned task, for which we had been especially trained after assignment to the staff, was to man operations plot, the nerve center of fleet operations. There was no electronic gadgetry in place here. Instead, we simply placed large paper overlays on plywood panels and sketched in each day's estimated location and direction of movement for all naval vessels. The job was a general combination of mechanical drawing, block printing, arithmetic, filing, geography, navigation, and information processing. (I have always been amused by the highly romanticized versions of operations plot rooms in war movies.)

We stood round-the-clock watches, and one of the four of us was on duty at the plot board at any time. We reported directly to the operations officer or his assistant, senior members of Nimitz's staff, during regular daytime hours and, at night, to the operations watch officer, a rotating sleep-in role assumed by all senior staff members. In the early months critical decisions were largely confined to those involving waking the operations watch officer upon receipt of dispatch information, made sometimes more critical by the observed inebriation of the late-reporting senior officer.

We did not track and position Japanese ships, either surface or submarines. We did not have direct access to intelligence information on these matters. This gap in the picture was filled in by Commander Eddie Layton, who came into the plot room early each morning with orange colored pencils and put dots around the map where Japanese units were estimated to be.[1]

In the early months of my tenure on the staff, the operations officer was Captain Delany, but the real work was done by Commander Roscoe Good, who formally succeeded Delany in mid-1942. Roscoe Good was a man whom I came to admire greatly, and from whom I learned much. Good, who after leaving the staff advanced to flag rank, was something of a tyrant in direct dealings with his inferiors. He could not tolerate either incompetence or laziness, and his tongue lashings left scars. But his compensating qual-

---

1. Layton was the staff intelligence officer during the whole period of my service. He was respected by all those who knew him. His posthumously published book, Edwin T. Layton, *And I Was There* (New York: William Morrow, 1985), fills in many of the gaps in information that even those of us who were there, at least part of the time, had always missed.

ity of unquestioned loyalty and support for all members of his staff when criticism from outside emerged erased, at least for me, all of the remembered internal suffering. If you were Good's man, you did as he directed; if you screwed it up, you were soundly thrashed; but woe be unto those who came in from beyond and attacked. In such a case, there was no prouder sense than to be "Good's man."

Roscoe Good was phenomenal in his retention of information about ships and all things relating to ships. He could recite tonnages, speeds, drafts, gun emplacements, dates of commission and records of service for what seemed to be each and every ship in the fleet. Even his seniors on the staff acknowledged this and deferred to his genuine expertise. In this sense Good was the most intelligent senior officer with whom I was associated over the course of the war. I have no comparable data on his strategic wisdom or other qualities. But, that much said, had I chosen to go to sea and had I been allowed to pick my ship's captain, Roscoe Good would have been my choice.

The headquarters location at the submarine base was temporary and, even before we arrived, construction had commenced on a permanent site at Makalapa, up the hill from Pearl Harbor on the edge of a long-inactive volcanic crater. By late 1942, we had moved to this genuine fortress with airtight security and impregnable layers of reinforced concrete. The operations plot was well below ground, and here our work setting did resemble somewhat more closely that which was so many times fictionalized. There was still no electronic gadgetry, and the work was done with paper, pencils, pens, pins, dividers, string, files, and manual typewriters. But we did have adequate space, and there was now room for Admiral Nimitz and members of his senior staff to crowd around the large central maps during periods of crisis.

Admiral Raymond A. Spruance took over as chief of staff to Admiral Nimitz near the time of the locational shift to Makalapa. He spent most of his working day, which was long, at a stand-up desk in a small room adjacent to our plot room with the adjoining door usually open. Such proximity guaranteed that I would come to know Spruance well—better than any other of the flag rank officers whom I variously encountered. My recollection is that of a man of intense concentration, who exemplified the work ethic and whose passion was for the task at hand—victory over the enemy. There was very little small talk, almost no joking, but there was a sense of inner confidence that was conveyed to those of us around him.

The operations plot was, of course, the one place where a generalized vision of fleet operations could be captured, and, hence, our central room was on the tour for all senior visitors who possessed the requisite clearances. These admirals who passed through Pearl Harbor on their way to taking over commands of fleets, task forces, divisions, and squadrons were usually accompanied by Spruance. And I distinctly recall the day when Spruance introduced me as follows: "This is Buchanan, who is mighty fast and fairly accurate." I have always considered "mighty fast and fairly accurate" to be an appropriately descriptive title for an autobiography. Even from my days as a plowboy, and extending through my years as a student, midshipman, Ph.D. candidate, and, finally, writer of papers and books, I have been able to work more rapidly than most peers, even if with less than perfect accuracy. Admiral Spruance did, indeed, know me well.

III. *Midway*

The Pacific war did not go well for our side in early 1942. Military action was largely confined to the South Pacific, and the only significant battle, Coral Sea, calls up recollections of our own losses in lives and ships rather than damages inflicted on the enemy. I recall the early reports of failures during those early months of the torpedoes on our submarines on patrol and of the inadequacy of our fighter planes in combat with the more maneuverable Japanese Zeros.

At headquarters, we did our best to track events as they occurred thousands of miles away and with limited radio contact. But confusion is more descriptive than precision in referring to our efforts. We lived in an atmosphere of uncertainty and doubt. The objective was to stop the southward Japanese advances, but at the same time to retain an ability to defend the middle Pacific. There was the sobering recognition of the months required for new construction and replacement of major units of the fleet. There was a felt sense of "holding out," a sense that "if we can only get through a few more months, things will begin to turn our way." And I recall that even as a very junior officer on the staff, a communitarian sharing in these anxieties.

The Battle of Midway was the event that tipped the scales. And this event in early June 1942 marks a divide between two quite separate wars, at least for those of us who were fortunate enough to share in some understanding of the grand strategies.

We knew that the Japanese planned to attack Midway; we knew (or thought we knew) when, how, and most of the other relevant details. As I noted earlier, as junior officers in the operations plot, we did not directly share intelligence information, but we did know that the Japanese codes had been broken and presumably without Japanese knowledge. The advance warning gave Admiral Nimitz time to order our carrier task force from the South Pacific. Admiral Halsey, task force commander, was to stop over in Pearl Harbor for only a few days and was then to proceed to positions off Midway in anticipation of the attack.

At this point, something happened that affected our attitude about Admiral Halsey. He contracted some sort of strange illness that made it necessary to give up his command. At the time (and now) this sequence of happenings seemed cloudy. Let me say only that those of us on the headquarters staff did not quite share in the worldwide adulation for "Bull" Halsey that later came his way. In any case, Admiral Spruance, who had not yet reported as chief of staff, was detached and assigned command of the task force that proceeded to Midway on schedule.

The hours of the battle itself were dramatic for those of us at headquarters. We stood double watches in the operations plot, and our room was continually occupied by Admiral Nimitz and other senior officers as we all tried to match limited information as it came in with times and places on the maps. Confusion rather than order describes the atmosphere, but, as the hours passed, it came to be clear that despite our own major fleet losses in men, planes, and ships, the back of the Japanese naval force had been broken. Never again would the Japanese be able to mount a major naval offensive. In this sense the war was over.

It would be folly on my part to try to reconstruct from my own recollections the course of events at the Battle of Midway itself.

Trained naval historians have sifted through the evidence, and many accounts are on record. But I did have a small part in the history that is worth recalling at this point in my narrative. Immediately after the battle was over, it seemed clear that some sorting out was required, some genuine research effort directed toward sifting through the many dispatches, written and oral reports, and other accounts. This task was urgent since Admiral Nimitz was expected to provide an official report of the battle to his superiors in Washington within a relatively short time.

The research report was assigned to Commander E. M. Eller, who had been on the staff for a period as an assistant gunnery officer.[2] I was taken off the operations plot watch routine and assigned to Commander Eller as his assistant. Perhaps for the only time in my life, I was plunged into genuine research into raw data. Our task was to make as much sense as possible out of what seemed to be a maze of confusion among conflicting reports made so hurriedly by so many. I do not recall just how many days we worked, at breakneck speed and very long hours, but we got the report finished. Once the report was edited, it did, indeed, become the official record of the Battle of Midway. And it was this report, as modified and edited, that was hand-carried by Admiral Nimitz and a senior aide to Washington. There was a slight mishap en route—the plane dunked its passengers in San Francisco Bay—but both passengers and the report survived.

IV. *After Midway*

After Midway things other than those of military moment assumed some importance. Curfews were lifted; blackouts were relaxed. Fear no longer seemed to be omnipresent. There was no discounting of the long way ahead; we knew that more battles must be fought, more lives must be lost, more ships sunk. But while we were getting on with it, there seemed to be time to look at creature comforts. In our off-duty days we looked for, and found, some feminine companionship. We rounded up used-car transportation and seized our

---

2. Many years later, as rear admiral, Eller served as director of naval history.

rations of gasoline. We began to enjoy Oahu's beaches, both familiar and remote. We enjoyed the facilities of the various officers' clubs, and, especially, the parties that were organized for the express purpose of "drinking up the profits."

The Pacific war was concentrated in the south, with defeats as well as victories. But the long buildup of the fleet finally began to take shape. Plans were laid for the western military thrust, island by island, atoll by atoll. Admiral Nimitz became supreme commander of the Central Pacific theater of war, and he was placed as a coequal with General Douglas MacArthur, commander of the Southwest Pacific theater. And thereby hangs a tale worth telling. Before and even after Midway, Nimitz and the navy generally were not much interested in public relations, in PR. The entire public relations staff consisted of one retired regular commander, as I recall it, and one junior officer. I think it is proper to say that Nimitz and the navy generally were primarily interested in winning the war, rather than in any personal plaudits back home in the United States.

But, after Midway, when we had time to look around a bit, we realized that MacArthur was winning the PR battle. Whereas we had a public relations staff of two officers, MacArthur had, so we were told, a PR staff of more than sixty colonels. And we could see their effectiveness. As information addressees of the dispatches sent back to Washington from Australia, we could read about the forays made by MacArthur's patrols up the New Guinea coast. A chance encounter with one or two starving Japanese stragglers (as reported in the actual dispatches), somehow became "MacArthur's forces advance against enemy fire up New Guinea coast." To a man, each and every one of us on Nimitz's staff, including, I am sure, the admiral himself, took on a passionate hatred for MacArthur and knew him for the near-fraud that, to this day, I think that he was. Years later, when President Truman summarily fired MacArthur in Korea, there was joy indeed for all those who remembered.

MacArthur did have supreme authority over the naval forces in the Southwest Pacific, the Seventh Fleet. And one of our tasks, as operations officers, was to assign to this fleet the dictated numbers of ships. Let me confess, here and now, that we did not allocate ships by criteria of efficiency; we tried our best to insure that MacArthur got and kept the least effective ships possible, always within the limits allowed to us. That seemed only small compensation for the losses we continued to suffer in the public relations war.

In 1944, as the island-hopping campaign continued and was successful in its own objectives, plans were made for the final stages of the ultimate victory over the Japanese. President Roosevelt and General MacArthur came to Makalapa for a meeting with Admiral Nimitz. I mention this event only to record my personal shock and surprise at the sight of Roosevelt from a few yards away. His basket-case disability had been so effectively concealed for so many years that I had grown up thinking Roosevelt was as fit as any other man. He was not; he was a severely crippled person who was totally dependent on his nurses. This sight remains stamped in my memory.

V. *My Shooting War*

But I get ahead of my story. At some stage of the war, I do not precisely recall when (probably in the spring of 1943) and in what sequence, Captain Tom Kelliher became staff operations officer and, hence, our immediate superior. Kelliher was a crusty salt with a twinkle in his eye and one very good principle for naval operations: Recall that ships need to go into port occasionally to "whore the crew." By the time Kelliher was on board, we had been around long enough to take over other responsibilities beyond record keeping. We had become assistant operations officers—first in fact, and finally in name. Kelliher was appalled at the sight of junior reserve officers writing out orders to ships of the line, officers who had never been to sea. As a partial corrective, he had us choose, by lot, an order by which we would be assigned short-term assignments on naval ships.

This prospect did not seem onerous, and indeed it had its own interest, especially since the first two chosen were allowed to proceed with open orders, to be written more or less as they chose. Unfortunately for me, the third in line, my immediate predecessor wrote his own orders to include an extended spell of stateside leave, to the dismay of Captain Kelliher. Needless to say, the offender was assigned full-time sea duty. But his offense affected me in that I was no longer allowed the option to proceed as I chose. I was assigned directly to temporary duty with the staff of Admiral Spruance, who was in command of the Fifth Fleet, and located aboard the cruiser *Indianapolis*. By this time in the island-hopping campaigns, Halsey with the Third Fleet and Spruance with the Fifth Fleet were alternating commanders, with many ships overlapping in both forces.

I was, of course, already well-acquainted with Spruance, and I also knew other members of his operations staff. I spent four weeks on the *Indianapolis*, followed by a week on a new battleship and a week on a destroyer before returning to Pearl Harbor. Sea duty, as such, was not onerous, and I mainly recall the hours of boredom. But it was on the *Indianapolis* that I had my one and only experience near any shooting. During the assault on Kwajalein Atoll in the Marshall Islands (February 1944), the cruiser participated in bombarding the landing beaches, and we were close in enough to hear the guns and see the fires. This was the extent of my involvement with guns, and my direct observation of war's effects was limited to one wounded Japanese soldier or sailor who was brought aboard the ship for medical treatment, only to die and be buried at sea.

In my weeks on the *Indianapolis*, I observed Admiral Spruance in a setting quite different from that which had described his role as chief of staff only a year or so earlier. On board, Spruance was commander, Fifth Fleet, with a staff of his own. And I was led to draw comparisons with Admiral C. W. Nimitz, as a commander, administrative organizer, and leader. Spruance does not stand up well in some important aspects of this comparison. Nimitz, in sharp contrast with Spruance, did not work very hard; there was no sense of a work ethic there. He took long lunch breaks and enjoyed playing horseshoes and engaging in social chatter. But Nimitz was, on balance, a better leader than Spruance for a very elementary reason. He had an ability to pick men, like Spruance (and McMorris, Carter, and others), as senior staff members and to delegate to them appropriate shares in responsibility. By contrast, Spruance, himself a model chief of staff, apparently lacked an ability to pick senior assistants. His senior staff was, to me, barely up to minimal standards for competence. As a result, Spruance, as commander, was saddled with almost all of the responsibilities that fell to the Fifth Fleet headquarters. As we know, of course, Spruance proved himself in battle; but the merits here go to Spruance alone, not to an organization.

VI. *On to Guam*

As I noted earlier, my responsibilities increased as the fleet expanded, along with the headquarters staff. As the highest rank among the four plot officers, I was relieved of watch duty early, and my designation was changed to that of assistant operations officer, with a desk of my own. Fleet operations was the action arm or agency of the whole headquarters. When a grand strategy was chosen, when plans were made and selected, there fell to operations the tasks of assignment and allocation.

Our office chose the ships to assign to that or this fleet, task force, division, or area command. We sent orders directly to ships, telling them to report for operational control to particular commanders. Our office determined which ships returned to which ports for repairs and on what dates. Participation in this operational enterprise for the whole Pacific theater was exciting and interesting, and it represented a major extension beyond the record-keeping chores that I had assumed on arrival in early 1942, a time that seemed a long time back by war's end.

For more than three years I had seen men, whom I had come to know quite well and whom I respected, make central decisions that would affect the lives of thousands of others. I knew these decision makers as ordinary men, little or no any different from the rest of us. They were simply doing the best they could given the situations into which they were placed. Had they all been like Roscoe Good, things might have been different for me, since Good was, indeed, a "superior" man in many respects. But observing quite ordinary persons making decisions critical to so many lives gave me a sense of the relative importance of things that I have never lost. This experience was surely important in my education. And, as I have noted in another chapter, this experience allowed me to relegate to the third order of smalls most matters that seem to occupy the minds of so many members of the academies of the land. And, of course, the enterprise of participation in decisions of operational command gave me personal confidence that has served me in good stead throughout a long career.

By late 1944, I had been on the staff for two and one-half years, and, indeed, if measured by time alone, I was quite "senior" given the turnover rate of most regular navy officers. Surprisingly, this "seniority" was widely respected on the staff itself, and reserve officers who were formally my superiors in rank were placed under my overall supervision. In December 1944, for the first time since early 1942 and before reporting to the staff, I was granted home leave. And after a few weeks in Tennessee, I returned to Pearl Harbor to participate in the movement of advance headquarters to Guam, where we remained until war's end. A staff was left at Makalapa, but, at least in operations, we essentially shifted all activities westward.

Sometime before the shift, a fortunate event happened. Captain James (Jimmy) Carter, our former Naval War College instructor, was appointed to head up the operations staff. We were, of course, delighted to renew our acquaintance, and I am sure that Carter himself took considerable pride in seeing that two of "his boys" had survived and prospered in the tasks for which he trained us. The senior staff had also expanded with the size of the fleet. And, as reorganization took place in preparations for the move to Guam, Carter was promoted to the little-used rank of commodore and his title changed to, chief of staff for operations. Directly beneath Commodore Carter, Captain Harold Krick took over as operations officer. As assistant operations officer, I reported directly to Krick, but I maintained contact also with Carter. Harold Krick was a true gentleman who had confidence in himself while at the same time remaining fully conscious of his own limitations. With Commodore Carter and Captain Krick, the operations staff in Guam was, indeed, a "happy ship" for the last nine months of the war. The hassles, snafus, and foul-ups that had seemed so frequent at Makalapa did not arise. This relative tranquillity was, of course, partially due to the commonly shared knowledge that the war was winding down. But it was also due to the presence of mutual respect between the senior and the junior staffs.

Carl Soden, who had been a high-school football coach in Kansas before the war, was the only member of the original four who had shared with me all of the stages since midshipmen's school in New York in 1941. By war's end, the two of us were among the most "senior" of the whole of Admiral Nimitz's staff, as measured in months-on-board. This shared experience, along with other compatible interests, provided the basis for a personal friendship that has continued. Soden is the only person from my "easy war" years with whom I have maintained contact. Any autobiographical account on my part would be seriously incomplete with no mention of his role as my compatriot, in matters both military and beyond, some of the latter being best left unreported here.

By the spring of 1945 the European war was over; only the Pacific war remained. The world's attention shifted in our direction after four years of neglect. There were several effects on my own experience. Naval forces from the Atlantic theater, including major ships from the British navy, joined the Pacific fleet under Nimitz's command. And I found that my own chores had somehow expanded to include several visits of welcome to flagships that put in at Guam en route to their final assignments. To be piped aboard a ship of the British navy—and to be offered a gin and squash in the wardroom, in the morning—meant that my world had indeed been very substantially enlarged.

On one such occasion I was authorized, as a welcoming gesture, to invite eleven British officers of their own choosing to a formal officers' club dance at our headquarters. The local naval hospital, Guam, was directed to provide twelve nurses as party partners. The twelfth nurse was, of course, to be my recompense for my role as host to the visitors. Suffice it here to say only that good times were had by all.

As attention shifted to our war, and especially as the dangers of enemy exposure lessened, the journalists sought to make theater visits. By this time (1945), Nimitz and the navy had come to be fully conscious of public relations, and, at our advance headquarters on Guam, sufficient space was allotted for visiting journalists who were provided lodging and food at the level of staff officers. We were forced to live with this alien breed.

I learned perhaps too much from this experience, and I became perhaps too prejudiced by the long exposure to an undisciplined set of persons in unfamiliar surroundings. But let me say that the group variously assembled at Guam over the course of several months in 1945 was the most obnoxious assortment of persons with whom I have ever been closely associated. They were, almost to a man or woman, surly, crude, loud, inconsiderate, alcoholic, arrogant, and insensitive. I realize the unfairness of guilt by association. But some judgments must be made by group identification. I have known farmers, country folk, naval personnel (officer and enlisted), undergraduate and graduate students, professors, economists, philosophers, bureaucrats, business men and women, southerners, easterners, westerners, Italians, British, German, Japanese, and many, many others over a long and interesting career. Of all the groups I have encountered, I place journalists at the bottom of my listing. These persons are, as a group, those with whom I should least prefer to share an island or an island headquarters in the Western Pacific, then or now.

VII. *War's End*

After the Battle of Midway, there was no uncertainty as to the ultimate outcome of the Pacific war. But there were many questions unanswered concerning when and how victory would come to be accomplished. As the attrition went on, month by month, year by year, we came to have increasing respect for Japanese tenacity, and the final assault of the Japanese main islands was predicted to be both bloody and protracted. By early 1945, there was no Japanese navy, and the size of the submarine fleet was minimal. With Okinawa seized, the island-hopping campaign was done, and preparations were made to implement the long-held plan for the main island invasion.

Operational attention came to be focused almost exclusively on troop transport, landing craft, and supply, along with the organization of support forces in offshore bombardment and in carrier air strikes. The main assault was scheduled for November 1945. And this date meant that both troop and ship movements commenced in late spring and early summer. In Fleet operations these tasks occupied all of our time during those months, but we felt that the organizational and assignment processes were well in hand, at least at our level of responsibility.

I was, personally, sufficiently close to the planning and organization of this major assault to have a sense for the magnitude of the effort. We knew how the war would end; but we dreaded the loss of life that seemed ahead of us, both for military personnel on our side and theirs and for the Japanese civilian population which had already suffered the fire bombing. Anyone who had a feel for the costs of the assault to come can only describe as "imbecilic" the tiresome and continuing postwar condemnations of President Truman and the United States for using the nuclear bomb to end the war. A decision to proceed with the assault while holding the bomb would have been criminal. The failure of Truman's critics to consider the alternative to his choice must reflect either irresponsible stupidity or deliberate use of emotional argument for ideological purpose.

But, again, I stray from my narrative into areas of discourse beyond my ken. I played a small role in the war's end, and I can provide a brief account.

I did not know that a war-ending weapon was anticipated. I knew that in Oak Ridge, Tennessee, there were rumors of a new sort of weapon that would have major impact. But I knew this from my trip back home in December 1944, not from any filter through operations on Guam. I do not think that there were more than a very few, very senior officers on Admiral Nimitz's whole staff who were privy to the atomic experiments. My guess, and only a guess, would be that, at the most, three to five members of the senior staff may have been partially informed.

I do know only that in July 1945 our office received a message from COMINCH more or less as follows: "Direct *Indianapolis* proceed Mare Island for special cargo and, when loaded, proceed at flank speed to Saipan for unloading." The *Indianapolis*, on which I had spent some weeks in 1944, was completing repairs in California and, as I recall, was at sea locally for shakedown, when the message came. I recall being a bit puzzled by the rather unusual order, but one of us in the office proceeded to write out the required dispatch. (I cannot recall whether or not I actually wrote out the dispatch or whether I saw it cross my desk as written by someone else.) The order from COMINCH was unusual because, upon completion of stateside repairs, large ships would normally have been directed or allowed to stop over for a few days at Pearl Harbor before proceeding to the Western Pacific. But I made no connection between the unusual order and the Saipan location, which was that of the airbase from which the B-29 raids on Japan were launched.

The bomb worked; the Japanese announced surrender. And, it was some days later, and only then, that I made a connection between all this and the *Indianapolis*. After offloading the materials in Saipan, the cruiser reported to port director, Guam, for routing to Leyte Gulf, Philippines. Tragically, it did not finish the trip. Knowing of war's end, the ship's captain failed to follow standard zigzag procedures, and, not knowing of war's end, the commander of a straggler Japanese submarine chanced upon a fine target on a moonlit night. The *Indianapolis* sank with major loss of life; many of those who died were my acquaintances. The failure to establish radio contact before sinking prevented possible rescue efforts.

When we first heard about the *Indianapolis* sinking and before we knew about the submarine, I remember, we were surprised by the unusual order and the Saipan destination. And it is indicative of my state of knowledge of things atomic that I then surmised that perhaps the special cargo was indeed so dangerous that residues somehow "burned through" and caused the sinking.

Those hectic days immediately after the Japanese announcement of surrender produced one small dashed expectation. Initially, plans were made to transport Admiral Nimitz and several of his staff members, fifteen in all, to Tokyo Bay by ship for the formal surrender ceremonies on the USS *Missouri*. Due to our long extended tour of duty on the staff, both Soden and I, although junior officers, were selected to be included in the fifteen chosen to make the trip. But this participation in history was dashed when a change in plans necessitated that the admiral and a much reduced group should fly to Tokyo Bay rather than proceed by ship. We remained behind and thought about what might have been.

VIII. *Opting Out*

With war's end, I faced a critical decision. I had served in the navy for four full years; it had been my life. I had no position to return to and no family fortune to think about spending. My career options were severely limited. I knew that I could continue in graduate school and work toward my Ph.D. degree; I had sufficient confidence in my ability to think that this task would present no difficulties. Two friends among the reserve officers I had met on the staff had made very provisional offers of job opportunities, one in investment banking, the other in publishing. Neither seemed attractive enough to follow up. But I could have planned to stay in the navy. My record was good; I had been awarded a Bronze Star for distinguished service; and, importantly, I had met all of the very important senior officers, along with many who would become more senior in the years immediately ahead. Both Commodore Carter and Captain Krick, but especially Carter, strongly recommended to me that I consider this option seriously.

The decision was whether to continue in graduate school and to become an economist, and presumably an academician, or to remain in military service as a naval officer. This choice was not an easy one. I remained reluctant to leave the navy. I had enjoyed my years in service; I felt comfortable with the military personality; I enjoyed the social life; I respected the attention to order and the place of standards. But I also recognized that, as a reserve officer rather than an officer in the regular navy, I should always face some residual prejudice. I also recognized that, although technically I was a line officer, the absence of sea duty early would make it more difficult to secure advancement. But the navy did represent ordered security; academia represented maximal uncertainty. As things have turned out for me, I made the correct choice. Had my abilities and talents been such that I could have achieved only run-of-the-mill positions in academia, with little or no research and publication prospects, I am not at all sure that my choice would have been correct. To return to my rankings when I referred to journalists, I should, even today, prefer naval officers, as a group, to academicians.

I did not linger long in Guam after war's end. I flew to Pearl Harbor, and I checked out the operations staff office at Makalapa. I recall being upset by the sloppiness that had been allowed to take over the place in our absence. And I am sure that the junior officers and enlisted ranks on board consider that I had indeed learned from Roscoe Good. Perhaps I had done so, for the "dressing down" I delivered was up to Good's own standards and was not, I suspect, soon forgotten.

After the Makalapa stopover, I flew on to San Francisco in late September 1945. There I joined forces, literally, with Ann Bakke, whom I had met in 1943 when she was working at Hickam Field, Oahu, with the Army Air Transport Command. We were married in

San Francisco in early October, and, after proceeding through Los Angeles, we crossed the country by train to New Orleans, where I reported for temporary duty to await discharge. After a few weeks in New Orleans, we proceeded to Memphis, Tennessee, where I was finally released in November 1945.

I judge it appropriate that I include the United States Navy under *Education* on my biographical forms. For me, the years of service were educational, interesting, and exciting. I came out with considerably more confidence in myself than I had when I entered. But in late 1945 it was time to change streams and to embark on a different career. On balance, it had been, for me, an easy war.

CHAPTER

5

Born-again Economist

I. *Introduction*

I HAVE BEEN TEMPTED to expand this chapter's title to "Born-
again Economist, with a Prophet but No God." Both parts of
this expanded title are descriptive. In the initial presentation at
Trinity University, I was specifically asked to discuss my evolution as
an economist, an assignment that I could not fulfill. I am not a "natural economist" as some of my colleagues are, and I did not
"evolve" into an economist.[1] Instead I sprang full-blown, upon intellectual conversion, after I "saw the light." I shall review this experience below, and I shall defend the implied definition and
classification of who qualifies as an economist.

The second part of my expanded title is related to the first. It is my
own play on the University of Chicago saying of the 1940s that
"there is no god, but Frank Knight is his prophet." I was indeed converted by Frank Knight, but he almost single-mindedly conveyed
the message that there exists no god whose pronouncements deserve elevation to the sacrosanct, be this god within or without the
scientific academy. Everything, everyone, anywhere, anytime—all
is open to challenge and criticism. There is a moral obligation to

1. See James M. Buchanan, "The Qualities of a Natural Economist," in *Democracy and Public Choice*, ed. Charles Rowley (New York: Blackwell, 1987), 9–19.

reach one's own conclusions, even if this sometimes means expos-
ing the prophet whom you have elevated to intellectual guruship.

In chapter 1 I identified two persons who were dominant intellectual influences on my own methodology, selection of subject
matter, attitude toward scholarship, positive analysis, and normative position. One of these, Knut Wicksell, influenced me exclusively through his ideas. I used the occasion of my Nobel Prize
lecture (1986) to trace the relation between Wicksell's precursory
foundations and later developments in the theory of public choice,
and notably in its constitutional economics component with which
I have been most closely associated.[2] By comparison and contrast,
this chapter offers me the opportunity, even if indirectly, to explore
more fully the influence of the second person identified, Frank H.
Knight, an influence that was exerted both through his ideas and
through a personal friendship that extended over a full quarter-
century.

II. *Pre-Chicago: Standards without Coherence*

From 1940, I called myself an "economist," as my military records
will indicate. I did so because, after graduating from Middle Tennessee State Teachers College in June 1940, I was awarded a graduate fellowship in economics at the University of Tennessee, for the
academic year 1940–41, and I earned a master's degree in 1941. By
the academic counters, I took courses labeled "economics," and I
made good grades. But as I have noted, however, I learned little or
no "economics" in my preferred definition during that Knoxville
year. I surveyed the workings and structures of the institutions of
Roosevelt's New Deal; I came to understand central banking theory
and policy; I learned something about taxing and budgeting processes; I learned a bit of elementary statistics, especially in practice.
But neither in any of these courses, nor in prior undergraduate
experience, did I have proper exposure to the central principle of
market organization. I remained blissfully ignorant of the coor-
dinating properties of decentralized market process, an ignorance

2. James M. Buchanan, "The Constitution of Economic Policy," *American Economic Review*, 77 (June 1987): 243–50.

that made me vulnerable to quasi-Marxist arguments and explanations about economic history and economic reality but also guaranteed that my mind was an open slate when I did finally get the exposure in question.

During the Knoxville year, I did learn to appreciate the dedication of the research scholar though my association with Charles P. White, whose course in research methods was the intellectual high point. White instilled in me the moral standards of the research process. My experience with him, as both a graduate student and a research assistant, gave me something that seems so often absent in the training of the economists of the postwar decades, whose technology so often outdistances their norms for behavior.

By subject matter, by terminology, and with a bit of technique, I left Knoxville as an "economist," but I lacked the coherence of vision of the economic process that I should now make the sine qua non for anyone who proposes to attach such a label to himself. I have often wondered whether or not I was relatively alone in my ignorance, or whether something akin to my experience has been shared by others who purport to pass as professional economists without the foggiest notion of what they are about.

III. *Chicago, 1946*

I enrolled in the University of Chicago for the Winter Quarter, 1946. I had chosen the University of Chicago without much knowledge about its faculty in economics. I was influenced almost exclusively by an undergraduate teacher in political science, C. C. Sims, who had earned a doctorate at Chicago in the late 1930s. Sims impressed on me the intellectual ferment of the university, the importance of ideas, the genuine life of the mind that was present at the institution. His near-idyllic sketch appealed to me, and I made the plunge into serious study for the first time in my life. In retrospect, I could not have made a better selection. Sims was precisely on target in conveying the intellectual excitement of the University of Chicago, an excitement that remains, to this day, unmatched anywhere else in the world.

During the first quarter, I took courses with Frank Knight, T. W. Schultz, and Simeon Leland. I was among the very first group of graduate students who returned to the academy after discharge from military service during World War II. We swelled the ranks of the graduate classes, at Chicago and elsewhere.

Within a few short weeks, perhaps by mid-February 1946, I had undergone a conversion in my understanding of how an economy operates. For the first time I was able to think in terms of the ordering principle of a market economy. The stylized model for the working of the competitive structure gave me the benchmark for constructive criticism of the economy to be observed. For the first time I was, indeed, an economist.

I attribute this conversion directly to Frank Knight's teachings, which perhaps raises more new questions than it answers. Knight was not a systematic instructor. More importantly, he remained ambiguous in his own interpretation as to what economics is all about. He was never able to shed off the allocating-maximizing paradigm which tends to distract attention from the coordination paradigm that I have long deemed central to the discipline.[3] But Knight's economics was a curious amalgam of these partially conflicting visions. And, for me, the organizational emphasis was sufficient to relegate the allocative thrust into a place of secondary relevance. In this respect I was fortunate in my ignorance. Had I received "better" pre-Chicago training in economics, as widely interpreted, I would have scarcely been able to elevate the coordination principle to the central place it has occupied in my thinking throughout my research career. Like so many of my peers, aside from the few who were exposed early to Austrian theory, I might have remained basically an allocationist.

There are subtle, but important, differences between the allocationist-maximization and the catallactic-coordination paradigm in terms of the implications for normative evaluation of institutions. In particular the evaluation of the market order may depend critically on which of these partially conflicting paradigms remains dominant in one's stylized vision. To the allocationist, the market is efficient, *if it works*. His test of the market becomes the comparison with the abstract ideal defined in his logic. To the

---

3. For an extended discussion of Knight's ambiguity in this respect, see James M. Buchanan, "The Economizing Element in Knight's Ethical Critique of Capitalist Order," *Ethics*, 98, no. 1 (October 1987): 61–75.

catallactist, the market coordinates the separate activities of self-seeking persons, *without the necessity of detailed political direction*. The test of the market is the comparison with its institutional alternative, that of politicized decision making.

There is, of course, no necessary implication of the differing paradigms for identifying the normative stance of the practicing economists. There are many modern economists who remain firm supporters of the market order while at the same time they remain within the maximizing paradigm. I submit here, however, that there remain relatively few economists whose vision is dominated by the catallactic perspective on market order who are predominately critics of such an order. Once the relevant comparison becomes that between the workings of the market, however imperfect this may seem, and the workings of its political alternative, there must indeed be very strong offsetting sources of evaluation present.

The apparent digression of the preceding paragraphs is important for my narrative and for an understanding of how my conversion by Frank Knight influenced my research career after Chicago. Those of us who entered graduate school in the immediate postwar years were all socialists, of one sort or another. Some of us were what I have elsewhere called "libertarian socialists," who placed a high residual value on individual liberty, but who simply did not understand the principle of market coordination. We were always libertarians first, socialists second. And we tended to be grossly naïve in our thinking about political alternatives. To us, the idealized attractions of populist democracy seemed preferable to those of the establishment controlled economy. It was this sort of young socialist, in particular, who was especially ready for immediate conversion upon exposure to teachings that transmitted the principle of market coordination.[4]

An understanding of this principle enabled us to concentrate our long-held antiestablishment evaluative norms on politics and governance, and at least to open up the prospect that economic interac-

4. For a discussion of two kinds of socialism in this setting, see the title essay in James M. Buchanan, *Liberty, Market and State: Political Economy in the 1980s* (Brighton, Eng.: Wheatsheaf Books, 1985; New York: New York University Press, 1985).

tion, in the limit anyway, need not embody the exercise of man's power over man. By our libertarian standards, politics had always been deemed to fail. Now, by these same standards, market may, just may, not involve exploitation.

An important element in Knight's economics was his emphasis on the organizational structure of markets, and it was this emphasis that elevated the coordination principle to center stage, despite Knight's continued obeisance to economizing-maximizing, as such. Once attention is drawn to a structure, to process, and away from resources, goods, and services, as such, many of the technical trappings of orthodox economic theory fall away. Here Knight's approach became institutional, in the proper meaning of this term.

It is useful at this point to recall that Frank Knight's career shared a temporal dimensionality with the seminal American institutionalists: Clarence Ayres, John R. Commons, Thorstein Veblen. He treated their technical economics with derision, but he shared with them an interest in the structure of social and economic interaction. Knight did not, himself, extend his institutional inquiry much beyond the seminal work on human wants that exposed some of the shallow presuppositions of economic orthodoxy. He did not, save in a few passing references, examine the structure of politics, considered as the only alternative to markets.

IV. *Public Choice and the Catallactic Paradigm*

Public choice is the inclusive term that describes the extension of analysis to the political alternatives to markets. It seems highly unlikely that this extension could have been effectively made by economists who viewed the market merely as an allocative mechanism, quite independently of its political role in reducing the range and scope of politicized activity. I can, of course, speak here only of my own experience, but it seems doubtful if I could have even recognized the Wicksellian message had not Knight's preparatory teachings of the coordination principle paved the way.

The point may be illustrated by the related, but yet quite distinct, strands of modern inquiry summarized under the two rubrics: "Social Choice" and "Public Choice." I have elsewhere identified the two central elements in public choice theory as (1) the conceptualization of politics as exchange, and (2) the model of *homo economicus.*[5] The second of these elements is shared with social choice theory, which seeks to ground social choices on the values of utility-maximizing individuals. Where social choice theory and public choice theory differ, and dramatically, lies in the first element noted. Social choice theory does not conceptualize politics as complex exchange; rather politics is implicitly or explicitly modeled on the age-old conception that there must exist some unique and hence discoverable "best" result. This element in social choice theory, from Arrow on, stems directly from the allocative paradigm in orthodox economics, and the maximization of the social welfare function becomes little more than the extension of the standard efficiency calculus to the aggregative economy.

By contrast, the extension of the catallactic paradigm, the emphasis on the theory of *exchange,* rather than allocation, to politics immediately calls attention to the institutional structure of political decision making. Without Frank Knight as teacher, and as role model, would Knut Wicksell's great work have been discovered by the fledgling economist that I was in 1948? I have strong reasons for doubt on this score.

V. *The Evolution of Confidence*

When I reflect on my own experiences over a tolerably long academic career, I come back again and again to identifiable events and persons who built up or bolstered my confidence, who made me, always an outsider, feel potentially competent among my academic peers. The first such event came with the release of academic records at the end of my second year at Middle Tennessee State Teachers College in 1938. My name led all the rest. For the first time I realized that, despite my rural origins, my day student status, and my graduation from a tiny struggling high school, I could compete with the town students, the live-in students, and all those whose earlier education was acknowledged to be superior to mine.

A second such event occurred in January 1942 when I finished a

5. James M. Buchanan, "The Public Choice Perspective," *Economia delle scelte publiche,* 1 (January 1983): 7–15.

three-month stint as a midshipman and was commissioned an ensign in the United States Naval Reserve. Again, despite my Tennessee heritage, despite the mediocre academic experience at both Middle Tennessee and the University of Tennessee, I ranked sixth or seventh in a midshipman class of some six hundred college and university graduates from across the land. The Tennessee country boy could, indeed, hold his own.

After a successful, interesting, exciting, and easy four years on active military duty in the Pacific theater of war, which I spent for the most part on the staff of Admiral Nimitz at Pearl Harbor and at Guam, my confidence was once again put to the test when I entered graduate school at the University of Chicago in January 1946. Here the test was of a totally different dimension. I knew that I could compete successfully in terms of the ordinary criteria—academic grades, degrees, and honors. I do not recall ever entertaining the slightest doubt about my ability to finish doctoral requirements. What I did not know was whether or not I could go beyond these criteria and enter the narrowed ranks of producing scholars who could generate ideas worthy of the serious attention of their peers.

At this point, Frank H. Knight again enters my narrative. Had my Chicago exposure been limited to the likes of Jacob Viner and Milton Friedman, both of whom were also my teachers there, I doubt that I should have ever emerged from the familiarly large ranks of Ph.D.'s with no or few publications. Jacob Viner, the classically erudite scholar whose self-appointed task in life seemed to be that of destroying confidence in students, and Milton Friedman, whose dominating intellectual brilliance in argument and analysis was such as to relegate the student to the role of fourth-best imitation—these were not the persons who encouraged anyone to believe that he or she, too, might eventually have ideas worthy of merit.

Frank Knight was dramatically different. In the classroom, he came across as a man engaged always in a search for ideas. He puzzled over principles, from the commonsensical to the esoteric, and he stood continuously dismayed at the arrogance of those who spouted forth the learned wisdom. Knight gave us who bothered to listen the abiding notion that all is up for intellectual grabs, that much of what paraded as truth was highly questionable, and that the hallmark of a scholar was his or her courage in cutting through the intellectual haze. The willingness to deny all gods, the courage to hold nothing as sacrosanct—these were the qualities of mind and character that best describe Frank Knight. And gods, as I use the term here, include the authorities in one's own discipline, as well as those who claim domain over other dimensions of truth. Those of us who were so often confused in so many things were bolstered by this Knightian stance before all gods. Only gradually, and much later, did we come to realize that in these qualities it was Frank Knight, not his peers, who attained the rank of genius.

As he was the first to acknowledge, Frank Knight was not a clever or brilliant thinker. He was an inveterate puzzler; but his thought process probed depths that the scholars about him could not realize even existed. To Knight, things were never so simple as they seemed, and he remained, at base, tolerant in the extreme because he sensed the elements of truth in all principles.

There were many graduate students, both in my own cohort and before and after my time, who could not take in or relate to the Knightian stance before the gods. To these "outsiders," Knight seemed to be a bumbling and confused teacher, whose writings mirrored his thought and whose primary attribute seemed to be intellectual incoherence. To a few of us, what seemed confusion to others came across as profundity, actual or potential, and despite the chasm that we acknowledged to exist between his mind and our own, Knight left us with the awful realization that if we did not have the simple courage to work out our own answers, we were vulnerable to victimization by false gods.

My own understanding, appreciation, and admiration for Frank Knight were aided and abetted by the development, early on, of a close personal relationship. Some three or four weeks after enrollment in his course, I visited Knight's jumbled office. What was expected to be a five-minute talk stretched over two hours, to be matched several times over the two and one-half years at Chicago, and beyond. He took an interest in me because we shared several dimensions of experience. Both of us were country boys, reared in agricultural poverty, well aware of the basic drudgery of rural existence, but also appreciative of the independence of a life on the land. Knight left his native Illinois in his teens for rudimentary college instruction in my home state of Tennessee, and he enrolled in graduate studies at the University of Tennessee, where I, too, had first commenced graduate work. These common threads of experience established, for me, a relationship that I shared with no other professor. We shared other interests, including an appreciation of the gloomy poetry of Thomas Hardy, and the fun of the clever off-color joke.

Of course, I was a one-way beneficiary of this relationship. Knight was, for me, the adviser who told me not to waste my time taking formal courses in philosophy, who corrected my dissertation grammar in great detail, who became the role model who has never been replaced or even slightly dislodged over a long academic career. In trying to assess my own development, I find it impossible to imagine what I might have been and become without exposure to Frank Knight.

Let me return to confidence, lest I digress too much. Both T. W. Schultz and Earl J. Hamilton deserve inclusion in this narrative account. Schultz encouraged students by his expressed willingness to locate potential merit in arguments that must have often approached the absurd. I was never a formal student of Earl Hamilton. I did not enroll in his economic history courses at Chicago. Nonetheless, during my last year at Chicago, 1948, Hamilton sought me out and took a direct personal interest in my prospects. As with Knight, the sharing of common experience in rural poverty created a personal bonding, supplemented in this case by a passion for baseball, reflected by trips to both Cubs and White Sox home games. Hamilton enjoyed giving advice to those whom he singled out for possible achievement, and, with me, two separate imperatives stand out in recall: the potential payoff to hard work, and the value of mastery of foreign languages.

Perhaps Earl J. Hamilton's most important influence on my career came after 1948, during his tenure as editor of the *Journal of Political Economy*. First of all, he forced me to follow up on his recommendation about language skills by sending to me French, German, and Italian books for review. Secondly, he handled my early submissions of articles with tolerance, understanding, and encouragement rather than with brutal or carping rejections that might, in my case, have proved fatal to further effort. Hamilton was, indeed, a tough editor, and each and every article that I finally published during his tenure was laboriously transformed, and dramatically pared down, through the process of multiple revise-resubmit stages. Without Hamilton as an editor who cared, my subsequent writing style would never have attained the economy it possesses, and my willingness to venture into subject matter beyond the boundaries of the orthodox might have been choked off. With Earl J. Hamilton as editor, by the mid-1950s, I had several solid papers on the record, a number sufficient to enable me to accept the occasional rejection slip with equanimity rather than despair.

I noted earlier how Friedman's analytic brilliance exerted a negative effect on those whom he instructed. An event occurred early in my post-Chicago years that tended to erase this negative influence by placing Milton Friedman, too, among the ranks of those who take intellectual tumbles. A relatively obscure scholar, Cecil G. Phipps, of the University of Florida, located and exposed a logical error in one of Friedman's papers, an error that Friedman graciously acknowledged.[6] To this day, I have never told Milton how this simple event contributed so massively to my self-confidence.

VI. *The Relatively Absolute Absolute*

I have already discussed how Frank Knight's willingness to challenge all authority—intellectual, moral, or scientific—indirectly established a confidence in those for whom he served as role model. Any account of such an influence would be seriously incomplete, and indeed, erroneous, if the philosophical stance suggested were one of relativism-cum-nihilism against the claim of any and all authority. It is at precisely this point that Frank Knight directly taught me the philosophical principle that has served me so well over so many years and in so many applications. This principle is that of the *relatively absolute absolute*, which allows for a philosophical way station between the extremes of absolutism on the one hand and relativism on the other, both of which are to be rejected.

Acceptance of this principle necessarily requires that there exist a continuing tension between the forces that dictate adherence to and acceptance of authority and those very qualities that define freedom

6. Cecil G. Phipps, "Friedman's 'Welfare' Effects," *Journal of Political Economy*, 60 (August 1952): 332–34. Milton Friedman, "A Reply," *Journal of Political Economy*, 60 (August 1952): 334–36.

of thought and inquiry. Knight's expressed willingness to challenge all authority, the characteristic of his intellectual stance that I have emphasized earlier in this chapter, was embedded within a wisdom that also recognized the relevance of tradition, in ideas, in manners, and in institutions. This wisdom dictates that, for most purposes and most of the time, prudent behavior consists in acting as if the authority that exists does indeed possess legitimacy. The principle of the relatively absolute absolute requires that we adhere to and accept the standards of established or conventional authority in our ordinary behavior, whether this be personal, scientific, or political, while at the same time and at still another (and "higher") level of consciousness we call all such standards into question, even to the extent of proposing change.

In relation to my own work this principle of the relatively absolute absolute is perhaps best exemplified in the critically important distinction between the postconstitutional and the constitutional levels of political interaction. More generally, the distinction is that between choosing among strategies of play in a game that is defined by a set of rules, and choosing among alternative sets of rules. To the chooser of strategies under defined rules, the rules themselves are to be treated as relatively absolute absolutes, as constraints which are a part of the existential reality but which, at the same time, may be subject to evaluation, modification, and change. In this extension and application of the Knightian principle to the political constitution, and particularly by way of the analogy with the choices of strategies and rules of ordinary games, I was stimulated and encouraged by my colleague at the University of Virginia, Rutledge Vining, who himself had also been strongly influenced by the teachings of Frank Knight.

VII. *Why "Better than Plowing"?*

I wrote the summary autobiographical essay, "Better than Plowing" (chapter 1), in 1985, and I borrowed the title directly from Frank Knight, who used it to describe his own attitude toward a career in the academy. To me, the title seemed also descriptive both for that essay and for this book. This title does, I think, convey my sense of comparative evaluation as between "employment" in the academy and in the economy beyond. To me, this title also suggests, even if somewhat vaguely, the sheer luck of those of us who served in the academy during the years of the baby boom educational explosion, luck that was translated into rents of magnitudes beyond imaginable dreams.

To my surprise, constructive critics have challenged the appropriateness of the "Better than Plowing" title for my more general autobiographical essay. To these critics, this title seems too casual, too much a throw-away phrase, too flippant a description of a research career that, objectively and externally considered, seems to have embodied central purpose or intent. The Trinity University invitation provided me with an opportunity to respond to these critics, while, at the same time, offering additional insights into my development as an economist.

The many books and papers that I wrote and published between 1949 and 1990 make up an objective reality that is "there" for all to read and interpret as they choose. These words and pages exist in some space analogous to the Popperian third world. There is a surprising coherence in this record that I can recognize as well or better than any interpretative critical biographer. As Robert Tollison and I have suggested in our analysis of autobiography, the autobiographer, himself, is in possession of a record over and beyond that which is potentially available to any biographer.[7] The person whose acts created the objective record lives with the subjective record itself. And such a person, as autobiographer, would be immoral if he relied on the objective record to impute to his life's work a purpose-oriented coherence that had never emerged into consciousness.

I recognize, of course, that my own research-publication record may be interpreted as the output of a methodological *and* normative individualist, whose underlying purpose has always been to further philosophical support for individual liberty. In subjective recall, however, this motivational thrust has never informed my conscious work effort. I have, throughout my career and with only a few exceptions, sought to clarify ambiguities and confusions, to clear up neglected pockets of analysis in the received arguments of fellow economists, social scientists, and philosophers. To the extent that

7. James M. Buchanan and Robert D. Tollison, "A Theory of Truth in Autobiography," *Kyklos*, 39 (1986): 507–17.

conscious motivation has entered these efforts, it has always been the sheer enjoyment of working out ideas, of creating the reality that is reflected finally in the finished manuscript. My own proof of normative disinterest lies in my failure to be interested in what happens once a manuscript is a finished draft, a failure that accounts for my sometimes inattention to choice of publisher, promotional details, and the potentials for either earnings or influence.

I look on myself as being much closer in spirit to the artist who creates on canvas or stone than to the scientist who discovers only that which he accepts as existing independently of his actions. And I should reject, and categorically, any affinity with the preacher who writes or speaks for the express and only purpose of persuading others to accept his prechosen set of values.

In all of this, once again, Frank Knight has served as my role model. His famous criticism of Pigou's road case exemplifies.[8] By introducing property rights, Knight enabled others to see the whole Pigovian analysis in a new light. Something was, indeed, created in the process. I like to think that, perhaps, some of my own works on public debt, opportunity cost, earmarked taxes, clubs, ordinary politics, and constitutional rules may have effected comparable shifts in perspective. The fact that these efforts have been commonly characterized by a reductionist thrust embodying an individualist methodology is explained, very simply, by my inability to look at the world through any window other than an individualist one.

It is as if the artist who only has red paint produces pictures that are only that color. Such an artist does not choose to paint red pictures and then, instrumentally, purchase red paints. Instead, the artist uses the instruments at hand to do what he can, and must, do, while enjoying himself immensely in the process. The fact that others are able to secure new insights with the aid of his creations, and that this, in turn, provides the artist with a bit of bread—this gratuitous result enables the artist, too, to entitle his autobiographical essay "Better than Plowing."

---

8. Frank H. Knight, "Fallacies in the Interpretation of Social Cost," *Quarterly Journal of Economics*, 38 (1924): 582–606. Reprinted in *The Ethics of Competition* (London: Allen and Unwin, 1935), 217–36.

6

Italian Retrospective

I. *Introduction*

THE FULBRIGHT YEAR in Italy (September 1955-August 1956) was critically important in influencing the development of my interest in political decision structures and processes and particularly in the participation by individuals in these structures and processes. It is not exaggeration to state that the Italian year allowed me to cross the threshold into what would much later come to be called the research program in "public choice," and, particularly, the more narrowly defined program in "constitutional political economy."

The Italian year was also important in setting off and stimulating my interest in the theory of public debt, which came to be the focus of my efforts immediately on my return to Virginia in 1956. In a more comprehensive, and external, assessment of my work this public debt effort may be viewed, as it has been by some critics, as a digression from the direct public choice emphasis, as initially suggested in my pre-Italy papers in 1949 and 1954 and carried forward

The translation of an early version of this chapter was printed under the title, "Ricordo di un anno in Italia," as part of the Italian translation of my *Freedom in Constitutional Contract* (College Station: Texas A & M University Press, 1977). *Libertà nel contratto costituzionale*, ed. di Paolo Martelli (Milan: Arnoldo Mondadori Editore, 1990).

in much of my later work.[1] However, in an internal assessment, the work on public debt falls squarely within the more inclusive research program that describes my career, and particularly with regard to my expressed aim of reducing changes in macroaggregative variables to individually identified utility gains and losses.

I can, indeed, locate precisely the moment when the "theory of public debt burden" became clear to me. This moment occurred near the end of my Italian visit, during a sojourn at the Albergo d'Ingleterra in Rome. Even more precisely, the moment of "enlightenment" came while I was walking down the marbled stairs between floors on the occasion of a mechanical failure of the lift. I treasure the memory of that moment because we rarely are able to locate the emergence of ideas so distinctly. I waxed so enthusiastic over the "discovery" that I commenced writing what later became my book on stationery picked up from the hotel writing room.[2]

II. *Before Italy*

I commenced my professional academic career as a straightforward public finance economist, whose concerns were about taxes, budgets, federalism, and fiscal policy. The public finance that I learned included goodly doses of Edgeworth-Pigou normative utilitarianism, of Marshallian incidence theory (of taxes, not of spending), of Keynesian inspired denial of debt burden. In this public finance orthodoxy for the 1940s, government was implicitly postulated to be exogenous to the economy or, when normative discourse commenced, was presumed to take the form of a monolithic and benevolent decision maker. In one of my first papers, I had challenged this presumption; in so doing I had already been stimulated and sup-

1. James M. Buchanan, "The Pure Theory of Public Finance: A Suggested Approach," *Journal of Political Economy*, 57 (December 1949): 496–505. James M. Buchanan, "Social Choice, Democracy, and Free Markets," *Journal of Political Economy*, 62 (April 1954): 114–24. Reprinted in James M. Buchanan, *Fiscal Theory and Political Economy* (Chapel Hill: University of North Carolina Press, 1960), 75–89; and in *Public Finance: Selected Readings*, ed. Helen Cameron and William Henderson (New York: Random House, 1966), 158–75.
2. James M. Buchanan, *Public Principles of Public Debt* (Homewood, Ill.: Irwin, 1958). Knut Wicksell, *Finanztheoretische Untersuchungen* (Jena: Gustav Fischer, 1896).

ported by Wicksell's seminal effort and by an English translation of De Viti De Marco's *First Principles of Public Finance*.[3]

My motivation in seeking a Fulbright Research Scholarship for study in Italy was a mixture of the scientific and the personal. I did, indeed, want to learn more about what the Italian masters in public finance had written about political decision structures, as these might affect the pattern of results observed. I was curious as to how the Italians had managed to integrate their analyses of taxes and spending, both positive and normative, with the alternative models or theories of collective or political decision making. But I also wanted some exposure to, some involvement in, a European cultural experience. As a Tennessee native whose World War II experience had been exclusively in the Pacific theater and whose graduate training had been in mid-America at Chicago, I sought to "jump over" the cultural atmosphere of the American East, and to acquire, within limits, some sense of the intellectual and cultural sophistication that only Europe seemed to, and did, offer.

Earl J. Hamilton, a professor at Chicago, had encouraged me to seize all opportunities to acquire language skills, and spurred by my initial reactions to De Viti De Marco, I tried to pick up minimal reading competence in Italian. Let me also acknowledge that I estimated my chances for success in the Fulbright competition to be higher in Italy than they might have been for a European year in the United Kingdom.

My application was successful, and from early 1955 I knew that the Italian year was settled. I had minimal personal contacts. Through earlier correspondence, I had exchanged views with Professor Lello Gangemi of Naples, who had encouraged me in my project. My personal assistance in the United States came from a surprising source. I got an unsolicited letter from Professor Oskar Morgenstern of Princeton, whom I had met only once, but who helped me greatly by listing acquaintances of his own whom I might look up when I arrived in Rome. It was Morgenstern who was responsible for my subsequent relationship with both Giannino Parravicini and Sergio Steve.

3. Antonio De Viti De Marco, *First Principles of Public Finance*, trans. E. P. Marget (London: Jonathan Cape, 1936).

III. *Culture Shock*

My wife and I sailed for Naples on the SS *Independence* in September 1955. At Naples, we—the whole group of American Fulbright recipients, professors, scholars, and students—were bused to Perugia, where we were enrolled for a month at the Universitá per Stranieri, with an intense concentration on learning to speak Italian.

We were lodged with the Giugliarelli family, in the oldest part of Perugia, near the center. The rules required that our hosts speak to us only in Italian. The month was personally rewarding because it helped us to get a sense of Italian family life and a taste for authentic Italian cuisine and to enjoy genuine Italian hospitality. Within a day of arrival we were, almost literally, made a part of the family, taking all our meals in the kitchen that served as the household center. My wife learned to cook Italian while I learned Italian conversational skills from a master instructor, Professor Guarnieri. And Perugia itself offered a fine base for the initial weeks of an extended Italian visit. The Umbrian hill towns—Perugia, Assisi, Gubbio, and others—remain, for me, the best of Italy.

In early October 1955 we were ready for Rome, and I was anxious to commence work on the project that had motivated the visit. Housing was difficult to find, and provisionally we found accommodations as paying guests in the lovely home of Signora Laura Guidi, the widow of a professor of Arabic languages at the University of Rome, and herself a distinguished Roman matron. Her home was ideally located in the Aventino, just across the street from the church of San Sabina, and only a short distance from the famous keyhole of the garden that frames St. Peter's across the Tiber. From my desk in the professor's study, surrounded by many volumes of Arabic grammar, I could look across at St. Peter's and reflect on the grandeur that was Catholic Rome.

IV. *Research Setting*

Finding a location where I might conduct my research was even more difficult. I was frustrated early by the limits on days and hours of library opening and on restrictions on the borrowing of books.

After some comparisons of the alternatives available, I settled in at the library of the Bank of Italy, on the Via Nazionale. This library had a good collection of books relevant to my inquiry and, importantly, also kept up to date with journal issues in all languages. In addition the research and clerical staff was cooperative and appreciative of my efforts. In part, my decision to locate at the bank was due to my early contact with Parravicini, who served on the research staff of the bank while, at the same time, holding down the chair of public finance, as professor-in-charge, at the University of Pavia. It was Parravicini who introduced me to the morning ritual of espresso or cappuccino at the nearby bar, always accompanied by good talk on economics.

Officially, I was attached to the University of Rome, but my physical presence there was limited to regular attendance at the seminar organized by Professor Ugo Papi every few weeks, always with presentations by visiting scholars from around the world. These were pleasant and informative occasions, made notably so by the postseminar dinners, always at an excellent restaurant on Piazza Colonna. Professor Papi, even in 1955, was quite a senior figure; I was more impressed by his extensive network of acquaintances among economists worldwide than by his contribution to ongoing discussion. But Papi was, indeed, a fine host figure, and the Italian year would have been less memorable in the absence of those seminars.

In terms of my own research purposes the most helpful Italian scholar was Professor Sergio Steve, who lived and worked in Rome, and whom I had also contacted early as a result of Morgenstern's indirect introduction. Steve remains closer to being a "pure professor" than any Italian I have ever met, and he proved invaluable in pointing me in productive directions. His wide-ranging scholarship and knowledge of the history of doctrine in "scienza delle finanze" saved me from hours of fruitless search.

While in Rome, I also visited with Professor Cesare Cosciani, whose textbook I had read. He was helpful, but my contact with him was limited to one or two visits.

V. *Procedure and Routine*

My research agenda was comprehensive but formless. I carried with me no provisional hypotheses to be tested. I sensed only that the Italian masters in "scienza delle finanze," because of their explicit attention to political decision structures, had worked at a level of analytical sophistication above and beyond that attained by their English-language counterparts. My immediate objective was to *read* the relevant materials, necessarily on a selective basis but broadly enough to give me some grounds for evaluation. My procedure was straightforward. Quite simply, I read and made notes on the trea- tises, books, monographs, and papers by Ferrara, Mazzola, De Viti De Marco, Pantaleoni, Ricca-Salerno, Puviani, Montemartini, Barone, Einaudi, Fasiani, Fubini, Cosciani, Griziotti, De Maria, Arena—and many others. In this process, at least in its early stages, I had no sense of what the structure of a final evaluation of the whole "tradition" might be, or if indeed a final evaluation would be forthcoming at all.

My routine was one of ordered scholarship, perhaps for the one and only time of my whole career. I arrived early at the library, and I worked a long half-day, almost never returning after the siesta, an institution that I came greatly to respect, then and now. Aside from the cappuccino breaks on those days when Parravicini was in resi- dence (he spent two days per week in Pavia), my personal contacts with fellow economists were minimal. I met the other economists of the bank's research staff, but on little other than a cursory basis. I kept my attention on the books, at least sufficiently to satisfy myself that work was being done.

VI. *When in Rome*

I was also *living* in Rome, and enjoying it. Perhaps more than in most cities of the world, there is a categorical distinction there between visiting and living. After two months as paying guests at Signora Guidi's, my wife and I subleased the flat of an economist from FAO (Food and Agriculture Organization) who took an American leave of absence. We moved across the Aventino, to Viale Giotto, only a short distance from Terme di Caracalla, the location of Rome's summer opera.

And we lived as Romans. The hard rolls delivered twice daily to our door spoiled forever our tastes for other breads. My wife made quotidian forays to the local markets, jug in hand, and returned with wines, pastas, fruits, and produce of the campagna. Vini dei Castelli, the wines of the Roman hills, were, for me, introductory to the pleasures of the grape. And the morning snack of the Roman shopper, focaccia or pizza bianca, remains a favorite after decades, so much so that my wife acquires a local reputation for its production wherever we locate for more than a few days.

We wandered about the city; we sampled its wares. We marveled at the delights of the "tavola calda," a glorious Italian precursor of the now ubiquitous fast-food franchise. We located the excellent, the good, the medium, and the bad trattorie; we learned the gustatory rewards of garlic, rosemary, oregano, basil, and so much else that was foreign to the mid-American palate, rewards without which we would now subsist nonexcitingly, if at all.

And, of course, we walked through the monuments of republican, imperial, medieval, and modern Rome, from the forum to the wedding cake. We did not neglect the churches, the museums, the fountains, or the galleries. We fed the communal cats at the Pantheon, those who sought out a bit of winter's sun on raw February days. We were in St. Peter's square on Easter Sunday, when the rain did stop to allow the Pope to appear on the balcony. But we did all this as Romans do, as if we were there rather than merely passing through.

VII. *Beyond the Walls*

Aside from Perugia, my academic experience beyond Rome was limited. (Touristic jaunts are quite another matter; both in the initial year, and later, we visited all of Italy's regions and most of its towns and cities.) I traveled to Naples early, and I presented a seminar at the university under Gangemi's sponsorship. My primary recollection is unrelated to the subject matter; it is about Gangemi's flat which was, literally, lined wall-to-wall with original paintings by Italian artists. And my viewing was accompanied by Gangemi's disarming honesty in admitting that his passion for economics had long since been replaced by that for art.

The primary academic extension of the Roman year was Pavia. As noted, Parravicini was professor-in-charge of the relevant courses at the university, and he invited me to come along for a lecture and/or seminar on, I think, two separate occasions during the year. The professorial chair at the University of Pavia had long been held by Professor Benvenuto Griziotti, who had just retired. Griziotti and his wife, herself a distinguished scholar in the history of economic ideas, entertained us graciously in their home. And they also introduced us to Francesco Forte, who remained in Pavia as Griziotti's very last assistant. Forte was assigned the task (perhaps a chore to him as a very busy young scholar) of acting as our tour guide, host, and life arranger during the whole course of a several-day visit to the Po Valley and its environs. We made the circuit, which included two days in Milan.

The Pavia visit is important for me largely in that it marked the start of my relationship with Francesco Forte, whom we came to know much better in later years, both personally and professionally. The young Francesco Forte of 1956 so impressed me that I subsequently invited him as a visitor to my university in Virginia, from which, in turn, there emerged several coauthored papers. For three decades we have counted Francesco and Carmen Forte among a relatively small number of friends for life.

During my initial year in Italy, 1955–56, I did not know Bruno Leoni, who was professor of political science at Pavia at the time. As I noted earlier, I was only beginning to venture beyond the disciplinary boundaries of economics, including public finance, and I had neither the excuse nor the courage to make research thrusts into legal and political philosophy, domains that later came to command much of my attention. Some five years later than my first Italian visit, and after my initial crossing of the disciplinary threshold, so to speak, I read some of Leoni's seminal pieces, and I subsequently invited him for a Virginia visit. This visit was followed up by my own later visits to Pavia, Stresa, and elsewhere under Leoni's auspices. And I maintained a personal and professional association with Leoni until his tragic death.

VIII. *A Meeting with Luigi Einaudi*

By late spring 1956, I had begun to block out a draft for a lengthy evaluative essay on the whole Italian tradition in "scienza delle finanze."[4] I had expressed to Giannino Parravicini a desire to meet, if at all possible, the only Italian master in the tradition who remained active. Luigi Einaudi had completed his tenure as president of the republic of Italy, and he had retired from both politics and the academy. But Professor Einaudi he remained to all who knew him, and during one of his periods of residence at his villa outside Rome he invited me to meet him. Parravicini accompanied me, and I recall a pleasant afternoon conversation in a sunlit and surprisingly well-stocked library of current periodicals in all languages and many subjects. Small in stature, but majestic in bearing, Einaudi greeted me with courtesy and respect, despite the awesome gulf between one of the free world's most respected leaders and an unknown, uncultured, and young American academic. Most importantly for me, however, was Einaudi's expressed and sincere interest in my research project. He agreed to read my provisional draft essay and to offer comments and suggestions. As soon as I could do so, I sent off a copy of the draft to him, and he did, as promised, make several constructive suggestions. I was perhaps more proud of my ability to make the footnote acknowledgment for Einaudi's assistance than for any other such attribution in any of my writings.

At several of Papi's seminars, I met Professor Gustavo Del Vecchio, who was also of Einaudi's generation, and who was widely respected as one of the most senior economists in Italy. Even though he had not worked directly in public finance theory, Del Vecchio knew personally many of those whose works I examined in the essay. He also agreed to read and make comments on my draft, and I was pleased to acknowledge his assistance as well in the same footnote.

IX. *The Italian Legacy*

A review of my summary essay, written in 1956 and 1957 and published in 1960, would not convey accurately the impact of the Italian

---

4. James M. Buchanan, "'La Scienza delle finanze': The Italian Tradition in Fiscal Theory," in *Fiscal Theory and Political Economy* (Chapel Hill: University of North Carolina Press, 1960), 24–74.

exposure on the direction and development of my own research program over the years subsequent to my visit. As noted, my scientific perspective as of the middle 1950s was that of a public finance economist who was only beginning to recognize the potential explanatory extension made possible by the abandonment of disciplinary constraints. I did not then appreciate that Knut Wicksell and the Italians had left me with an enduring intellectual legacy that insured personal differentiation of "my product" from that of most of my American peers.

This differentiation in perspective, on political economy generally, was in the process of emergence almost from the onset of my research career, as witnessed by the arguments in my 1949 paper and in my 1954 review of Arrow's work.[5] Despite these directional flags, however, my specific work in 1955, just prior to the Italian year, involved a strictly orthodox application of efficiency analysis to current policy, specifically to the financing, production, and pricing of highway or road services. The Italian leave of absence from this project convinced me that the whole argument of the book I had almost finished was both naïve and misleading, so much so that, upon my return, I gleefully abandoned all efforts toward completion.

Two things had happened during the twelve-month period. I had, while living and working in Rome, completed the final draft of the English translation (from the German original) of Wicksell's seminal essay.[6] (In this effort, I was aided and abetted greatly by Elisabeth Henderson, who lived in Rome only a short distance from my flat.) And, as narrated above, I had also read the Italian masters in "scienza delle finanze," who had emphasized the importance of modeling political decision structures for any exercise in political economy, whether positive or normative.

In retrospect, I do not think that a geographically detached or distanced experience of these two "readings" would have sufficed to push me fully and irrevocably beyond the mindset of the orthodox economists of the day. I was, in this sense, fortunate that these complementary "readings" occurred during residence in Italy. I ab-

---

5. Kenneth Arrow, *Social Choice and Individual Values* (New York: Wiley, 1951).
6. Knut Wicksell, "A New Theory of Just Taxation," in *Classics in the Theory of Public Finance*, ed. R. A. Musgrave and A. T. Peacock (London: Macmillan, 1958), 72–118.

sorbed what was, for me, an attitude toward "the state" that I could never have quite attained in America (or in Britain). Is it grossly inaccurate to claim that the Italian mind remained almost totally immune from Hegelian mythology, and that "the state" was always viewed through the observed activities of its all-too-human agents? What I might call this Italian perspective on politics, which now seems so natural to me, emerged definitively upon my return to American academia.

This perspective has much in common with eighteenth-century conceptions from which emerged both the ideas of the Scottish Enlightenment and those of the American Founding Fathers. After Italy, I was prepared, intellectually, psychologically, and emotionally, to join in an entrepreneurial venture with my Virginia colleague, Warren Nutter, a venture aimed at bringing renewed emphasis to "political economy" in its classical sense. And from these beginnings, the more directed research spin-off into the "economics of politics," initiated jointly with my colleague, Gordon Tullock, now seems as but a natural progression.

7

Virginia Political Economy
Some Personal Reflections

I. *Introduction*

IN THIS CHAPTER I shall discuss what has come to be known as "Virginia Political Economy" from my own personal, and very private, perspective. By "personal" I refer to a subjective vision of persons and events as they affected the academic matters to be discussed. I do not intend to treat details of private lives, either my own or those of others. The chapter is, therefore, autobiographical in an intellectual rather than in a behavioral, emotional, or psychological sense.

I have, of course, been pleased by the emergence of the appellation "Virginia" or "Virginian" applied or assigned to the particular research program in political economy with which I have been associated at three separate universities in the commonwealth, and over a period of more than three decades. I have not, and I do not, reject this appellation, and I have never felt embarrassed when my work has been described as its exemplar. I have come increasingly to accept the uniqueness of my perspective on political-economic-legal order. For many years I considered my perspective to be similar if not identical to that which was very widely shared by most if not all persons who emerged from the American culture; I now realize that my estimates of the number of persons who share my perspective were grossly exaggerated.

To the extent that "Virginia Political Economy" embodies the unfolding and developing articulation of my vision of social interaction, I am alone responsible for both the limits and the credits. In yet another, and quite interesting, sense, I have been placed in the position of being the "front man," the representative embodiment of intersecting strands of ideas that have been created by others with whom I have worked closely. The research program in Virginia Political Economy may be associated with me—properly so—but the program as it developed could never have emerged independently of the efforts and input of G. Warren Nutter, Rutledge Vining, Gordon Tullock, Leland Yeager, Winston Bush, Richard Wagner, Charles Goetz, Geoffrey Brennan, and other colleagues and students over the years. I shall, in this chapter, try to isolate and identify the separate contributions of these charter members, so to speak, of the "Virginia School." Those whose names enter my narrative explicitly may, of course, reject my interpretation both of ideas and of events. And those whose names are not explicitly noted deserve my apologies. I make no effort here to do other than present my considered, but still personal, reflections.

II. *Chicago, Charlottesville, and Thomas Jefferson*

Virginia Political Economy was born in the foyer of the Social Sciences Building at the University of Chicago early in 1948. In a casual conversation with a fellow graduate student, Warren Nutter, I discovered that we shared an evaluation and diagnosis of developments in economics, the discipline with which we were about to become associated as licensed practitioners. We sensed that economics had shifted, and was shifting, away from its classical foundations as a component element in a comprehensive moral philosophy, and that technique was replacing substance. We concurred in the view that some deliberately organized renewal of the classical emphasis was a project worthy of dreams.

Almost ten years later, in early 1957, Warren Nutter and I found ourselves in a position to actuate the idea we had discussed. We had simultaneously joined the faculty at the University of Virginia in Charlottesville, and we had more or less inherited a leadership role. With enthusiastic support from William Duren, then dean of the faculty, we established the Thomas Jefferson Center for Studies in Political Economy and Social Philosophy. The last three words were necessary to describe our purpose, but these soon proved too cumbersome for practical usage and were dropped.

I shall not, in this chapter, discuss the opposition we encountered; I have touched on this briefly elsewhere.[1] But we were not totally isolated, and we secured solid, and substantial, early support for our projected program. The William Volker Fund deserves special mention. An initial five-year grant enabled us to bring to Charlottesville a sequence of Distinguished Visiting Scholars for periods of a half-year each. We turned immediately to Frank H. Knight and F. A. Hayek and later added Michael Polanyi, Maurice Allais, Bertil Ohlin, Overton H. Taylor, T. W. Hutchison, Duncan Black, and Bruno Leoni. These political economists, defined in the broadest sense, graced the Charlottesville academic scene with formal lecture series as well as informal contacts with students and faculty alike. And, importantly for our purposes, their presence brought external attention to the Virginia program in political economy, attention that was necessary to suggest that the program was, in fact, different from the mainstream.

Let me pause here in my account and discuss briefly the Virginia program in economics that Warren Nutter and I found when we arrived in Charlottesville in 1956 and 1957. David McCord Wright had already departed for Oxford and McGill, but his presence was alive, and our proposal might not have been so well received locally without his preparation of the ground. But Rutledge Vining was very much in residence, before, during, and after the glory days. And Vining's influence on my own ideas in particular deserves consideration in some detail.

Vining had been trained at the University of Chicago, and he, too, had been greatly influenced by Frank Knight. This background made for a shared intellectual heritage that facilitated communication between us. But it was the particular set of Knightian ideas that Vining developed that was to affect me—and to stimulate me, too—to draw heavily on Knightian foundations. Rutledge Vining de-

1. See James M. Buchanan, Nutter Memorial Lecture entitled "Political Economy: 1957–82," reprinted in James M. Buchanan, *Liberty, Market, and State: Political Economy in the 1980s* (Brighton: Wheatsheaf, 1985), 8–18.

serves primary credit for initiating what was to become a centrally important component of Virginia Political Economy, the stress on *rules* as contrasted with the then universal stress on policy alternatives within rules. Vining repeatedly emphasized that relevant political choices are not among separate allocations or distributions, but rather are among alternative sets of rules, arrangements, or constraints, which along with the behavior of utility-maximizing persons generate patterns of outcomes or results that we call allocations or distributions. Vining, of course, went further than this initial statement of methodological principle. He also stressed the difficulty in diagnosing "failure" in economic order until the underlying stochastic patterns might be evaluated. This latter emphasis on the basic need for probability theory in any political economy did not attract my own attention except for peripheral acceptance. But the central emphasis on rules as the appropriate objects for political choice found in me a receptive audience.

I was predisposed to accept Vining's criticism of orthodoxy in this respect because I, too, recalled Knight's discussion of rules and, perhaps more significantly, came armed with Knut Wicksell's very practical admonition that, unless we do pay heed to the rules, to the structure of the incentives faced by political agents, we, as economists, were unlikely to exert any influence at all, even in some potential sense.[2] To my knowledge, Vining, in his own work, did not make the step from the emphasis on rules to the incentive structure of political agents. But his direct influence allowed me to pull out from Wicksell's more applied treatment the two-stage or two-level structure of political decision making that is perhaps the sine qua non of constitutional economics.

My own efforts, before Charlottesville, reflect the combined influences of Knight and Wicksell, as expressed in my criticism of orthodox method in normative public finance, my reaction to critics of Arrow's impossibility theorem, and my emerging discovery that, indeed, economists' understanding of the free society of interaction was divergent from my own. I recall my amazement when I found

---

2. I have discussed Wicksell's seminal influence on the development of public choice and, by inference, on Virginia Political Economy in my Nobel lecture. See James M. Buchanan, "The Constitution of Economic Policy," *American Economic Review*, 77 (June 1987): 243–50.

that no one had bothered to carry out the rather simple comparative exercise involved in relating individual choice in the market to individual choice in politics.

The generalized emphasis of the Charlottesville program in economics should not be neglected. Warren Nutter was a dedicated scholar and an outstanding price theorist. Leland Yeager, who joined us in 1958, was, and is, an outstanding independent scholar, who brooks no nonsense, whether spouted by dominant authority or by anyone else. These colleagues, along with Alexandre Kafka, Ronald Coase, and Andrew Whinston, all of whom joined us later, made for an exciting community of scholarship, one where ideas did matter, and where there was sufficient isolation from mainstream pressure to lend confidence to the unorthodox.

As I noted earlier, Warren Nutter and I were motivated to establish the Thomas Jefferson Center out of our shared conviction that mainstream economics was drifting away from its classical tradition. This conviction had normative foundations and normative implications. Economists seemed to be losing an understanding of the market order, and, particularly, to be losing any appreciation of the market's political function, which is to minimize the need for politicized control over and decisions concerning resource use. The Virginia emphasis was, from the outset, on the limits of political process rather than on any schemes to use politics to correct for market failures.

I cannot, of course, speak for my colleagues, but personally I do not ever recall consciously or unconsciously putting myself in the role of proffering advice to government, the stance that has characterized political economists, then and now, despite Wicksell's early admonition. Government, or politics, was, to me, always something to seek protection from, not something to exploit, either for my own ends or for those that I might define for the public at large.

III. *Gordon Tullock and the Economics of Politics*

An element in what was to become the "Virginia School" was, however, missing in the Knight, Wicksell, Nutter, and Vining influences emergent in my own work in the classically oriented academic atmosphere of Charlottesville in the late 1950s. This element was to be added when Gordon Tullock joined us in 1958, first as a post-doctoral fellow at the Thomas Jefferson Center, and, after a spell at South Carolina, as a faculty colleague. Tullock brought with him his near genius sweep of received knowledge in the sciences and in history, along with a rare ability to make dramatic leaps across intellectual bridges. In all this, however, Tullock acted as what I have called a "natural economist," who reduced any and all human behavior to that of *homo economicus*, at least as an initial working hypothesis.[3] This basically hard-nosed vision of the behavior of persons in bureaucratic roles allowed Tullock to "explain" and to "understand" what he had observed in his nine years of experience in the foreign service bureaucracy. And this basic behavioral model gave him an initial handle on analyzing the workings of majoritarian democratic process.

In a real sense Tullock's contribution to Virginia Political Economy was to harden the underlying behavioral model, to make the individualistic approach that I had long stressed more amenable to precise analytical manipulation. The important book in Virginia Political Economy was *The Calculus of Consent*, which Tullock and I actually wrote during the 1959–60 academic year, while I enjoyed the research potential offered by a Ford Faculty Fellowship and while Tullock was laboring in a foreign affairs department at the University of South Carolina.[4] Viewed in retrospect, this book effectively combined the two developing strands of inquiry, the emphasis on the rules within which choices are made, and the economists' model of the behavior of political agents. Furthermore, and importantly, these two strands of inquiry were imbedded in a normative framework that confused and irritated our critics. The book was as much political philosophy as it was either economics or political science, and we did not, then or now, deny or even apologize for its location within the Madisonian vision of the American experience.

In my own personal interpretation these two elements are the necessary components of the public choice research program generally, as I have argued elsewhere. And these two elements uniquely

3. See James M. Buchanan, "The Qualities of a Natural Economist," in *Democracy and Public Choice*, ed. Charles Rowley (Oxford: Basil Blackwell, 1987), 9–19.
4. James M. Buchanan and Gordon Tullock, *The Calculus of Consent: Logical Foundations of Constitutional Democracy* (Ann Arbor: University of Michigan Press, 1962).

emerged in the Charlottesville setting of the very early 1960s. My own role in this constellation of ideas lay in my entrepreneurial efforts in establishing the institutional structure within which such unorthodox political economy might grow and flourish. (I have already acknowledged Warren Nutter's share in this academic enterprise.) It was in my work that the two strands were integrated. Developed independently and in isolation, neither the Wicksell-Knight-Vining emphasis on rules nor the Tullock emphasis on *homo economicus* in politics could have emerged as the far-reaching and influential research program that Virginia Political Economy became after 1962.

IV. *From Political Economy to Public Choice:*
Positive Economics, Welfare Economics, and Welfare Politics

Lest we forget, it is useful to remind ourselves in the 1990s that the predominant emphasis of the theoretical welfare economics of the 1950s and 1960s was placed on the identification of "market failure," with the accompanying normative argument for politicized correction. In retrospect, it seems naïve in the extreme to advance institutional comparisons between the workings of an observed and an idealized alternative. Despite Wicksell's early criticism, however, economists continued to assume, implicitly, that politics would work ideally in the corrective adjustments to market failures that analysis enabled them to identify.

The lasting contribution of public choice theory has been to correct this obvious imbalance in analysis. Any institutional comparison that is worthy of serious considerations must compare relevant alternatives; if market organization is to be replaced by politicized order, or vice versa, the two institutional structures must be evaluated on the basis of predictions as to how they will actually work. Political failure, as well as market failure, must become central to the comprehensive analysis that precedes normative judgment.

To accomplish this, public choice theory had to be split off or divorced from its parent, political economy. This judgment is made from a quarter century's retrospective view; it was not at all explicit in our thinking in 1963. My own implicit understanding of the differential impact of the two complementary arguments was surely due to Wicksell's influence, and it should be noted here that this influence was exclusively exerted through my contributions to the research program. Political economy, interpreted as a return to the classical foundations, and always reflected in the work of Warren Nutter, emphasized the positive virtues of the market. As normative argument, this emphasis clearly has its limits. By contrast, public choice, which came to be increasingly identified with my own work and that of Gordon Tullock from the early 1960s, emphasized the failures of politics. This argument offered an appeal to many scholars who could never have been reached by political economy.

The institutional beginnings of this divorce or separation commenced in 1963, when Gordon Tullock and I organized what was to become the Public Choice Society at a small meeting in Charlottesville. For the next four years at Charlottesville, Tullock and I formed a splinter subgroup, one that was not fully appreciated by our peers in the more comprehensive program. But we were very successful externally; the small band of scholars increased rapidly in numbers, and the journal, finally named, *Public Choice*, began to attract attention.

During this period, we lived through a different sixties from the chaos that was developing in the other academies. There was a set of successive graduate classes with genuinely outstanding students. And these students were very successful in becoming published economists early, many even while still graduate students. This feat was accomplished, quite simply, because the public choice research program was new and there were many, many applications waiting to be analyzed. We could almost literally say to a student, "Pick any politically organized activity, and proceed to analyze its origins, its support, its operation, with the tools of public choice." Those were, indeed, exciting times.

V. *Blacksburg, Winston Bush, and Hobbesian Anarchy*

Had Gordon Tullock and I remained in Charlottesville, public choice would not have been divorced nearly so sharply from political economy as was, in fact, the case. But problems with the university administration insured that the initial research thrust could not survive in

Charlottesville. Gordon Tullock shifted to Rice University, and, one year later, I moved on to UCLA. But under the entrepreneurial efforts of Charles Goetz, public choice found a Virginia location of its own at VPI, separated from the Charlottesville context. Gordon Tullock moved to Blacksburg in 1968, and I joined in 1969. The independent public choice program in Blacksburg accentuated the developing differentiation in focus between the Buchanan-Tullock inquiry into political failures and the Nutter-classical-Chicago inquiry into market successes. At Blacksburg, we analyzed political rules, political institutions, and political behavior as affected by these rules and institutions; we did so almost exclusively.

Between Charlottesville and Blacksburg, however, other events in the outside worlds of academia had occurred that were also to have their influence and effects on the way in which the Virginia School developed. The Charlottesville research program, exemplified by *The Calculus of Consent* and by my *Public Finance in Democratic Process*, embodied an underlying positive evaluation of the basic institutions of governance in the United States.[5] Despite the recognition of the necessity of limits, and despite the diagnosis of political failures in many applications, there was an upbeat or optimistic quality to these heady years of public choice. Between Charlottesville and Blacksburg the character of the underlying diagnosis shifted, at least for me, influenced in part by the events that were taking place in our established institutions of social order, including the universities. Anarchy replaced order as the underlying model, as the title of one of my books suggested.[6]

The research problem seemed to be to explain and understand the emergence of order out of anarchy rather than to grasp the meaning of a stable order that already existed. Thomas Hobbes, whose work had seemed only peripherally relevant to me in 1960, moved to center stage as the political philosopher to be pondered. At precisely this point in its history, Virginia Political Economy discovered its brightest short-lived star. Winston Bush was, for two short but exciting years, the catalyst who helped us put it all to-

5. James M. Buchanan, *Public Finance in Democratic Process* (Chapel Hill: University of North Carolina Press, 1966).

6. James M. Buchanan and Nicos Devletoglou, *Academia in Anarchy: An Economic Diagnosis* (New York: Basic Books, 1970).

gether. Building on Hobbes as foundation, and using all the tools of
modern economic theory, Bush was able to formalize the model of
"social interaction" in genuine anarchy. He was the driving force in
organizing a series of weekly workshops in which the participants
wrote papers on anarchy that Gordon Tullock put together in two
small volumes, *Explorations in the Theory of Anarchy* and *Further Explorations.*[7] This research focus inspired both Gordon Tullock and
me, independently, to prepare full-length books, Tullock's *The Social
Dilemma* and my own work, *The Limits of Liberty.*[8] After Bush's tragic
death in 1973, it was difficult to recapture the Blacksburg spirit that
had been so alive for the winter in which we studied anarchy.

My book *The Limits of Liberty* was treated by some constructive
critics as complementary to works by both John Rawls, whose seminal book *A Theory of Justice* had been published in 1971, and Robert
Nozick, whose *Anarchy, State and Utopia* appeared in 1974.[9] These
works marked a rebirth, of sorts, of political philosophy, and one of
the continuing strands of my own interests has been in constructing
elements of the contractarian position in varying applications and
extensions. This interest, joined with the earlier Wicksellian influence, provides the roots of "constitutional economics" or "constitutional political economy," the term coined in the 1980s to differentiate this area of inquiry from the more positivistic and more
empirical interest-group theory of politics.

VI. *Constitutional Economics in Application:*
The Fiscal Constitution

From the early 1970s, public choice, defined comprehensively,
came to embody two separate and distinct research programs. The
first, constitutional economics, finds its precursors in the work of

7. *Explorations in the Theory of Anarchy*, ed. Gordon Tullock (Blacksburg, Va.:
University Publications for Center for Study of Public Choice, 1972). *Further Explorations in the Theory of Anarchy*, ed. Gordon Tullock (Blacksburg, Va.: University Publications for The Center for Study of Public Choice, 1974).

8. Gordon Tullock, *The Social Dilemma: The Economics of War and Revolution*
(Blacksburg, Va.: University Publications for The Center for Study of Public Choice,
1974). James M. Buchanan, *The Limits of Liberty: Between Anarchy and Leviathan*
(Chicago: University of Chicago Press, 1975).

9. John Rawls, *A Theory of Justice* (Cambridge: Harvard University Press, 1971).
Robert Nozick, *Anarchy, State, and Utopia* (New York: Basic Books, 1974).

Wicksell and its modern representatives in those of Vining, Buchanan, Wagner, Brennan, and Vanberg. And, as I have noted, my own emphasis has been almost exclusively limited to this program. The second research program within public choice falls more appropriately under the rubric "the economic theory of politics" and involves the extension of *homo economicus* to behavior under observed institutional rules. A neglected precursor is Schumpeter, and its modern representatives are Gordon Tullock, who is in a sense the primary influence, along with the Chicago-based interest-group theorists, George Stigler, Sam Peltzman, and Gary Becker, and also some Virginia second-generation scholars, notably Robert Tollison and his coworkers.

I shall not, in this chapter, discuss contributions of this second research program to what may be interpreted as the Virginia School of Political Economy. This neglect is not indicative of any relegation of this program to second-rank importance. Especially in the theory of rent seeking, first advanced by Gordon Tullock in the late 1960s, major insights into the workings of politicized arrangements have been secured. My neglect here is motivated exclusively by my own relationship to the other program in constitutional economics. And recall that I promised to present here my private, personal reflections on Virginia Political Economy rather than a comprehensive interpretation or history. This chapter should be taken to be neither of these.

Within constitutional economics itself, two substrands of inquiry can be identified, and my own works since the early 1970s can readily be classified as falling variously within these two separable areas. First, there is the continuing attempt at integration of the analysis into the more general contractarian political philosophy. Second, there is the effort to derive implications of the analysis for issues of practical public policy.

It is perhaps not at all surprising that the public policy applications that have been most thoroughly developed are those in public finance, since this was Wicksell's initial focus, and since I came to all this from training as a public-finance economist. As early as 1954, before both the Virginia initiative and any specific emphasis on what was later to be public choice, I had written and circulated a draft paper in which I argued that the Keynesian theory of economic policy was developed in a political vacuum and that the precepts of this theory were unworkable in democratic settings. For better or worse, I heeded the advice of colleagues who warned me against trying to publish such an argument in the climate of ideas that described the early 1950s; there are costs to being branded a heretic too early in one's career. By the mid-1970s this climate was totally different, and Keynesian dominance had at least been partially punctured. In addition simple observation of the workings of politics suggested that the persistence of deficits had already become a problem that would only get more serious in the 1980s. In Richard Wagner I found a colleague and coauthor who shared my views on the political efficacy of the Keynesian fiscal policy nostrums, and we wrote *Democracy in Deficit*, a book that had less impact than it should have had due to the bad choice of publisher on our part.[10] This book made one central point; politicians enjoy spending and do not enjoy taxing. These natural proclivities must emerge so long as politicians are responsive to constituents. I have often used this example as the simplest possible illustration of public choice logic. The normative implications are clear; ordinary politics contains a procedural flaw that can only be corrected by the imposition of constitutional constraints. The argument of *Democracy in Deficit* became increasingly relevant in the decade after it was published, as the deficits of the 1980s emerged to dwarf those of the 1970s in size. And, in some indirect sense, we can, I think, legitimately suggest that both the Gramm-Rudman-Hollings legislation and the movements toward approval of the constitutional amendment requiring budget balance find their intellectual foundations in the Buchanan-Wagner book.

This book was "closer to" current policy discussion than any other of my works, earlier or later. There were other elements of the fiscal constitution that seemed to warrant examination, but at a somewhat more remote distance and in idealized abstraction from fiscal reality. Behind an appropriately defined veil of ignorance and/or uncertainty, when asked to select among alternative rules to be imposed on governmental fiscal authorities, how much taxing power would be assigned? Again I was fortunate to find a colleague and coauthor who could assist me in working out the answer to this

10. James M. Buchanan and Richard Wagner, *Democracy in Deficit: The Political Legacy of Lord Keynes* (New York: Academic Press, 1977).

challenging question. Geoffrey Brennan was equipped with the orthodox tools of the trade for a modern public-finance economist,
and these tools when mixed with the public choice-constitutional
economics emphasis of my own produced two books, *The Power to
Tax* and *The Reason of Rules*.[11] Without Brennan's influence I would
never have "jumped out" of the central public choice model of politics, even for the purpose of constitutional exercise, and without this
intellectual leap *The Power to Tax* would never have emerged. What
was required in order to answer the question posed above was a
model of how ordinary politics works in the use of the taxing power.
Orthodox public choice models could produce a multiplicity of results. We needed something much more amenable to analysis. The
revenue-maximizing model of government gave us the "handle"
upon which to hang the whole constitutional analysis. We recognized, of course, that the workings of politics in democratic societies
are complex. But, if the purpose is one of drawing the constitutional
limits on the taxing power, would it not be meaningful to utilize a
worst-case scenario and to see model governments, anywhere and
everywhere, as revenue-maximizing? That is, given any revenue
source, would it not be best to assume maximal exploitation? With
this model the book almost wrote itself. There were readily discernible constitutional limits to the taxing power that could be laid down,
and the "principles" that emerged from the analysis turned orthodox
normative tax theory on its head in many cases.

VII. *Constitutional Economics*

The constitutional exercise that was the motivating purpose of *The
Power to Tax* was not understood by many of our critics, who took
our model of revenue maximizing government to be descriptive of
fiscal reality rather than a worst-case model introduced explicitly
for the aim of constitutional design. The second Brennan-
Buchanan book, *The Reason of Rules*, is best summarized as a response to these critics. In this book we move beyond the fiscal appli-

11. James M. Buchanan and Geoffrey Brennan, *The Power to Tax: Analytical Foun-
dations of a Fiscal Constitution* (Cambridge: Cambridge University Press, 1980). James
M. Buchanan and Geoffrey Brennan, *The Reason of Rules—Constitutional Political
Economy* (Cambridge: Cambridge University Press, 1985).

cation and discuss the constitutional approach generally, an approach that has characterized my own work since the initial Wicksellian influence, and particularly since *The Calculus of Consent*.

I have come increasingly to think that the constitutionalist-contractarian methodological framework is, indeed, the central feature of Virginia Political Economy, a framework that, from the start, I have found to be appropriately described locationally in the commonwealth that produced James Madison and the other Virginia Founders. I can, I think, make a plausible case that this framework would be out of place in California, Illinois, or Massachusetts. Despite the opposition that we encountered in Virginia's academies, especially in Charlottesville, I like to think that it was our research program that was, indeed, indigenous and that our antagonists were the aliens.

We owe the precise name "Constitutional Economics" to Richard McKenzie, a former student and colleague, who organized a conference and published a book under this title in the early 1980s. I have often used "contractarian political economy" as an alternative designation. Much of my own work during the decade of the 1980s has been in methodological defense of this approach to issues of social philosophy.

In one sense we may pose the challenge of the 1990s and beyond in terms of the struggle between the practical implications of the two separate strands that I have identified as describing Public Choice and the Virginia research program in an inclusive way. Positive public choice theory suggests that the rent seekers are indeed to inherit our earth, that our polity is already described by the "churning state" metaphor used by Anthony de Jasay in his book, *The State*.[12] Constitutional reform offers the only escape from this gloomy projection. But until and unless the rent seeking potential embodied in the nonconstrained institutions of governance is fully appreciated, it remains impossible to secure the requisite constitutional attitude or constitutional wisdom that will make reform a realistic alternative.

I have often stated that I feel a moral obligation to hope that such reform can indeed take place. Underneath its abstract analysis, the

---

12. Anthony de Jasay, *The State* (Oxford: Basil Blackwell, 1985).

Virginia research program has always embodied a moral passion that our adversaries have fully appreciated. The program has advanced our scientific understanding of social interaction, but the science has been consistently applied to the normatively chosen question. How can individuals live in social order while preserving their own liberties? Scholars associated with the program have consistently eschewed the question: How can the state exert more effective control over individuals? Those scholars who associate themselves with the interests of "the state" have never found, and will not find, Virginia Political Economy congenial. This differentiation in ultimate normative purpose is a feature of Virginia Political Economy that I value positively and strongly.

In conclusion let me stress again what I stated at the outset. These remarks have contained my private and personal assessment of Virginia Political Economy, of its origins, its history, and its development, along with some reference to people and institutions that describe the research program. Other participants will, of course, write a different story and offer a different assessment.

The beauty of the country besides, the pleasures of a country life, the tranquility of mind which it promises, and whenever the injustice of human laws does not disturb it, the independency which it really affords, have charm that more or less attract every body; and as to cultivate the ground was the original destination of man, so in every stage of his existence he seems to retain a predilection for this primitive employment.

ADAM SMITH, *The Wealth of Nations*

. . . no other creature was so conditionally and undivinely mortal as man, for none was so capable of perjury, and the more abject he was the more mortal he became, but most perjuring and most mortal was he whose foot had estranged itself from the earth and touched nothing but pavements, the man who no longer tilled and no longer sowed, for whom nothing took place in accordance with the circling of the stars, for whom the forest no longer sang, nor the greening meadows; verily nobody and nothing was so mortal as the mob in the great cities, grovelling, sneaking, swarming, through the streets, having staggered so long that it had forgotten how to walk, upheld by no law and upholding none, the re-scattered herd, its former wisdom forfeited, unwilling to have knowledge, submitting like the animal, like something less than the animal, to every chance, and at last to a chance extinction without memory, without hope, without immortality . . .

HERMANN BROCH, *The Death of Virgil*

Country Aesthetic

I. *Introduction*

THIS CHAPTER IS a narrative of discovery, not of some external truth waiting to be revealed, but of an element of myself that I might have once deemed impossible. It is also an expression of appreciation for the exogenous events of personal history that combined to offer me the understanding that emerged independently of purpose or preference. Finally, the subject is "country" which, for me, takes on the form of an encompassing, and continuing, aesthetic experience.

As chapter 2 should have made clear, my early life could scarcely have produced in me some romanticized yearning for the drudgery of the yeoman farmer. And, through the middle decades of my life I felt no yearning to return to the soil, to seek out my roots, to engage with nature directly in some continuing struggle to transform the wild into the fruitful. Nor did I lapse into the opposing green absurdity, the abstracted longing for some return to nature, even if red in tooth and claw. I was, for three full decades, willing to live simply in the complex and interdependent world of modernity, content to purchase my necessaries at the market from income earned in peddling my academic wares in the markets of their own. I sensed no foregone fulfillment in my failures to walk among golden daffodils, and neither in painting nor in poetry did the idealizations of nature's wonders stimulate my notice.

I lived variously as others lived—in a row house in Chicago, in an apartment and a starter house in Knoxville, Tennessee, in a detached house in Tallahassee, Florida. And, as fortunes grew, I enjoyed the status of upper-scale suburbia in Charlottesville, Virginia, interspersed by sojourns in Rome and London flats. In Los Angeles I lived cheek-by-jowl with strangers in an artificially constructed environment that maximized interdependent mobility. And initially, after my return to Virginia (this time in Blacksburg), I sought to avoid my small-town neighbors whose backyard barbeques taxed the limits of my tolerance. In a larger sense all of my livings were of a piece, habitats that became necessary inputs to my survival as an emerging academician—instructor, scholar, entrepreneur—for whom the aesthetics of location seemed of little matter.

A new world opened in the 1970s, a world that I had not anticipated, a world that I had not known even to exist, for me or for others, save in the accounts of fiction. I came to know what "land" means to one who owns and walks upon it. I came to sense the silent deepness of mountain woods. I came to live the wonder and the glory of things that grow and to participate fully in the annual cycle of fertility. And with all this, there came the wider and more satisfactory understanding and appreciation, indeed a happiness, that independence offers. My own account was toted to a higher value; my net worth increased manyfold when reckoned in inner shekels.

This chapter is a stumbling effort to convey something of this new world, something of my serendipitous discovery, its presumed origins for me, along with a brief narrative of its development. And finally, and most importantly, my purpose here is to express, as best as I am able, an appreciation for that which so many others cannot achieve in an increasingly interdependent world. Fortune smiled upon me, in this as in other ways, and by my own internal counters made me a rich man indeed.

II. *Unexamined Living in an Examined Order*

From Chicago forward, I accepted the role laid out for me by Frank Knight, and before him, by Adam Smith. My raison d'être, as an economist, rests first in the understanding and then in transmission of the principles of economic order among autonomous persons, each of whom is capable of thought, choice, and action. In such an enterprise I have never seen myself as a mere teacher of that which passed for wisdom because, to me, the confusion and error in such claimed wisdom suggested that the achievement of understanding was, in itself, a major challenge. (Whether I should have attained such a stance before my professional peers without exposure to Frank Knight is a question without an answer.) But I most surely did not pause to reexamine the most elementary of all the economists' precepts: There are mutual gains from trade. Within any community of persons, each can secure more of the "goods" that are privately valued by combining specialization in production with trade than by remaining self-sufficient. This much I thought I understood, at least sufficiently to file away into the category of "uninteresting truths."

I achieved what seemed, for me, an understanding of the economic order of a society of free and responsible individuals, along with a critical ability to recognize where, how, and in what respects existing societies, my own and others, failed to meet the imagined standards. In the broadest, but at the same time very practical, sense I examined the *political economy*, and I tried to persuade my professional peers in the social sciences, along with my students, to join in my vision of the integrated order of economic interdependence, both that which was to be observed, now and in historical development, and that which might be within the possible.

I shared with my economist peers the intellectual smugness that accompanies any scientific or specialized understanding. I have often recalled, and have used, a citation from the 1930s that Frank Ward had posted on his office door when I first arrived at the University of Tennessee in 1940. "The study of Economics won't keep you out of the breadline; but at least you'll know why you're there." Economists, too, enjoy a shared sense of "expertise"; we think, rightly or wrongly as the case may be, that there are relationships in observed social reality that we know more about than our noneconomist fellows.

At the same time, most of us, in our purely participatory roles within the complex patterns of social interaction, think, choose,

and act no differently from anyone else. Very few economists, I suspect, are amateur psychologists or psychiatrists who engage in serious examination of their own choice behavior, who seek to sort
out and unravel the arguments that enter into their own preference
functions. I can, of course, speak only for myself here, but I have
never been an explorer of my own psyche. I have instead, for the
most part, been a reactive chooser among the opportunities that
have emerged to confront me. Any entrepreneurial or creative urges
that I might have exhibited and acted upon have been strictly within
my role as an academic, scholar, and professor and not at all within
my privately organized existence.

III. *The 1960s Happened*

This personal resignation before the elements that described my
quotidian existence makes the transformation effected in the early
1970s (I was in my early fifties) both surprising and significant. But
such a change in my personal outlook on the world might not have
occurred at all without the intervening decade of the 1960s. The impact of the events of that decade offers some explanation of my own
readiness to seize upon that which was fortuitously offered in the
1970s.

"My world" was radically shifted in the 1960s. Chaos replaced
order along several dimensions, or so it seemed from my private
window on events, and I found myself forced to search for new har-
bors in which to drop anchor. There need be no rekindling of old
fires here, but some statement of "where I stood" when and as the
1960s happened, to me, is necessary if I am to expect any measure of
success in securing some understanding of my newly discovered
country of the 1970s and beyond. And I stress that my aim is to be
understood; I do not seek, or desire, either agreement or approval.

In mid-1960, Gordon Tullock and I completed the draft of *The
Calculus of Consent*, the book that was destined to become a classic, of
sorts, in the emerging subdiscipline of public choice.[1] We were internally pleased with our joint product, even if there was no elation
that might accompany newly discovered wisdom. At base we were

1. James M. Buchanan and Gordon Tullock, *The Calculus of Consent: Logical Foundations of Constitutional Democracy* (Ann Arbor: University of Michigan Press, 1962).

optimistic because we had succeeded in our effort to reconcile the economists' model of utility maximizing behavior and the Madisonian vision of constitutional political order. The book conveyed the positive, if also normative, message: "Democracy works, if organized along the lines of the American constitutional republic."

The manuscript had scarcely been mailed off to the press when, to some of us, American democracy seemed demonstrably to fail in preventing a rich man's purchase of the presidency for his son. The conceptual break between observed reality and analyzed possibility was sharpened, and we pulled back into the caves of nonestablishment academia as the best and brightest sought to rule us all. But there was to be no escape. We were not allowed, at least in Charlottesville, Virginia, to pursue the grand endeavor that was Madison's, even in our abstracted research inquiry. We were chastised, scorned, and differentially damaged by our stated refusals to ride with the gathering winds of Camelot. How could we, as rational beings, fail to sense the glory of the hour? Our external academic successes, both in training graduate students and in professional publications of our research, were as nothing when matched against our alleged "fascist" and "right-wing" zealotry by those who made decisions for the corporate actor that was the University of Virginia.

Our academic enterprise had failed, even before the bloom was gone from Camelot, and in the selfsame year (1963) that Tullock and I set up the founding meeting of what was to become the Public Choice Society, the University of Virginia was establishing, *secretly*, its own investigative inquiry into the biased attitudes of those of us who were identified as participants in the programs of research and instruction in economics and political economy. The sometimes cozy world from which *The Calculus of Consent* had emerged was disintegrating. And I soon discovered that I could not so readily separate my personal from my professional experience. I could not maintain self-respect in a setting of institutional idiocy.

All of this happened on the "inside" in Charlottesville before, during, and after the sequence of external events that transformed America so dramatically, along with everyone within it. The assassination of the president, the cowardly cover-up of the Warren Commission, the early Berkeley riots, the Johnson landslide, the Great Society, the escalation of Vietnam, the draft dodgers, the generalized erosion of academic order, the breakdown in manners, morals, and social convention, the emerging generational gap, the commencement of a drug culture, Woodstock, the follow-on assassinations of 1968, the Chicago convention, the Nixon agonies, the Cambodian spring, Kent State. Do not examine this remembered listing; accept my simple point that the decade was turbulent, even for those of us who remained on the outside of the events themselves.

I felt myself lost before these external events. I was estranged from my potentially stabilizing academic base, and the order of the external world seemed to be eroding toward anarchy. I could not understand at all the behavior of my peers in the nation's academies, and I came down squarely on the "law and order" side of most of the critical issues that surfaced, both inside and outside university communities. At the same time, I sensed the contradiction between such a stance and my long-held libertarian principles.

By necessity, I retreated professionally into the insulated shells of academic scholarship as I sought out a more congenial university environment. My ultimate choice to join the excellent, and highly professional, department at UCLA was a personal mistake because I had not reckoned on the importance of effective university administrative leadership on those campuses that were vulnerable to disruption. In Charlottesville my problems lay with the attitudes of the university leadership toward the enterprise in political economy developed by me and my colleagues. In Los Angeles my problems were different; they involved my unwillingness to stand by and observe a university leadership that was incapable of opposing the demands of those whose protests reached to the limits of theatrical absurdity.

My return to Virginia in 1969, this time to Blacksburg in the southwest mountains, to VPI, was a self-acknowledged "hunkering down," an attempt to salvage a personal tranquillity of sorts, isolated maximally from turmoil in an industry that seemed bent on self-destruction. There was an acute awareness that there were to be no finer hours and that I should find tolerance only in the netherlands of academia, only in those sites that had been subjected to the sneers of those who now found their ivy poisoned.

IV. *Explorations of Anarchy*

The return to Virginia was not a new mistake, and I was to be dramatically surprised, both professionally and personally, by the genuine achievement of finer hours, made more so by their violation of all expectations. I was impressed by the importance for productive effort generated by the presence of a university administration that lent support and by the smallness of the number of complementary research scholars required for effective work. Gordon Tullock's presence helped me immensely during those early Blacksburg years, and Charles Goetz, who had been perhaps my best of all the Ph.D. students in Charlottesville, had the entrepreneurial vision to recognize Blacksburg's prospects.

I shall delay, until the following section, treatment of the personal, private impact of the mountains, which remains, as noted, the primary focus of this chapter. But a summary of a research program deserves inclusion because this program surely counted for something in the upscaling of my total balance that was to occur.

I had observed the eruption of anarchy in the universities, from afar in the middle 1960s, and from close-up at UCLA in 1968. I sensed an urge to stand and fight, to do battle in the quads, as I saw rules and conventions that embodied capital value fall undefended before the new barbarians. Failing to act out this urge, which, in truth, was never close to realization, I sought catharsis through analysis and examination. During my final months in Los Angeles, I wrote, jointly with Nicos Devletoglou, a small book, *Academia in Anarchy*, which presented an analysis of what we saw happening before our eyes.[2] I do not now rank this book high among my own works. For the only time in my career, I responded to the challenge of the current and engaged in argument with those who I should have known would remain immune to logic. I mention this book here only to note its title, and especially the word "anarchy."

This word in a title, and the feedbacks on my thought patterns, may have stimulated my entry into the more serious research program on anarchy that occupied us in Blacksburg in the early 1970s. But surely more important variables in the mix were the emptiness

---

2. James M. Buchanan and Nicos Devletoglou, *Academia In Anarchy: An Economic Diagnosis* (New York: Basic Books, 1970).

of a research program waiting to be occupied along with the emergence of a new star in our own research team, a young man who came equipped with the technical tools of economic theory, along with an interest in the deeper issues of political philosophy, all embedded within an attitude that reflected the unique independence of a populist redneck with self-confidence. Winston Bush galvanized our interests in the theory of anarchy, an organizational alternative that had never been seriously analyzed. What were the descriptive features of Hobbesian anarchy? Could something like an anarchistic equilibrium be defined?

Bush was instrumental in organizing a series of weekly workshops in 1972 during which each participant in turn presented papers on differing aspects of the theory of anarchy. As revised, these papers were published in *Explorations in the Theory of Anarchy*.[3] Those weeks were exciting because never before or since have I participated so fully in a genuinely multiparty ongoing research effort, one that we knew to be relevant in some ultimate sense, but which was not responsive to evanescent policy initiative, as conceived by some governmental agency, private foundation, or even university. For me this brief period of research activity was important because it gave me a new focus on my whole enterprise. I was able, once again, to get a "handle" on events, and I recognized that my comparative advantage lay in going behind the presumed presence of democratic order in the background of the analysis of *The Calculus of Consent*. I commenced with my own statement of the theory of anarchy in order to demonstrate how the leap into order might proceed along contractual lines. My book, *The Limits of Liberty: Between Anarchy and Leviathan*, took its initial shape and inspiration from the Bush workshops.[4] Gordon Tullock's book, *The Social Dilemma*, had similar origins, along with some comparable arguments.[5]

Winston Bush's tragic death snuffed out a research program that was, perhaps, destined to be short-lived in its institutionalized form.

3. *Explorations in the Theory of Anarchy*, ed. Gordon Tullock (Blacksburg, Va.: University Publications for the Center for Study of Public Choice, 1972).
4. James M. Buchanan, *The Limits of Liberty: Between Anarchy and Leviathan* (Chicago: University of Chicago Press, 1975).
5. Gordon Tullock, *The Social Dilemma: The Economics of War and Revolution* (Blacksburg, Va.: University Publications for the Center for Study of Public Choice, 1974).

But armed with an internally satisfying way of thinking anew about the sociopolitical reality that I observed, I was, by the early 1970s, sufficiently confident to go forward to develop variations on the bundle of related themes that beckoned.

V. *Virginia Mountain Land*

The two preceding sections of this chapter may appear to represent a digression from my announced purpose of discussing personal discovery rather than professional experience. But without the events of the 1960s and the explorations into anarchy, my reactions to the 1970s would have been very different, and my private world of "country" need not have been revealed at all.

Southwest Virginia is a part of Appalachia, and there are thousands of acres of secondary growth forest, both publicly and privately owned, interspersed with clearings where self-sufficient farms existed well into this century. There are few, if any, full-time, self-sufficient farmers now, and the few old homesteads that remain are owned, and operated, by persons variously employed in the scattered towns in the vicinity. Ugly clusters of modern mobile homes appear at the road crossings in the valleys.

Much of the acreage itself is heavily wooded, steep, and almost inaccessible. Most of this land is walked over only in the very active deer-hunting season in late November.

My introduction to ownership took place in 1970, when Gordon Tullock and I jointly purchased, for a song, an abandoned mountainside farm from four Norfolk deer hunters. There were some one hundred twenty acres, and the farm was located in Giles County on the road down from the Mountain Lake Resort.

The stone foundations of the burned-out house remained, a haven for rattlesnakes; the ruins of the barn were nearby; the old spring house over the running stream still stood. The cherry trees produced fruit in springtime abundance, and some of the shrubs still bloomed. Up the very steep road toward the top of the property, where the access road was located, there stood a well-ruined, one-room schoolhouse, last used, perhaps, in the 1930s.

This old farm provided the beginnings of my feelings for owned land, for property to be enjoyed, something that had never been present, for me, in my nominal ownership rights in the postage-stamp habitats in city, suburb, or town. I learned what it really meant, in inner psychological contentment, to walk about on ground where others did not tread, beyond sight or sound. I learned the joy of picking wild berries from the territory and cutting winter's firewood without permit, market, or even "please."

VI. *A Cabin on Dry Run*

The initial experience with ownership of mountain land did little more than whet my appetite. Here was a potential source of utility that I had not known existed. I realized that the opportunity for personal gratification in this direction had been only minimally exploited. I commenced a search for more accessible holdings, closer to my academic base in Blacksburg and with some potential for second-home development.

My search paid off, and in 1971 we purchased, this time on our own, a nonproducing ninety-acre farm only a few miles out of Blacksburg. Again most of the acreage was wooded, but this time the slopes were not so steep, and near the country road there stood a marginally usable cabin in such a state of disrepair that the realtor advised me to assign it a zero value in any evaluation of the property.

The weeds were shoulder high in June; the rats roamed freely between the old house and the garbage dump in the unused trench silo; the fireplace had collapsed; the upstairs porch of the two-story log cabin was rotted through; the septic field was flooded; the outbuildings were unused; there were tangles of wire where there had once been fences; that which had once been a pigpen was a swamp. A summary description might have been "Appalachia at its worst."

But the log cabin itself was picturesque, as it stood beneath two mighty Norwegian spruce; the lilac bushes were higher than the weeds; the front porch seemed made for rocking chairs; there was a garden spot where vegetables and flowers might one day grow. From the very start I saw the place as it might be rather than as it was or had been. And I entered on a voyage of self-discovery in a permanent location, in a setting that might be shaped to my own liking, with absolutely minimal feedback from the attitudes of others, whether these be friend or foe. It is adequately descriptive to say that, from 1971 forward, in that place I have felt as a plant would feel, anchored firmly in one location but putting forth branches here and there with the developing shape only roughly discernible. For the first time I located myself personally to match the location of myself professionally-scientifically that had been fixed two decades before.

I now had a personal project, one that could and did command my physical, mental, financial, organizational, and creative energies. I lay awake thinking of choices to be made along many dimensions—what, where, and when to plant; what fence to build and how to build it; how much repair and reconstruction to undertake and with whom to contract; how much time to spend on these matters so removed from the activities of the academy.

And, slowly, the setting was transformed. The rotten logs were spliced; the fireplace and the porch were reconstructed; the rats were countered with some cats and rat wire; the garbage dump was bulldozed over; the weeds were bushhogged; the drainage was fixed; pieces of old furniture were bought at auctions; the cabin became plausibly functional.

The first winter came, and I learned what I had long forgotten, that heat from open fires and from kitchen woodstoves is more satisfying than that from any central system. I learned how wood would split on a cold morning, and I also learned that water pipes and heaters freeze readily in unheated houses. Spring followed, and, with the aid of Winston Bush, I tilled and planted vegetables and built crude fences. As summer's heat arrived, I spent increasing days and hours at the cabin and less at the house in town. Vegetables ripened; then they were eaten, canned, frozen, and transferred. Mountain blackberries challenged me to brave the steep slopes, the thorns, and the prospects of rattlesnakes. The fruit, once picked, was eaten, canned, frozen, transferred, and made into quite drinkable wine.

Each passing season brought developments with new dimensions—a picket fence along the road dictated by the loss of a loved fox terrier, more cats, a storage shed built by student helpers, a modernized bathroom, a second and third garden plot, the added acreage of still steeper slopes, shrubs, trees, perennials (especially peonies), and a growing list of things grown. This cabin became much more than a second home. It was home itself—holiday seasons, summers, weekends, summer evenings—I came to begrudge chores at the house in town, chores that seemed necessary only to please the prying neighbors. There was never a conscious cost to work at the country place.

A two-car garage replaced a battered open shed; more and better fences were made; a modern bedroom was added, along with a new red tin roof for the whole house. More land was purchased, and a local neighbor joined in a venture to graze cattle on the open pastures. A second extension now took shape in the addition of a self-contained guest suite that doubled as a reading-writing room for me. Again more land was added, this time with the acquisition of acreage across the road, which included a house up the slope in the woods, just far enough away to be close enough for comfort. Arrangements were made with a young family to manage my "estate" while they lived in the house in the woods. This scheme now allowed for animals, dogs and cats, to be permanently kept at the cabin, something that would not have been possible after my academic relocation across Virginia to Fairfax in 1983.

Later, in 1990, the kitchen was modernized. But a woodstove remains, and the cabin on Dry Run increasingly becomes my single home, with the Fairfax townhouse offering interim residence for the academic duties that still call. More changes will be made, and, as I write this chapter, I think about plans for yet another independent guest suite to be added, yet more acreage to be purchased, yet more fences to be built.

Dry Run itself warrants some mention. Directly across from the log cabin a strong spring comes forth from the mountainside. This spring becomes the origin of Dry Run, a truly burbling brook that runs along the lower edges of my garden and allows for irrigation in dry times. The run offers a rough boundary of the property for a half-mile and includes a waterfall that all my visitors enjoy. Further downstream the run goes underground in dry seasons, only to resurface again; hence "Dry Run."

VII. *"That Undiscovered Country"*

I must again apologize for the narrative description of my own mundane existence as sketched out in the preceding section. I ask myself again why anyone would find interest in the private dimensions of my own history. But the narrative does have the purpose noted at the outset; country living taught me things about myself that are worth some effort at generalization.

The first point concerns knowledge, and specifically knowledge possessed by the individual who chooses among alternatives, whether these be goods in a marketplace, courses in a college, professions or jobs that are available, marriage partners, ballot levers for candidates or parties in an election, or any of the extendable listing that might be put down here. Some economists define their discipline as "the science of choice," but they rarely engage themselves in an analysis of preferences. Most economists, most of the time, are quite content to assume that individuals have well-defined preferences that remain stable over the course of the behavior subjected to examination. In simpler terms economists presume that individuals know what it is they want before they make the choices among the options faced.

For some everyday, routinized, and repeatedly made choices, the economists' model may be acceptable. The unimaginative housewife knows that the family needs one pound of coffee per week, along with two gallons of milk, a dozen bananas, and other standard items. But, in this model, how is genuine choice ever exercised? How does a new good enter the consumption pattern? For analysis of interesting choice behavior, the economist must allow preference orderings to be open-ended, that is, individuals must be presumed to make some choices before they know what the consequences will be. The realm of exploratory or creative choice must be assigned its own place, alongside the reactive choice that dominates the analytical models.

Creative choice results in discovery, the finding out of something that was not known before. But even the word "discovery" is misleading; that which is "discovered" by creative choice may not come into existence until the choice itself is made. The analogy with geographic "discovery" is perhaps dangerous here. Creative choice is closer to that of the sculptor who "discovers" the statue in the stone, but who also knows that the statue does not and will not exist at all until and unless it is created.

The relevance of this epistemological detour for my discussion of country life should be clear. There were no arguments in my preference function before 1970 that told me to look for ways and means to satisfy a demand for hobby farming, for rural tranquillity, for physical engagement with the earth itself. There was, instead, a willingness on my part to explore a life-style, the consequences of which were beyond the knowable. My log cabin on Dry Run, and everything that goes with this living, involves creative choice applied to personal rather than scientific enterprise.

VIII. *"The Independency Which It Really Affords"*

The "personal enterprise" that my life and living in Dry Run became over two decades proved to be productive of happiness beyond any limits of my earlier imagination. My life in this country setting arrived at a stability that had been absent. Why did this result occur? Why did I find myself transported to a higher plane of personal realization? These are questions that seem worth a bit of speculation.

Those who work and live in ideas rarely, I suspect, have need for hobbies that challenge. I am no exception here, and I have never felt the urge to become a collector, of anything, a model builder, a fisherman, a golfer, or any of the thousand-and-one other activities that come to dominate the off-work existence of so many. And, in this sense, growing my vegetables and making my wine, or even building my fences, are not hobbies in any dictionary-type definition. I take no particular pride in growing larger cabbages than my neighbor. A hobby farmer I am not.

There is a "tranquillity of mind" indeed, but this very tranquillity is more the explanandum than the explanans. There are, to be sure, particularly satisfying moments of repose to be gathered in a front-porch rocking chair on a summer's eve or by a blazing fire on a darkened winter's afternoon. But quiet locations for contemplation and reflection can always be found; there is something over and beyond reclusion that my mountain farm provides.

I identify this "something" by reference, once again, to the evocative statement by Adam Smith with which I commenced this chapter. The statement reflects an inclusive understanding of country living, and it mentions natural beauty, simple pleasures, mental tranquillity, and engaged cultivation of the earth as sources of potential satisfaction. Each of these features, along with others that might be added, does contribute its share in the increment to my well-being that my country living offers. But Adam Smith's statement includes another feature that, for me, surely dominates all of the others, "the independency which it really affords."

This "independency" deserves discussion because it is both the most important and the most surprising of the elements that enter into the aesthetics of country life, as I experience it. The degree of surprise in my evaluation of "independency" is related to my disciplinary identification as an economist, and especially as an economist who had never so much as paused to question the most basic of all principles—that which demonstrates the mutuality of gains from trade and specialization. The whole enterprise of economics, from its eighteenth-century origins, is an elaboration of the principle that through specialization and trade, that is, through becoming *dependent*, persons can achieve greater material wealth. What this enterprise, and its practitioners, failed to emphasize sufficiently is that the increase in material goods secured by the increasing dependence is purchased by a sacrifice of *independence*, which itself is a highly valued source of personal satisfaction. I could not have appreciated or understood this simple principle without having experienced country living, because it has been only in that living itself that I have been able to enjoy the increased satisfaction that each and every move toward greater independence offers.

I noted earlier that the 1960s and anarchy were relevant to my discovery. In that turbulent decade, and for the first time in my life, there were riots in American cities; there were acts of terrorism against citizens; there were threats of even wider disruption in social order. Think, then, of what it did mean, personally, to me to be able to live, and to live well, without direct dependence on a municipal water supply, without externally purchased oil or gas as a heating or cooking source, without necessary dependence on an electricity distribution system. In my country setting I require neither water, fuel, nor power from external suppliers, although, of course, convenience dictates use of the available electricity. Who could possibly challenge my claim to a level of well-being that is, quite simply, beyond the reach of anyone who must, perforce, remain dependent on others for even the basic rudiments of living?

The pleasures derived from producing goods for my own consumption offer reinforcement and reminder of the values of independence. The vegetables that grow from the soil are different from those that come from the bins in the supermarket, not in taste and quality but in some deeper sense of inalienability. And the knowledge that, out of season, potatoes are in the cellar, canned goods are in the pantry, and meat is on the hoof yields me a security that is not to be reckoned lightly. The potential dangers posed by inflation, transitory or permanent unemployment, shifts in values of investment portfolios, or even personalized errors of major magnitude in market dealings do not loom so ominous when judged from a country perspective.

I recognize, of course, that the secondary, residual, or backup independence that my country living provides is of a different order from that which the self-sufficient farmer on my place a century ago "enjoyed." His primary and nonvoluntary independence left him vulnerable to exigencies that I need not face at all. If that farmer's potato crop failed, or if the floods destroyed his corn, his family remained hungry. He could not call on either his own financial resources or the facilities of modern markets to replace ordinary sources of supply. He would, indeed, have greatly valued the easy availability of the modern market's manifold abundance. Recognition of the difference between that farmer's lot and mine does not, however, dispel my central explanation of what it is that I discovered in my country living. Of course I would not swap places with that farmer of a century past. But neither would I swap places with the modern urban dweller, no matter what his financial resources. And, as between the farmer of a century past and the urbanite or suburbanite of 1990, my choice would not be easy.

IX. Market Independence, Liberty, and the Search for Community

As I reckon the counters in my own game, I am led to generalize by calling into question the wisdom of policies that, either in some explicit furtherance of collectively chosen objectives or in acquiescence before evolutionary drift, have allowed participants in modern societies to become overly dependent on institutional structures that are dangerously vulnerable to disruption. Modern man and woman, singly or in a family unit, have little or no residual ability to survive the shocks to ordered routine that might emerge from so many different sources.

In the idealized limits so beautifully presented in the economists' model of an active competitive world, persons are independent but in a sense totally different from the "independency" of the farmer, then or now. In the competitive setting, as idealized, a person depends on no *identified* other, for *anything* of value, because the working market offers a multiplicity of alternatives for each and every choice. There are many sellers for each good among whom any buyer may choose; there are many buyers for each good or service among whom any seller can choose, including the seller of his or her own capacity to produce that which is valued by others.

As observed social reality diverges from the economists' ideal model, the personal independence offered by market interaction is directly reduced. The person who specializes, and who indeed may prosper mightily in the ideally competitive world, may find that in the markets that he or she enters, either as seller or buyer, the exit option is foreclosed. Personal and/or institutional dependence replaces independence, and the talents for pleasing those with whom one interacts become more important relative to talents that produce value. "Politics," in this inclusive and relational sense, replaces impersonal exchange.

It is in this setting that the individual who recognizes the vulnerability of dependence searches out for others with whom he or she may join in community enterprise, which may, in turn, close off still other exit options for those who remain outside the memberships. The complex institutional structures of modern society emerge, but the individual participant does not escape from the abiding fear that something may go wrong, and he or she will be left with no capacity to produce value *independently*, the capacity that country living has indeed insured that I possess.

I should be naïvely romantic to believe that more than a very small number of persons in modern societies could achieve the degree of independency that I have attained in the Southwest Virginia mountains. As F. A. Hayek has emphasized in his latest book, *The Fatal Conceit*, a complex market economy is necessary to support a population at anything remotely close to current levels.[1] This much I acknowledge, but my own experience over two decades has impressed upon me the valuational content in Jefferson's ideal polity of yeoman farmers, latterly put forth by the Southern Agrarians of the 1930s. The country life, as I have lived and live it, cannot be enjoyed by many; but it is not, in any sense, a status "good" that attains a part of its "goodness" by being necessarily scarce.

An understanding of and appreciation for the country life allow me to sense anew the horror of Stalin's crushing of the kulaks, and indeed to assess the immeasurable losses suffered by all persons who have been placed in politicized-bureaucraticized dependence as both agrarian and market independency were replaced. The socialist epoch has run its course, but we have hardly commenced to reduce the necessary dependence imposed on individuals by the domination of political agency. We have not yet come to the generalized understanding that, for most persons, the independence offered by the presence of market alternatives offers the maximal liberty that is possible. But we have not yet designed institutions that will satisfy the individual's search for community in the impersonal settings of the market order without, at the same time, undermining the very independence that this order affords.

In latter parts of this chapter I have strayed into familiar territory, into discussion of issues in political and economic philosophy and away from my theme of country life. But there is a deep relation between my personal experience and my effort at understanding issues of constitutional order. Without my country life I would have continued to grope in even greater confusion after that which now describes my continuing inquiry. By understanding more, perhaps I can explain more of that which we see, which, in its turn, may offer grounds for suggested change.

6. F. A. Hayek, *The Fatal Conceit* (Chicago: University of Chicago Press, 1989).

9

Words Written Down

I. *Introduction*

THIS CHAPTER IS NOT an autobiographical essay, at least in any way that is analogous to most of the other chapters in this book. Save for this introduction, the words are not my own. They are, instead, words written by others that have attracted my attention sufficiently to prompt me to write them down in three small black notebooks. Indirectly, the chapter is autobiographical, of course, since much can be made of what it is that has been written down, or copied out, over a period of some forty years.

As the selections indicate, the substantive ideas expressed rather than their literary qualities have been the motivational influence in most cases, although particular aphorisms survive because of the how rather than the what of that which is said. The things written down are derivative from things that were read, and it is worthy of note here that the selections are not taken primarily from writings within my own discipline, economics, and only a few of the ideas expressed are relevant for this discipline's scientific enterprise. Most of the ideas are methodological, philosophical, or moral—relevant to the development and reinforcement of a generalizable personal philosophy for someone who just happens to have been trained professionally as an economist.

The classifications are arbitrary, and they have little independent meaning. They are imposed ex post on a previously selected subset of the contents of the three notebooks. I introduce the classification only to bring some sort of order to the structure. It is perhaps not surprising that the inclusive category labeled "Constitutional Rules, Politics, and the Law" should be the most extensive, since my interest has always been centered on the relations between the individual and the collective.

The selections were written down in the three black notebooks over four decades, roughly from the late 1940s through the late 1980s, with some weighting toward the middle years of this extended period. As I came to write more in the late 1970s and 1980s, the opportunity costs were measured in less time for reading and, hence, a smaller base from which statements of note might be chosen. Also, and admittedly, I have become more selective as my own ideas have matured.

I include this chapter partly for the simple purpose of ensuring the preservation of the selections. Beyond this purpose, however, there is the hypothesis that my own vision of myself and of the world about me may be quite accurately gleaned from these words of others.

II. *Analysis, Abstraction, and Education*

KNUT WICKSELL: I am ready to admit that one will be inclined to classify much of my discussion as armchair speculation. I accept this title gladly, for this is, in fact, the manner in which everything is able to be taken into account, and an inclusive, internally consistent, system constructed. And I, for this reason, never worry about the external consequences of carrying out my theory. How much of it—or whether any of it at all—may be practically applied in the near future, practical men may decide. I become the same as them if I try to take into account every conceivable practical criticism.

> Knut Wicksell, *Finanztheoretische Untersuchungen* (Jena: Fischer, 1896), Preface. (Translated by J. Buchanan)

LUIGI EINAUDI: The economist does not know, and should not know, and should not be concerned as to whether his theories, his models, his instruments of research, serve or should serve a few, many, all, or none. If they are not correct, others will expose the errors, modify them, perfect them. He can be happy if he has produced one small part of the edifice that continues always to become more majestic and beautiful.

Luigi Einaudi Inaugural Lecture for the
Academic Year 1949–50 at Torino, as cited in
Aldo Scotto, "Luigi Einaudi," *Economia
Internazionale* 15 (February 1962): 35.
(Translated by J. Buchanan)

MICHAEL POLANYI: Scientific knowing consists in discerning Gestalten that are aspects of reality.

Michael Polanyi, *Science, Faith, and Society*
(Chicago: Phoenix Books, 1964), 10.

KNUT WICKSELL: But it is not the purpose of science to describe the obvious in elaborate terms.

Knut Wicksell, *Lectures on Political Economy*
(London: Kegan Paul, 1934), 19.

FRIEDRICH NIETZSCHE: He is a thinker: that is to say he knows how to take things as being simpler than they are.

Die fröhliche Wissenschaft, as cited in
Ronald Hayman, *Nietzsche* (New York:
Penguin, 1982), 358.

IMMANUEL KANT: . . . if one denies him all understanding . . . , how can one make him understand that he has erred?

Immanuel Kant, *Metaphysik der Sitten* as cited
in M. J. Gregor, *Laws of Freedom* (New York:
Barnes and Noble, 1963), 190.

HERBERT SPENCER: Only by varied reiteration can alien conceptions be forced on reluctant minds.

Herbert Spencer, in the Preface to *Data of
Ethics*, as cited by Frank H. Knight in
"Professor Hayek and the Theory of
Investment," *Economic Journal,* 45 (March
1935): 94n.

LORD ACTON: Learn as much by writing as by reading; be not content with the best book; seek sidelights from the others; have no

favorites; keep men and things apart; guard against the prestige
of great names; see that your judgments are your own, and do
not shrink from disagreement; no trusting without testing; be
more severe to ideas than to actions; do not overlook the strength
of the bad cause or the weakness of the good; never be surprised
by the crumbling of an idol or the disclosure of a skeleton; judge
talent at its best and character at its worst; suspect power more
than vice; and study problems in preference to periods.

> Lord Acton, *Essays on Freedom and Power*
> (Glencoe: Free Press, 1948), 45.

III. *Choice, Imagination, Reality, and Time*

G. L. S. SHACKLE: Economic man is supposed to pursue his interest
by supplying reason to his circumstances. Since most of the circumstances that matter do not yet exist, but are waiting to be created by man's own choices, how does he know what his
circumstances are? What does he substitute for the knowledge
that is denied him by time itself, the elemental condition of men.

> G. L. S. Shackle, in a review of
> N. Rescher, *Unpopular Essays on Technological
> Progress* (1966), in *Journal of Economic
> Literature*, 19 (March 1980): 90.

JAMES JOYCE: Had Pyrrhus not fallen by a beldam's hand in Argos or
Julius Caesar not been knifed to death? They are not to be
thought away. Time has branded them and fettered they are
lodged in the room of the infinite possibilities they have ousted.
But can those have been possible seeing that they never were? Or
was that only possible which came to pass?

> James Joyce, *Ulysses* (London: Bodley Head,
> 1960), 30.

THOMAS SUTCLIFFE: The world doesn't just contain stories waiting to
be read out by writers, it is, as far as we know, formed by the ability to make plots.

> Thomas Sutcliffe, in a review, "Before the Art
> of Cunning," of Italo Calvo, *Adam: One
> Afternoon,* in *Times Literary Supplement*
> (London), September 2, 1983, 921.

ALFRED SCHUTZ: In terms of the past there is no possibility for choice. Having realized my work or at least portions of it, I chose once for all what has been done and have now to bear the consequences. I cannot choose what I want to have done.

> Alfred Schutz, *On Phenomenology and Social Relations*, (Chicago: University of Chicago Press, 1970), 71.

EDWIN LAND: Each step of human civilization is defined by our mental structures, the concepts we create, and then project upon the universe. They not only redescribe the universe but also in so doing modify it, both for our time and for subsequent generations.

> Edwin Land, Comments at Groundbreaking Ceremony, American Academy of Arts and Sciences, *Bulletin of the American Academy of Arts and Sciences*, 32 (May 1979): 6.

IRVING BABBITT: Words, especially abstract words, have such an important relation to reality because they control the imagination which in turn determines action and so "governs mankind."

> Irving Babbitt, *Democracy and Leadership* (Indianapolis: Liberty Press, 1979), 218.

LORD ACTON: The few have not strength to achieve great changes unaided; the many have not wisdom to be moved by truth unmixed. Where the disease is various, no particular definite remedy can meet the wants of all. Only the attraction of an abstract idea, or of an ideal state, can unite in a common action multitudes who seek a universal cure for many special evils, and a common restorative applicable to many different conditions. And hence false principles, which correspond with the bad as well as with the just aspirations of mankind, are a normal and necessary element in the social life of nations.

> Lord Acton, *Essays in Freedom and Power* (Glencoe: Free Press, 1948), 168.

A. GEOFFREY WOODHEAD: The man-in-the-street needs to have a moral reason and justification for doing what in fact he does do, or what he wants to do, even though he may not profess any high

standards of morality, or indeed, profess any morality based on
metaphysical or religious conviction; and he will feel this need
even though the actions themselves possess no inherent moral
connotation—when indeed they respond, on analysis, to laws
which are devoid of moral content.

> A. Geoffrey Woodhead, *Thucydides on the
> Nature of Power* (Cambridge: Harvard
> University Press, 1970), 152.

FRIEDRICH NIETZSCHE: Truth is the will to be master over the multiplicity of sensations. . . . In this . . . we take phenomena to be
real.

> *Der Wille zur Macht*, as cited in Ronald
> Hayman, *Nietzsche* (New York: Penguin, 1982),
> 357.

A. GEOFFREY WOODHEAD: If a man's life is essentially founded on
innocent falsehood, it is not correctly delineated or explained by
an analysis of the truth.

> A. Geoffrey Woodhead, *Thucydides on the
> Nature of Power* (Cambridge, Mass.: Harvard
> University Press, 1970), 159.

IV. *Constitutional Rules, Politics, and The Law*

THUCYDIDES: . . . as a general rule states are better governed by the
man in the street than by intellectuals. These are the sort of
people who want to appear wiser than the laws, who want to get
their own way in every general discussion, because they feel that
they cannot show off their intelligence in matters of greater importance, and who, as a result, very often bring ruin on their
country. But the other kind—the people who are not so confident in their own intelligence—are prepared to admit that the
laws are wiser than they are . . .

> Speech of Cleon, in Thucydides, *The
> Peloponnesian War* (Harmondsworth: Penguin
> Classics, 1977), 181.

ADAM FERGUSON: In free states, therefore, the wisest laws are never,
perhaps, dictated by the interest and spirit of any order of men:

they are moved, they are opposed, or amended by different hands; and come at last to express that medium and composition which contending parties have forced one another to adopt.

Adam Ferguson, *An Essay on the History of
Civil Society* (1767) (Edinburgh: Edinburgh
University Press, 1966), 128.

DAVID HUME: [It is] a just political maxim *that every man must be supposed a knave*: Though at the same time, it appears somewhat strange, that a maxim should be true in *politics*, which is false in *fact* . . . men are generally more honest in their private than in their public capacity, and will go to greater lengths to serve a party, than when their own private interest is alone concerned. Honour is a great check upon mankind: But where a considerable body of men act together, this check is, in a great measure, removed; since a man is sure to be approved by his own party . . . and he soon learns to despise the clamour of adversaries.

David Hume, "On the Independency of
Parliament," in *Essays*, 1:118–19, as cited in
Douglass Adair, *Fame and the Founding Fathers*
(New York: Norton, 1974), 102.

JOHN ADAMS: It will never be pretended that the men who set up the American governments had interviews with the gods, or were in any degree under the inspiration of Heaven.

John Adams, as cited by Herbert J. Muller,
Religion and Freedom in the Modern World
(Chicago: University of Chicago Press, 1963),
8.

RAYMOND ARON: Perhaps it will be otherwise. Perhaps the intellectual will lose interest in politics as soon as he discovers its limitations. Let us accept joyfully this uncertain promise. Indifference will not harm us. Men, unfortunately, have not yet reached the point where they have no further occasion or motive for killing one another. If tolerance is born of doubt, let us teach everyone to doubt all models and utopias, to challenge all prophets of redemption and heralds of catastrophe. If they alone can abolish fanaticism, let us pray for the advent of the skeptics. . . . Politics will always remain the art of the irrevocable choice by fallible men in unforeseen circumstances and semi-ignorance.

> Raymond Aron, *The Opium of the Intellectuals* (New York: Norton, 1955), 324 and 199.

FRANK H. KNIGHT: The economic view is rather superficial; the problem of conduct is less that of "satisfying wants" than one of making the rules of a game, a game that covers an infinite variety of component games. But it is both - and correspondingly complex and difficult.

> Frank H. Knight, "Virtue and Knowledge: The View of Professor Polanyi," *International Journal of Ethics*, 59 (July 1949): 281n.

R. G. ROSS: To insist that the majority is free, democratically, to do anything it pleases (and that a constitution in only the dead hand of the past) is like urging a man to behave on the impulse of the moment, not on the reflection of a lifetime.

> R. G. Ross, "Democracy, Party, and Politics," *International Journal of Ethics*, 64 (January 1954): 114.

LORD ACTON: Whenever a single definite object is made the supreme end of the State, be it the advantage of a class, the safety of the power of the country, the greatest happiness of the greatest number, or the support of any speculative idea, the State becomes for the time inevitably absolute: Liberty alone demands for its realization the limitation of the public authority, for liberty is the only object which benefits all alike, and provokes no sincere opposition.

> Lord Acton, *Essays on Freedom and Power* (Glencoe, Ill.: The Free Press, 1948), 184.

HENRY THOMAS BUCKLE: . . . the world has been made familiar with the great truth, that one main condition of the prosperity of a people is, that its rulers shall have very little power, that they shall exercise that power very sparingly, and that they shall by no means presume to raise themselves into supreme judges of the national interests, or deem themselves authorized to defeat the

44

wishes of those for whose benefit alone they occupy the post entrusted to them.

Henry Thomas Buckle, *History of Civilization in England* (New York: Hearst's International Library, 1913), 1:208.

W. A. Orton: It follows that a cardinal principle of policy is the elimination of coercion from all normal situations of social life and that the increase in coercion is too high a price to pay for no matter what collective ends. This is the point at which the defense of freedom begins to be called reaction by state planners, collectivists and militarists . . .

W. A. Orton, *The Economic Role of the State* (Chicago: University of Chicago Press, 1950), 105.

It is one of the central tenets of both liberal and Catholic doctrine that every person, great or small, cultured or lowly, every moment of time, every human generation, partakes of a significance that is absolute, second to no other; that to maintain the contrary in contemplation of a God who is supposed to be outside human time, or the divine presence, which is supposed to be inside human time, is, morally speaking, presumptuous, and, philosophically speaking, ridiculous. What any individual—even the weakest and meanest—is and becomes in himself, what he does by himself, with himself to himself, is not to be held of no account merely because, as is probably the case, it will make precious little difference to the state of society, the course of history or the fate of civilization. This is the true and fundamental basis of democracy; and if that institution tries to perpetuate itself on any other foundation than this, it will absurdly collapse—for there is none. To talk of states as if they were persons, endowed with the spiritual impulses and aspirations of human beings, and therefore morally accountable, is a piece of pure abstraction for which not even Hegel can be held responsible. It is a habit of modern journalism, catering to that mixture of vulgar passion and dominant materialism which renders unto Caesar the things that are God's because Caesar can be bribed.

W. A. Orton, *The Liberal Tradition* (New Haven: Yale University Press, 1945), 212 and 245.

ALDOUS HUXLEY: There was a time when I should have preferred to this rather sniffling enunciation of pious hopes and high ideals a more brutally "realistic" outburst in the manner of Mussolini. But that was long ago. I have outgrown my boyish admiration for political cynicism and am now an ardent believer in hypocrisy. The political hypocrite admits the existence of values higher than those of immediate national, party or economic interest. Having made the admission he cannot permit his actions to be too glaringly inconsistent with his professed principles. With him there are always "better feelings" to be appealed to. But the realist, the political cynic, has no "better feelings." To such a man it is obviously useless to talk about democracy.

The more cant there is in politics the better. Cant is nothing in itself; but attached to even the smallest quantity of sincerity, it serves like a nought after a numeral, to multiply whatever of genuine goodwill may exist.

> Aldous Huxley, in *Jesting Pilate,* as cited by G.
> G. Weinberg in a letter in *The Spectator,* July
> 31, 1971, 188.

JEREMY BENTHAM: To prevent our doing mischief to one another, it is but too necessary to put bridles in all our mouths: it is necessary to the tranquility and very being of society: but that the tacking of leading-strings upon the backs of grown persons, in order to prevent their doing themselves a mischief, is not necessary either to the being or tranquility of society, however conducive to its well-being, I think cannot be disputed.

> Jeremy Bentham, "Defense of Usury," in *Jeremy
> Bentham's Economic Writings,* ed. W. Stark
> (London: Royal Economic Society, 1952),
> 133.

WILHELM RÖPKE: When demanding assistance from the state people forget that it is a demand upon the other citizens merely passed on through the government, but believe they are making a demand upon a sort of Fourth Dimension which is supposed to be able to supply the wants of all and sundry to their hearts' content without any individual person having to bear the *burden.*

> Wilhelm Röpke, *Civitas Humana* (London:
> Wm. Hodge, 1948), 94.

JOHANN GOETHE AND FRIEDRICH NIETZSCHE: I think it is true that humanity will triumph eventually, only I fear that at the same time the world will be a large hospital and each will be the others' humane nurse.

> Johann Goethe, in a letter to Frau von Stein (1787). Cited in Walter Kaufmann, *Nietzsche* (Princeton: Princeton University Press, 1950), 323.

Because so much is done for others, the world is so imperfect.

> Friedrich Nietzsche, as cited in Kaufmann, *Nietzsche*, 323.

JOSÉ ORTEGA Y GASSET: Politics hurries to put out the light so that all these cats will be gray.

> José Ortega y Gasset, *Toward a Philosophy of History* (New York: Norton, 1941), 72.

ROBERT LOUIS STEVENSON: [Politics is] a wrongful striving after right.

> Robert Louis Stevenson, *The Lantern Blazers and Other Essays* (London: Chatto and Windus, 1988), 213.

DAVID MCCORD WRIGHT: You and I may both believe in planning, but my plan may be to kill you.

> David McCord Wright, *Democracy and Progress* (New York: Macmillan, 1948), xv.

JOHN DONNE:

> And though each spring do add to love new heat,
>   As princes do in action get,
> New taxes, and remit them not in peace,
> No winter shall abate the spring's increase.

> John Donne, in "Love's Growth," as cited in Jon Elster, *Ulysses and the Sirens* (Cambridge: Cambridge University Press, 1979), 170.

V. *Ethics*

ADAM SMITH: The qualities most useful to ourselves are, first of all, superior reasoning and understanding, by which we are capable of discerning the remote consequences of all our actions, and of foreseeing the advantage or detriment which is likely to result from them; and, secondly, self-command, by which we are enabled to abstain from present pleasure or to endure present pain, in order to obtain a greater pleasure or to avoid a greater pain in some future time. In the union of those two qualities consists the virtue of prudence, of all the virtues that which is most useful to the individual.

> Adam Smith, *The Theory of Moral Sentiments*
> (New Rochelle: Arlington House, 1969),
> 271–72.

T. H. HUXLEY: Social progress means a checking of the cosmic process at every step and the substitution for it of another, which may be called the ethical process; the end of which is not the survival of the fittest, in respect to the whole of the conditions which obtain, but of those who are ethically the best.

> T. H. Huxley, *Evolution and Ethics and Other
> Essays* (New York and London: Appleton,
> 1929), 81.

Frank H. Knight specifically recommended that I read T. H. Huxley and referred to this passage.

FRANK H. KNIGHT: There is a place, and a vital place, for an "absolute" science of ethics. Its dicta will not really be absolute, for they never cut loose entirely from the real world and its possibilities of growth and transformation, and they will always grow and change. But at least they are not "merely" relative; they must be beyond the immediately attainable, and will often lie in the field of the actually impossible, patterns to be approached rather than objectives to be obtained.

> Frank H. Knight, *The Ethics of Competition and
> Other Essays* (New York: Augustus M. Kelley,
> 1935), 44.

KARL POPPER: For those who have eaten from the tree of knowledge, paradise is lost. The more we try to return to tribal heroism, the more surely do we arrive at the Inquisition, at the Secret Police, and at a romanticized gangsterism. Beginning with the suppression of reason and truth, we must end with the most brutal and violent destruction of all that is human. There is no return to a harmonious state of nature. If we turn back, then we must go the whole way—we must return to the beasts.

It is an issue which we must face squarely, hard though it may be for us to do so. If we dream of a return to our childhood, if we are tempted to rely on others and so be happy, if we turn back from the task of carrying our cross, the cross of humaneness, of reason, of responsibility, if we lose courage and flinch from the strain, then we must try to fortify ourselves with a clear understanding of the simple decision before us. We can return to the beasts. But if we wish to remain human, then there is only one way, the way into the open society. We must go into the unknown, courageously, using what reason we have, to plan for security *and* freedom.

> Karl Popper, *The Open Society and Its Enemies*,
> (London: Routledge and Kegan Paul, 1945),
> 1:177.

JEAN PIAGET: The great difference between constraint and cooperation, or between unilateral respect and mutual respect, is that the first imposes beliefs or rules that are ready made and to be accepted *en bloc*, while the second only suggests a method—a method of verification and reciprocal control in the intellectual field, of justification and discussion in the domain of morals. It matters little whether this method be applied immediately to all rules imposed by the environment or only to one aspect of behavior: once it has come into existence it has the right to be applied to everything.

> Jean Piaget, *The Moral Judgment of the Child*
> (New York: Collier Books, 1962), 97.

RICHARD McKEON: A truth which is not subject to discussion is an impediment to the discovery of truth; an ideal which is used as an instrument is an impediment to the enrichment of values; a freedom of conformity is an impediment to the freedom of self-realization; an authoritarian society is an impediment to all processes of discussion and government by agreement.

> Richard McKeon, "Communication, Truth, and
> Society," *International Journal of Ethics*,
> 67 (January 1957): 94.

GEORG HEGEL: What is harmful is trying to preserve oneself from errors.

> Georg Hegel, as cited by Walter Kaufmann, in
> *Hegel: A Reinterpretation* (New York: Anchor
> Books, 1966), 157.

FRIEDRICH NIETZSCHE: Faith means not *wanting* to know what is true.

> Friedrich Nietzsche, in "Antichrist" as cited by
> Walter Kaufmann, *The Owl and the Nightingale*
> (London: Faber and Faber, 1959), 173.

FRANK KNIGHT: Truth is interesting chiefly because it is either "useful" or marvelous, or at least novel. "Mere" truth, completely established and beyond question, is a commonplace and a bore. Especially, truth is interesting because it is controversial, and in any case it is something to be pursued rather than to be possessed.

Truth itself is finally a value, and the will to believe the truth, rather than anything else that one might for any other reason wish to believe, is the foundation of all morality.

> Frank Knight, *Freedom and Reform* (New York:
> Harper, 1947), 342, 95.

FRIEDRICH NIETZSCHE: . . . a very popular error: having the courage of one's convictions; rather it is a matter of having the courage for an *attack* on one's convictions.

> Friedrich Nietzsche, *Der Wille zur Macht*,
> cited in Walter Kaufmann, *Nietzsche*
> (Princeton: Princeton University Press, 1950),
> 310.

PLATO: The philosopher sees that he has no ally with whose aid he might go and defend the right with a chance of safety. He is like a man in a den of wild beasts. Share their injustice he will not. He is not strong enough to hold out alone where all are savages. He would lose his life before he could do any benefit to the city or his friends, and so be equally useless to himself and the world. Weighing all these considerations, he holds his peace and does his own work, like a man in a storm sheltering behind a wall from the driving wind of dust and hail.

> Plato, *The Republic*, as cited in Elie Kedourie, *Nationalism* (London: Hutchison, 1961), 42n.

VI. *Intellectuals*

GEORGE ORWELL: You have to belong to the intelligentsia to believe things like that; no ordinary man would be such a fool.

> George Orwell, as cited by Robert Conquest in a letter to *The Times Literary Supplement* (London), July 8, 1965.

. . . perhaps when the pinch comes the common people will turn out to be more intelligent than the clever ones. I certainly hope so.

> George Orwell, *Collected Essays*, (London: Secker and Warburg, 1968), 1:410.

WALTER KAUFMANN (ON HEGEL'S "HALFWAY HOUSES"): . . . and those who inhabit them dim the lights and move around carefully lest they discover the limitations of their intellectual homes.

> Walter Kaufmann, *Hegel: A Reinterpretation* (New York: Anchor Books, 1966), 132.

VII. *Motive, Power, and Influence*

THOMAS HOBBES: . . . there is nothing not disputable, because it compareth men, and meddleth with their right and profit; in which as oft reasons is against a man, so oft will a man be against reason. And from hence it cometh that they that have written of justice and policy in general, do all invade each other, and themselves, with contradiction.

> Thomas Hobbes, *Elements*, Epistle Dedicatory, as cited in John W. Danford, *Wittgenstein and Political Philosophy* (Chicago: University of Chicago Press, 1978), 193.

SAMUEL JOHNSON: A man, who keeps his money, has in reality more use from it, than he can have by spending it. If it were certain that a man would keep his money locked up forever, to be sure he would have no influence; but, as so many want money, and he has the power of giving it, and they know not but by gaining his favour they may obtain it, the rich man will always have the greatest influence. He again who lavishes his money, is laughed at as foolish, and in a great degree with justice, considering how much is spent from vanity. Even those who partake of a man's hospitality, have but a transient kindness for him. If he has not the command of money, people know he cannot help them, if he would; whereas the rich man always can, and for the chance of that, will have much weight.

> Attributed to Samuel Johnson by James Boswell, in James Boswell, *The Journal of a Tour to the Hebrides with Samuel Johnson* (London: Everyman Edition, 1946), 83.

Power confers the ability of gratifying our desire without the consent of others. Wealth enables us to obtain the consent of others to our gratification. Power, simply considered, whatever it confers on one, must take from another. Wealth enables its owner to give to others, by taking only from himself.

> Samuel Johnson, *The Yale Edition of the Works of Samuel Johnson* (New Haven: Yale University Press, 1971), 94.

GEORGE ORWELL: Circus dogs jump when the trainer cracks his whip, but the really well-trained dog is the one that turns his somersault when there is no whip.

> George Orwell, as cited by John Wain, "Orwell and the Intelligentsia," *Encounter* 31 (December 1968): 72.

VIII. *Perspectives and Perceptions*

MOIRA ROBERTS: Loose talk about postulated ideal observers is out of place in philosophy, and indeed in any inquiry, and can be left to the special techniques of theology; for complete cognisance and ultimately true knowledge are matters of faith, not of logic.

> Moira Roberts, *Responsibility and Practical Freedom* (Cambridge: Cambridge University Press, 1965), 207.

Shirley Robin Letwin: Hopefulness is not only reasonable, but obligatory, because despair betrays an arrogant pretension to foresee the future with certainty, to know what mortal beings may not hope to know.

> Shirley Robin Letwin, *The Gentlemen in
> Trollope: Individuality and Moral Conduct*
> (Cambridge, Mass.: Harvard University Press, 1982),
> 63.

F. Scott Fitzgerald: The test of a first-rate intelligence is the ability to hold two opposed ideas at the same time, and still retain the ability to function. One should, for example, be able to see that things are hopeless and yet be determined to make them otherwise . . . I must hold in balance the sense of futility of effort and the sense of the necessity to struggle; the conviction of the inevitability of failure and still the determination to succeed.

> F. Scott Fitzgerald, in *The Crack-Up*, as cited in
> *The Times Literary Supplement* (London),
> March 29, 1974, 314.

Iris Murdoch: The humble man, because he sees himself as nothing, can see other things as they are.

> Iris Murdoch, as cited by Stephen Metcalf in
> *The Spectator* (November 1, 1968), 632.

Albert Camus: The important thing, as Abbé Galiani said to Mme. d'Epinay, is not to be cured, but to live with one's ailments.

> Albert Camus, *The Myth of Sisyphus* (London:
> Hamish Hamilton, 1955), 36.

Joseph Conrad: For every age is fed on illusions, lest men should renounce life early and the human race come to an end.

> Joseph Conrad, *Victory* (New York: Modern
> Library, 1932), 91.

Friedrich Nietzsche: . . . to look now out of this now out of that window, being wary of settling anywhere . . .

> Friedrich Nietzsche, *Der Wille zur Macht*,
> as cited in Walter Kaufmann, *Nietzsche*
> (Princeton: Princeton University Press, 1950),
> 61.

JAKOB BURCKHARDT: Greatness is all that we are *not*. To the beetle in the grass the hazel-bush (if he so much as notices it) may seem great just because he is a beetle.

> Jakob Burckhardt, *Reflections on History* (Indianapolis: Liberty Press, 1979), 303.

NORBERT WEINER: . . . our main obligation is to establish arbitrary enclaves of order and system. These enclaves will not remain there indefinitely by any momentum of their own after we have established them . . . we are not fighting for a definitive victory in the indefinite future. It is the greatest possible victory to be, to continue to be, and to have been. No defeat can deprive us of the process of having existed for some moment of time in a universe that seems indifferent to us.

> Norbert Weiner, *I Am a Mathematician* (Cambridge, Mass.: MIT Press, 1956), 325.

FRIEDRICH NIETZSCHE: Escape, my friend, into your solitude, where the air is fresh and strong. It is not for you to chase flies.

> Friedrich Nietzsche, in "On Flies in the Marketplace," as cited in Ronald Hayman, *Nietzsche* (New York: Penguin, 1982), 259.

F. SCOTT FITZGERALD: . . . life is much more successfully looked at from a single window, after all.

> F. Scott Fitzgerald, *The Great Gatsby* (New York: Scribners, 1925), 3.

JAMES JOYCE: It is an age of exhausted whoredom groping for its god.

> James Joyce, *Ulysses* (London: Bodley Head, 1960), 265.

T. H. HUXLEY: The constant widening of the intellectual field indefinitely extended the range of that especially human faculty of looking before and after, which adds to the fleeting present those old and new worlds of past and future, wherein men dwell the more the higher their culture. But the very sharpening of the sense and that subtle refinement of emotion, which brought such a wealth of pleasures, were fatally attended by a proportional enlargement of the capacity for suffering; and the divine faculty of imagination, while it created new heavens and new earths, provided them with the corresponding hells of futile regret for the past and morbid anxiety for the future. Finally, the inevitable penalty of over-stimulation, exhaustion, opened the gates of civilization to its greatest enemy, ennui; the stale and flat weariness when man delights not, nor woman neither; when all things are vanity and Vexation; and life seems not worth living except to escape the "bore of dying."

T. H. Huxley, *Evolution and Ethics and Other Essays* (New York and London: Appleton, 1929), 55.

JOHN UPDIKE: In the western world there are only two comical things, the Christian church and naked women . . . Everything else tells us we are dead.

John Updike, *Couples* (New York: Knopf, 1968), 146.

JAMES JOYCE: The high roads are dreary but they lead to the town.

James Joyce, *Ulysses* (London: Bodley Head, 1960), 250.

IX. *The Utility of Composition*

ST. AUGUSTINE: I am the sort of man who writes because he has made progress, and who makes progress—by writing.

St. Augustine, *Letters*, as cited in Peter Brown, *Augustine of Hippo* (Berkeley: University of California Press, 1967), 353.

ARNOLD SCHÖNBERG: Had this morning suddenly a great desire to compose. After a very long time! I had already envisaged the possibility that I might never compose again. There seem to be many reasons to give for this. The obstinacy with which my students tread on my heels, as they strive to outbid what I offer, puts me in danger of becoming their imitator, and prevents me from consolidating what I have built on the ground where I already stand. They raise everything at once to the tenth power. And it works! It is really good. But I do not know if it is necessary. That is why I am now forced to decide yet more carefully than before whether I must write. Since—I do not attach much importance of my originality; but it often gives me joy, and in any case I prefer it to unoriginality. Then came the occupation with theoretical questions. This decidedly dries one up. And perhaps that is why I suddenly after two years no longer feel so young. I have become remarkably tranquil. . . . What I lack is an aggressive spirit. The quick going-outside-oneself, and the ability to attack, to grab. Perhaps it will be better that I do, nevertheless, compose again. Or, indeed, it is better. I remember that I wrote a poem ten or twelve years ago in which I wanted to become old and without ambition, tranquil. Now I suddenly see the earlier possibilities of disquiet again, I almost long for them. Or, are they already there once more?

Arnold Schönberg, written on March 12, 1912, in his *Berliner Tagebuch*, ed. Joseph Rufer (Berlin: Propylaen, 1975), as cited in *The Times Literary Supplement* (London), November 7, 1975, 1335.

10

From the Inside Looking Out

I. *Introduction*

I N THE EARLY 1970s, I received a short and strange note from a woman whom I had met at a European conference. The note asked me, quite straightforwardly, to outline my philosophy of life in a single paragraph not more than a half-page in length. The challenge was sufficient to make me respond, and my outline summary was expanded into, first, a lecture, and, later, a brief chapter in a book.[1] I now interpret that response to be an adequate statement of what I should call my "public philosophy," a statement that requires little or no emendation after a decade's ripening. In this chapter I respond differently. Partly in order to differentiate the product and partly to meet what seems to have been the particular desires of the editors of the series for which this chapter was initially written, I shall here offer a statement of my "private philosophy," or, rather, a set of statements about separate attributes of my personal stance before my own gods.

I shall limit the autobiographical narrative here, because I have traced out portions of my life story in other chapters in this book. This chapter is personal rather than autobiographical. That is to say,

---

1. See James M. Buchanan, "Criteria for a Free Society: Definition, Diagnosis, and Prescription," in *Freedom in Constitutional Contract: Perspectives of a Political Economist* (College Station: Texas A&M University Press, 1977), 287–99.

I shall describe how I look out at the world beyond as opposed to any attempt to look on myself as an object of narrative exposition. There is a sense in which this sort of private or personal statement of a philosophy becomes almost the intellectual opposite of auto-biography.

II. *Is It My Task to Save the World?*

I shall commence this section with a lengthy citation from Frank H. Knight:

> It is intellectually impossible to believe that the individual can have any influence to speak of, . . . on the course of history. But it seems to me that to regard this as an ethical difficulty involves a complete misconception of the social-moral problem . . . I find it impossible to give meaning to an eth-ical obligation on the part of the individual to improve society.
>
> The disposition of an individual, under liberalism, to take upon himself such a responsibility seems to be an exhibition of intellectual and *moral* conceit . . . ; it is *un*ethical. Ethical-social change must come about through a genuine moral consensus among individuals meeting on a level of genuine equality and mutuality and not with any one in the role of cause and the rest in that of effect, of one the "potter" and the others as "clay."[2]

I have long felt a strong affinity for Knight's position. But I have found it difficult to go beyond affirmation of agreement and to mount persuasive argument in support. We face squarely the ques-tion: If no individual assumes responsibility for improving society, how can society ever improve, other than through the forces of evo-lutionary change? I am on record as rejecting acquiescence before the forces of cultural evolution. I have stated, on numerous occa-sions, that we have a moral obligation to think that we can con-structively design and implement reform in social arrangements.

Any appearance of paradox vanishes if care is taken to read and to understand what Frank Knight says in the statement quoted above. He is not advancing a logic of rationally grounded abstention from discussion about changes in the rules for social order. He is de-fining the limits or constraints under which any individual must place himself as he enters into such discussion. The moral conceit

---

2. Frank H. Knight, "Intellectual Confusion on Morals and Economics," *Interna-tional Journal of Ethics*, 45 (January 1935): 218.

that bothers Knight arises when any individual, or group, presumes to take on the responsibility for others, independently of their expressed agreement in a setting of mutuality and reciprocity. The underlying principle is indeed a simple one: Each person counts equally. And even if this principle counters observed empirical reality in terms of measurable criteria, adherence to the principle must remain relatively absolute, even on an acknowledged "as if" basis.

This principle has been a central element in my own approach to political economy. I have always thought it to be my task to develop and create ideas and to enter these ideas into the discussion matrix. Once this step is taken, my task is done. I have felt, and feel, no moral obligation to promulgate my own ideas, or those of others. In this attitudinal dimension I differ sharply from many of my disciplinary colleagues in economics. I have never been didactically motivated, despite reasonable career success in teaching, especially at the graduate level. For me utility enhancement stems from working out ideas for myself and with sufficient clarity to enable me to present a coherent and aesthetically satisfying argument. Ultimate publication reconfirms initial judgments in this respect. If my ideas succeed in persuading others to view the social world in a fashion similar to my own way, I secure secondary utility gains. But if my ideas fail to persuade, and the implied reforms in social arrangements do not occur, my private utility losses are no greater than those of persons who do not enter the discussion. I do not, in any sense, accept responsibility for the results of the interaction process in which I am only one among many participants. I cannot as Knight suggests, move the world unaided, and it is morally arrogant of me to imagine myself in a position of power sufficient to enable me to act unilaterally.

Respect for the individual, as one among many participants in the social network of interaction, imposes a necessary humility on the social scientist. This humility is a stance that must be deliberately maintained. The natural scientist faces no comparable choice; he works within the constraints imposed by the almost total exogeneity of the subject matter that he explores. The social scientist must acknowledge the endogeneity of the structure of social interaction, at least within broad limits. But the endogeneity applies to the whole community of participants, including the scientist. Imagined, and potentially realizable, structures of social interaction alternative to that which is observed to exist are within the set of those that are made feasible by physical and natural limits, including the nature of man. The social scientist defaults on his duty if he fails to model structures of interaction "that might be." As the social scientist makes predictions about the working properties of imagined alternative structures, he becomes both internally and externally vulnerable in a manner unknown to the natural scientist. Precisely because the direct linkage between observed reality and theories about that reality is abandoned, the discipline imposed by potential testability (falsifiability) is weakened. The social scientist is internally tempted to bias his argument toward structures that reflect his normative values. And even if he succeeds in thwarting this temptation, his critics will charge that he has not done so.

The fact-value distinction so beloved by second-rate methodologists confuses rather than enlightens. The social scientist who predicts "what might be" is not working within the realm of facts that may be observed in historical reality. The often observed pitiful efforts to milk empirical data to reinforce hypothetical predictions reflect misunderstanding of the whole enterprise.

III. *Science or Art?*

I have never been attracted to enter the sometimes complex upper reaches of the philosophy of science, and particularly the discussion of "economics as a science." I have not shied away from presenting my own methodological position, which does, indeed, ensure that I remain an outsider in this as in so many other aspects of my endeavors.[3] But discussion among philosophers of science, per se, has always seemed to me to use the natural sciences as a model and to embody a failure to appreciate the distinguishing features of social science, only some of which I noted in the previous section.

It is precisely because of my conviction that social science is different from natural science that I find myself more sympathetic to the interpretist critique than most of my economist peers, save for a

3. See James M. Buchanan, "Positive Economics, Welfare Economics, and Political Economy," *Journal of Law and Economics*, 2 (October 1959): 124–38; "What Should Economists Do?," *Southern Economic Journal*, 30 (January 1964): 213–22.

few who locate themselves among modern Austrians. Yet while I am more sympathetic to the criticism, I should insist that the social scientist hold fast to the truth directed morality of his natural science counterpart. My position can perhaps be clarified by examining, in comparison and contrast, the scientist and the artist, with the former described in the role normally assigned to the natural scientist. I return to the exogeneity of the subject matter with which the natural scientist works, the reality that is, independently of his own understanding of its inner workings. The behavior of the scientist is *discovery*; he finds that which exists, and his imaginative talents are deployed in the search process. There is, and should be, no pretense that something new is created.

By comparison and contrast, consider the artist. He is, of course, constrained by the physical limits of his medium, be this paint or stone. But it is totally misleading to model the artist's act as discovery. The artist creates something where there was nothing. Both the act of scientific discovery and that of artistic creation are intensely private as they are carried out. But the products divide sharply along the public-private dimension, once the acts are done. Scientific discovery is public in the classical sense; once made available to anyone it can be available to everyone. Artistic creation is available to everyone once it is done; but that which is created may be privately interpreted in many and varied ways.

This comparative sketch should suggest that social science, as an activity, falls somewhere between the two models. Because the social scientist must explore the working properties of imagined alternatives to that which may be observed, constrained only by the natural limits of the material with which he or she works, his or her activity has elements that are more akin to those that inform the artistic process than the scientific. On the other hand, the ultimate motivation matches that of the scientist, not the artist. The social scientist works in the hope that improvement in the processes of social interaction may finally emerge upon agreement on both diagnosis and effective reform; aesthetic experience plays little role.

My own subdisciplinary prejudices should be evident. Within economics, I look on the efforts of the general equilibrium theorists, even if these efforts are sometimes extended to unnecessarily rarified abstraction, to be potentially more productive of insight than the works of those empiricists who behave as if the reality of social interaction embodies an exogeneity comparable to that of the physical world.

IV. *Normative and Positive Political Economy*

Critics have charged that my work has been driven by an underlying normative purpose, and, by inference, if not directly, they have judged me to be mildly subversive. As I noted earlier, anyone who models interaction structures that might be is likely to be accused of biasing analysis toward those alternatives that best meet his personal value standards. Whether or not my efforts have exhibited bias in this sense is for others to determine. I shall acknowledge that I work always within a self-imposed constraint that some may choose to call a normative one. I have no interest in structures of social interaction that are nonindividualist in the potter-clay analogy mentioned in the earlier citation from Frank Knight. That is to say, I do not extend my own analysis to alternatives that embody the *rule* of any person or group of persons over other persons or group of persons. If this places my work in some stigmatized normative category, so be it.

The individualist element in my vision of social reality, actual or potential, has been an important component of my substantive criticism of the work of others in political economy. I have remained unable either to share in the enthusiasm for the social welfare function of formal welfare economics or to participate putatively in proffering advice to a presumed benevolently despotic government. There are at least three distinguishable sources of my criticism of orthodox political economy. First, I have been influenced by Frank Knight and by F. A. Hayek in their insistence that the problem of social order is not scientific in the standard sense. Second, I was greatly influenced by Knut Wicksell's admonition that economists should cease acting as if government were a benevolent despot. Third, I rejected, very early in my thinking, the orthodox economist's elevation of allocative efficiency as an independent standard of evaluation.

These three sources seem internally consistent, and properly combined they have provided me with my own window on the political economy. From this window I found it relatively easy to mount criticism of much of the conventional wisdom. There seemed to be no shortage of matters to be straightened out, and I have been quite happy to leave to others the classification into normative or positive categories.

Wicksell's was perhaps the most significant influence, but without Knight's teaching and without my conversion to a catallactic perspective, Wicksell's message might not have been so compelling to me. However, once Wicksell's advice is heeded, once we acknowledge that governmental or political outcomes are, themselves, produced by an interaction of persons, acting in varying roles, the political economist necessarily must extend analysis to the process of interaction and to the relation between process and patterns of results. The theory of public choice, at least my own version of this theory, was an almost natural consequence of my absorption of the Wicksellian message.[4]

Conceptualization of political reality as emergent from the interacting behavior of many persons immediately suggests that patterns of results depend on the rules or institutions within which behavior takes place. Constitutional political economy, in both its normative and positive variants, replaces the political economy of policy at center stage. The shift of focus to rules comes quite naturally to the economist who has been exposed to the approach of modern game theory. But concentration on processes rather than outcomes does not fit well within the orthodoxy of political science, the premodern origins of which involve idealizations of parliamentary regimes. Despite our expressed intent to model the logical foundations of constitutional democracy, roughly corresponding to the Madisonian enterprise, Gordon Tullock and I found a very mixed reception to our book, *The Calculus of Consent.*[5]

There seemed to be a surprising reluctance of modern social scientists, economists and political scientists alike, to accept the two stage decision structure which constitutional understanding re-

4. The relationship between the precursory ideas of Wicksell and later developments in public choice theory was the subject of my Nobel Prize lecture in December 1986. See James M. Buchanan, "The Constitution of Economic Policy," *American Economic Review*, 77 (June 1987): 243–50.

5. James M. Buchanan and Gordon Tullock, *The Calculus of Consent: Logical Foundations of Constitutional Democracy* (Ann Arbor: University of Michigan Press, 1962).

quires, and which all game theorists necessarily adopt. For over a quarter-century, I have found myself trying to clarify the constitutional perspective on policies, and on the economy as well, with demonstrable but quite limited success.

V. *An Outsider Comes Inside*

Nonetheless, the dialogue has been shifted. "Constitutional economics" or "constitutional political economy" has emerged as an entry in *The New Palgrave*. My own emphasis on the importance of the rules of the socio-economic-political game was recognized in the Nobel award citation in 1986. No longer could I claim status as a genuine outsider, whose efforts continue to be largely ignored by my peers in the academy. Within limits, and despite my stance of relative indifference noted earlier, my ideas now begin to have consequences. I do not yet know how I shall react when and if specific changes in rules are more or less directly traceable to my influence. I do not welcome becoming an "insider" in any sense, and my own efforts over four decades can only be understood in terms of the outsider image of myself that has been an integral part of my personal luggage.

The outsider appellation explains the somewhat singular type of self-confidence that I have always had to a degree, and that has been reinforced over four decades. I have been academically successful, far beyond any plausibly predictable range, more or less "in spite of" my limitations rather than "because of" my capacities. I would never have been really surprised had my work failed to prove acceptable for publication, had my published work been neglected more than it was, had my career advancement been less rapid, had there been no series of alternative opportunities in the competitive academic environment of the United States, had I not been awarded the Nobel Prize in 1986. I have never felt, nor do I feel today, that there is much that is unique or special about what I have done or what I do, write, and say. My surprise, and this surprise has continued for four decades, is not at all that my own work is relatively neglected; my surprise is, instead, at the failure of other economists to have acknowledged the simple and the obvious, which is all that I have ever claimed my work to be. In a sense I have felt embarrassment of sorts at being placed in the role of telling my far more clever peers that the emperor really has no clothes.

Why was it my task to point out that economists should postulate some model of polices before proffering policy advice? Why, among the many critics of Arrow's important work on the general impossibility theorem, did it fall on me to point out that the satisfaction of his plausible conditions would amount to political tyranny rather than effective democracy? Why was it necessary for me to demonstrate that classical public debt theory was logically valid, in face of the Keynesian macroaggregation absurdities? Why was it required to show that genuinely sacrificed opportunities must be measured in a utility dimension? These and other "contributions" attributed to me might not have been made if I had worked as an "insider," involved in the complexities of analytical discussion along the heated cutting edges of economics. Such an insider may have found himself unable to take the comprehensive perspective on elements of subject matter that my outsider position allowed me to assume, almost as a matter of course.

It is in this respect that I do not especially welcome the increasing academic respectability-popularity of my own ideas. As a critic of prevailing orthodoxies, I had no reason to back up and respond to critics of my constructions, which seemed, in any case, to be triturations of the obvious. As my ideas approach mainstream, at least in some aspects, I find myself being challenged to defend foundational normative sources that I had long considered to be widely shared. The fact that my own acknowledged normative starting points do not seem so widely accepted as I should have expected may possibly account for the apparent oversight of propositions that seemed so obvious to me. In other words, my normative mindset may be more important than I have ever realized.

VI. *Why Not Sit in My Rocking Chair?*

I resist, and resist strongly, any and all efforts to pull me toward positions of advising on this or that policy or cause. I sign no petitions, join no political organizations, advise no party, serve no lobbying effort. Yet the public's image of me, and especially as developed through the media after the Nobel award in 1986, is that of a right-wing libertarian zealot, who is antidemocratic, antiegalitarian, and antiscientific. I am, of course, none of these, and am, indeed, the opposites. Properly understood, my position is both democratic and egalitarian, and I am as much a scientist as any of my disciplinary peers in economics. But I am passionately individualistic, and my emphasis on individual liberty does set me apart from many of my academic colleagues whose mindsets are mildly elitist and, hence, collectivist. And, to these colleagues, I can never be forgiven for having contributed to the development of a subdiscipline, public choice, that has exposed the operation of collectivist-political institutions to serious scrutiny for the first time in well over a century.

Why do I continue to work? Why do I not retire gracefully to my mountain farm in Virginia, sit in my front porch rocking chair and stand bemused at the follies of the world? Since I have acknowledged that I do not presume to move the world unaided, and that I have no urge to do so, what inner forces drive me? My answer, as adumbrated, is simple and straightforward. I work because I enjoy it! I get utility in ideas, in thinking, in organizing my thoughts, in writing these thoughts in coherent argument, in seeing my words in manuscript and in print. In some real sense I am a writer, who enjoys living in my own world, a world that some critics claim to be fictional, but which I defend as feasibly attainable territory. I am also a lecturer, perhaps a century out of date, and I get utility from the receptive feedback from an intellectually competent audience. Here again, my ultimate purpose, either in writing or in lecturing, is not so much to convince readers or listeners of the merits of my argument as to engage them in ongoing discussion.

Above all, perhaps, I am an intellectual reductionist who seeks to cut through the complexities of argument and to understand points in simple terms and homely examples. As noted earlier, much of my work has been in the form of exposé, and hence of a sort that is rarely welcomed by those who are natural obscurantists.

When all is said, I have faced few genuine choices between work and play because there is really no distinction. My work is my play, and I am surely among the fortunate in this as in so many other aspects of a happy and well-ordered life. I have not been plagued by psychological hangups that make me try to respond to the "whys" of existence or the "whats" beyond. I hope that I seem what I think I am: a constitutional political economist who shares an appreciation for the Judeo-Christian heritage that produced the values of Western culture and institutions of civil order, particularly as represented in the Madisonian vision of what the United States might have been and might still become. Am I grossly naïve to think this definition is sufficient unto itself??

C H A P T E R
11

Nobelity

I. *Introduction*

ON OCTOBER 17, 1988, it was announced that Maurice Allais had been awarded the 1988 Nobel Memorial Prize in Economic Sciences. I was delighted by the selection of Allais, whom I had come to know well during his semester-long visit with us at the University of Virginia in 1959–60, and whose work I had considered to have been too much and too long neglected. With this announcement, however, came another reaction. A full two years had passed since my own unexpected telephone call from the Royal Academy of Sciences in Stockholm on October 16, 1986. The second anniversary of that event seemed to offer me a time for reflection and reassessment, a time to pursue, at least partially, a "before" and "after" comparison, a time to respond in a considered way to the question so often posed to me: How did the Nobel award change my life?

I must acknowledge that change has occurred, despite my professed early statement of intent reinforced by continuing personal resistance. It is only small exaggeration to state that I have been dragged, kicking and screaming, into the celebrity status that all Nobel laureates necessarily come to occupy. And, for reasons that I shall note later, this dramatic dislocation involved relatively more "social distance" for me than for most of my Nobel peers, a fact that, in itself, exerted its own feedback pressures on academic tranquillity.

II. *Before October 1986*

Other autobiographical chapters in this book summarize backward-looking accounts of several stages of my academic and nonacademic life experience. I shall limit discussion in this section to points in this long experience that seem directly relevant to the subject at hand, the Nobel Memorial Prize in 1986.

First, I can state, and categorically, that any directed or targeted objective such as "winning the Nobel Prize" was never within the remotest horizon of my vision. I suspect that this total absence of "Nobelity" from career objectives describes almost all of my peers within the discipline, if for no other reason than the relative youth of the prize in economic science. Economists of my generation, or of the one immediately preceding or immediately following, matured as professionals well before a Nobel Memorial Prize in Economic Sciences came into existence. We could scarcely have dreamed of such an award.

Quite apart from such necessary absence from my own psyche, however, and even after the economics prize came into being, there was no intrusion into my own consciousness of even the slightest prospect that, one day, I might be selected. Motivational stimuli did not exist. There were, I think, good reasons for my shutting out that which later emerged as possible. As I have noted in other essays in this book, I have never lacked self-confidence, and this quality has extended to ideas, including those that counter the conventional wisdom of my discipline. But the nonorthodoxy of my ideas, both in subject and in method, my ideological distance from the dominant mindset, and the provinciality of my institutional-locational experience seemed more than sufficient to insure against any potential achievement of serious consideration for a Nobel Prize. This self-apologist attitude was also reinforced by an honest assessment of my intellectual limits.

I was, of course, pleased throughout my career by the external recognition of my contributions, as instanced by attractive employment opportunities that were not realized, by elevation to offices in regional, national, and international professional associations, and, particularly, by pre-Nobel awards of honorary doctorates by the University of Giessen (Germany) in 1983, and the University of Zurich (Switzerland) in 1984, and the Frank Siedman Award in Political Economy (1984). Finally, I was pleased, if amused, when in the early 1980s, colleagues, more in Europe than in the United States, began to mention nominations for the Nobel Memorial Prize.

Prospects that I might be seriously considered emerged quite suddenly in mid-1984. Rumors abound in international academia, and I came to be aware that my name emerged often in casual conversations at conferences. Requests for interviews by the press, again notably in Europe, seemed to have become more frequent. And, importantly, at a Stockholm conference in August 1984 on the growth of government, itself sponsored by the Nobel Foundation, I seemed to be placed in a position that commanded unusual personal deference. Predictions that I would, indeed, be awarded the Nobel Memorial Prize in 1984 seemed to have been widely made, and occasionally my name was noted in print. At the least by August 1984 I arrived at the awesome realization that, like it or not, prepared or not, I was in some considerable danger of getting myself "psyched up," of allowing expectations to build up which could only serve to impose possibly severe psychological damage in the event of ultimate disappointment.

I have never experienced psychological hangups, at least at any level of rational recognition. But my situation in August 1984 did threaten to be of such portent that I began to fear my own reactions. I recognized full well that somehow, in some way, I needed to get my own psyche bottled up; I needed to stifle the positive expectations that had been thrust upon me. To the maximum extent possible, I needed to prepare myself for possibly dramatic disappointment, made so, in part, surely by the unexpected and sudden build up in positive expectations.

I was in Europe during all of the weeks when this crisis developed. Immediately after the Stockholm conference I was scheduled to participate in the Alpbach European Forum in Alpbach, Austria, a fine location in the Tyrolian Alps, and surely one of the world's most attractive quasi-academic events. I knew in advance that a longtime friend from Dallas, Texas, Marsha Ard, and a longtime Alpbach devotee, would be a participant in the forum. Immediately on arrival, I sought Marsha out and asked her, simply, to listen to my story. I shall always be grateful to Marsha Ard for serving as my amateur psychiatrist, who allowed me to talk my way out of my dilemma. A sympathetic and appreciative listener who understood the magnitude of the issues involved was precisely what I needed. I was able to get on top of myself with newfound respect for the role of the analyst, and, from that point forward, I was able to survive the ensuing two months with reasonable tranquillity.

And it was well that I did. For, as I had feared, I was not selected in 1984. The recipient of the Nobel Memorial Prize in Economic Sciences that year was Richard Stone, a British pioneer in national accounting who had largely been forgotten. I was, of course, personally disappointed that the earlier rumors were unfounded. But my self-sensed warnings that had been heeded served me well. There was no shock, no profound sadness, sorrow, regret, or feeling of injustice. I was able to ride well with the punch, to consider myself fortunate to have been considered seriously, if at all, and to go about my ordinary affairs of academia.

I do not know what did happen in 1984. Were the rumor mills simply totally wrong? Or do such rumors emerge two years out of time phase? Or was my nomination vetoed by some member or members of the Swedish committee? Or was the committee's nomination overruled by the foundation? I was, and remain, content to remain unenlightened.

I can attest only to my own attitudes. Having been, quite surprisingly and suddenly, elevated into prominence as a possible Nobel Prize awardee in 1984, I held out no post-1984 hope of selection. The most plausible scenario, from my personal perspective, was that my name had been proposed with some support, but that I had failed to meet the requirements somewhere during the rather mysterious selection process. And, once having come close, in my own reading of the matter, I presumed, and without any knowledge at all, that my prospects were no longer alive.

I was, therefore, pleased for Franco Modigliani when his name was announced in October 1985, as I would have been pleased for any one of several other fine prospects. There was, for me, a total absence of any sense of disappointment save for those days-weeks in August-October 1984, when suddenly all things seemed to be within the possible.

I could not, then, have been better prepared for the telephone call on October 16, 1986. I experienced the exhilaration that only accompanies total surprise, while, at the same time, the 1984 events had served to bring my selection within the realm of the possible. The updated 1984 imaginings of what might be offered me elements of stability in the 1986 realization of what had come into being.

III. *October–December 1986*

I am an early riser, and I had finished my breakfast, brushed my teeth, and was on the way out the door of my Fairfax townhouse when the telephone call from Stockholm came at 6:32 A.M. on October 16, 1986. My schedule called for a half-day's work at George Mason University before driving down the Shenandoah Valley in October's colorful splendor to my country place, tucked deep in Virginia's Appalachians. My wife, Ann, had been at the country place all summer; we had not yet made the semiannual, quasi-move from the country place to Washington's suburbia, a move that we delay each year as long as possible.

The telephone call changed all such plans. I called Ann, then Betty Tillman, my long-time girl Friday, and escaped from the townhouse after only one other call, from CBS Morning News. On arrival at the office shortly before 7 A.M., it was already abundantly clear that October 16 would not be an ordinary day. Representatives from the print, sight, and sound media had commenced to arrive, and the parking lot was soon filled with sending towers and dishes. The phones went wild, and Betty rounded up all of the building's clerical staff, plus graduate students as they arrived, for assistance. Helen Ackerman, the university's public relations director, came to help with press contacts. We hastily organized a news conference for 11 A.M., which went on for an hour with perhaps one hundred in attendance.

In part this unexpected concentration of attention on my selection for the Nobel award was temporal and locational. Congress was not in session, and the Iran-Contra scandal was bubbling just beneath the surface of exposure. The Washington suburb, Fairfax City, is only a half-hour from the district. I was "the news" of the day, and quite in contrast with Robert Solow, who a year later, was named as the 1987 Nobel Memorial Prize recipient on the day after Black Monday's stock market crash.

Basically, the early releases were informationally accurate and largely biographical. Who is James Buchanan? Where and what is George Mason University? What is Public Choice? Perhaps I responded too quickly to the last of these questions, and perhaps in my eagerness to be understood I jumped too readily into the application of public choice analysis to the budget deficit. As a result, all sophistication in evaluation was lost, and the secondary journalistic accounts that appeared in the days immediately after October 16 were simplistic, grossly misleading, and could have been taken to be insulting to me personally. Along with most of the other Nobel laureates in economics, my selection was ridiculed by the media ignoramuses, in my case on the grounds that any fool knows that public choosers seek to promote their own interests. This type of criticism, stemming from uninformed journalistic arrogance, is unique to economics, and it is a cross that we bear in a science that has never isolated itself sufficiently from the public discourse. Every man his own economist—this has proved to be the scourge of rational public discourse for the lifetime of political economy.

Tertiary accounts, both positive and negative, that appeared in the weeklies and monthlies were more thoughtful, since they were written by journalists who made at least some effort to understand the award by reading my books rather than the reports of other journalists.

It was apparent, very soon after October 16, that, had I chosen to do so, I could have "enjoyed" widespread media exposure on the Washington-based talk shows that are centered on economic and political events. My very early reactions were surely the correct ones. Aside from a first day appearance on the McNeil-Lehrer PBS Newshour, I turned down all invitations for TV, radio, and guest column slots. I am not a policy analyst, and my views on current issues should carry little more weight than those of anyone else. I was determined not to become an "instant expert" on everything merely because I had achieved the notoriety of the Nobel Memorial Prize.

A full day did not pass before I came to realize that my selection was special in its own way and unrelated to me in a directly personal sense. As I suggested earlier, I had never entertained the prospect of Nobel Prize status, despite considerable academic acclaim, because I held myself, my work, and my affiliation to be too far outside the mainstream of both my own discipline and American academia. (And I know that I would never have been selected for such an award had the selection committee been drawn from senior American economists!) But this very distance from the central thrusts in subject matter, research method, ideology, institutional affiliation, regional location, and personal history also insured that, once the distinguished Swedish committee chose me for the Nobel award, I would become, in a real sense, "representative" of all members of the several intersecting sets of scholars and students. As I stated (chapter 3) on my return to a celebration in my honor in Tennessee in early 1988, "If Jim Buchanan can be selected for a Nobel Prize, anyone can." And I felt that this sentiment was indirectly expressed in the hundreds of calls, telegrams, and letters of congratulations that poured into Fairfax from all corners of the globe during those weeks in late 1986.

In a sense I do embody something of the American myth of social mobility. For how many farm boys from Middle Tennessee, educated in tiny, poor, and rural public schools and at a struggling state-financed teachers college have received Nobel prizes? How many scholars who have worked almost exclusively at southern universities have done so, in any scientific discipline? How many of my economist peers who are laureates have eschewed the use of both formal mathematical techniques and the extended resort to empirical testing?

When the singularity of my position along these and several other dimensions is recognized, it is perhaps not surprising that so many seemed to sense that my selection was, indeed, a vindication of the outsider. And the simple fact that my selection offered hope and encouragement to so many among the "great unwashed" scattered throughout the academic boondocks has been, when all is said and done, the most gratifying aspect of the whole experience of "Nobelity."

I was not surprised at all, of course, by the outpouring of congratulations from my research peers in public choice with whom I had worked for decades. As I emphasized at the first day's press conference, I recognized that I did represent this whole group. There was no single or unique contribution attributable to me, alone, that provided the basis for the committee's action. The award was, I think correctly, bestowed in recognition of an important research program in political economy, a program that involved many participants, including many colleagues, students, and coauthors. I was presumably singled out as representative because of the extended period of my research concentration, the leadership role that I had assumed, and the increasing emphasis on the constitutional implications of the program, implications that I have always particularly stressed.

The good wishes of so many warmed my heart, but these messages were accompanied by a surprisingly large number of calls, telegrams, and letters from the world's self-proclaimed saviors. I had encountered the occasional kook previously, but the Nobel Prize announcement offered a focus upon which many more could direct their efforts at persuasion. Boxes piled high with pleas; if I would only endorse this or that scheme (economic, military, moral, philosophical, political, or religious) the world would surely come right. And these pleas covered the whole spectrum of rationality, ranging from the ravings of the near insane to the entirely plausible petitions of sincerely devoted rational-if-romantic reformers.

Once again, and early, I imposed an internal rule for my own behavioral responses. The notoriety of "Nobelity" did not elevate me to the peaks of wisdom, and a pronouncement by me or any other laureate or any collection of laureates should command no more respect than pronouncements by anyone else. I resolved to abjure all invitations, whether for signatures of support, or for participation in congresses, conferences, or meetings, that carried the aura of Nobel identified intellectual-scientific elitism. This resolution was surely inspired, in part, by my observations of the common folly of scholars and scientists who pretend to be wise beyond their own borders.

IV. *The Nobel Week—Stockholm, December 1986*

Sweden is the optimal country to administer the Nobel prizes. The awards and events would be buried among other current agenda items claiming attention in a large country. And a smaller nation could scarcely attract the external world's notice by nothing other than a set of handsome prizes and elaborate ceremonials. Sweden commands attention in the world, both public and scientific, through its uniquely concentrated national interest in the Nobel awards and events. All of those who are associated with the prizes are placed at center stage for the Nobel Week in one of the world's most attractive capital cities.

This week becomes Sweden and Stockholm at its splendid best, and even the weather cooperated in 1986. The fact that the whole occasion is offered in tribute to academic-scientific achievement stirs the souls of scholars everywhere. I can state without fear of challenge on the part of any of those who have participated as Nobel laureates that there is and can be no remotely comparable experience. The Nobel Foundation, along with the several academies and institutes that cooperate in all stages of the nomination-selection-announcement-award process, carry on with the aplomb that accompanies a long experience of pride in success.

From the moment of arrival at Stockholm Airport the sense is conveyed that the Nobel Week is special, and that you, a Nobel laureate, are deserving of the acclaim. Customs, luggage, immigration —these entering chores are taken away, and a young attaché of the Swedish Foreign Office becomes your personal escort for the whole set of related functions during the week ahead. A chauffeured limousine, all your own, awaits, and jet lag seems to disappear as you and yours are installed in splendor at the Grand Hotel, directly across a small boat harbor from the Royal Palace.

The first organized event was an informal reception at which we were given instructions as to the full schedule, and at which we also met the Nobel laureates for 1986, from other disciplines, other countries, other cultures. In my own case two separate instances suggest the smallness of the world. John Polanyi, of Toronto, was one of the 1986 laureates in chemistry. I had known his father Michael Polanyi well, and I had invited Michael to spend a semester's visit with us at the Thomas Jefferson Center for Political Economy at the University of Virginia in 1961. The second instance was even less within the probable. Stanley Cohen, from Vanderbilt University in Nashville, Tennessee, was one of the 1986 corecipients in medicine. As things turned out, his mother-in-law, who was in his party, lived in Franklin, Tennessee, and was an acquaintance of Angela Tillman, the proprietress of Windy Hill Kennels and one of the leading breeders of smooth fox terriers in the United States, from whom we had purchased three: Topper, Brother, and Sister (and I pause here to state that, for me, dogs are important).

A private dinner at the home of Lars Werin, a member of the Royal Academy's committee of economists who nominate candidates for the Memorial Award in Economic Sciences, allowed me to meet a few prominent Swedish economists, including other members of the committee, in an informal and relaxed within discipline atmosphere. Here we were, partners in the genuinely international community defined by our discipline, and talk could range over personalities, policies, prizes, and programs for research. A day later came both the formal luncheon at the American Embassy hosted by the United States ambassador and the grand reception at the Royal Academy of Sciences, which cooperates with the Nobel Foundation in the physics, chemistry, and economics prizes. Notables from all of Sweden's academy were in attendance at the latter event, along with the Nobel laureates and their guests. A more selective dinner at the academy followed, amusingly remembered because the caterers prepared two too few servings of soup.

The Nobel lectures are decentralized, with specialized audiences in differing locations. My own lecture, at the Stockholm School of Economics, was a huge success. A standing-room-only audience seemed to maintain its interest in my subject matter and argument—appropriately so, since I had deliberately designed the lecture for the Swedish performance. I concentrated on the relation of Knut Wicksell's work to my own research agenda. For me this lecture was an opportunity seized rather than exploited because Wicksell surely deserved tribute in his own country as the single most important precursor of the ideas that public choice, particularly in its constitutional implications, embodies.

The Swedes are industrious, generous, and gracious people, but their senses of humor are heavy-handed and seem to emerge from forced effort. The skit by the Stockholm students following my lecture was not, for me, amusing. And I failed completely to get the point allegedly conveyed by the monstrous contraption that they had constructed in some mockingly abstract representation of my work and of public choice generally. But the choir at the Stockholm School was outstanding, and the lunch hosted by the administration and faculty made up for the awkwardness of the skit.

The day, December 10, the anniversary of Alfred Nobel's death, had arrived. A scheduled morning rehearsal of the afternoon's formal ceremony went off without a hitch, and all was finally in order for the big event. Pomp and circumstance were in the air. The white-tie costume was mastered, and I managed to get in place on the concert hall's stage with only a minor difficulty in learning to sit with tails on. The music was fitting to the occasion, the audience enrapt, the hall itself magnificent, and the queen elegantly beautiful. As the Nobel Memorial Prize in Economic Sciences was only added in 1968 and remains the only addition to the specific listing of disciplines in Nobel's will, the economics laureate comes last in all the proceedings. This lowly position in the pecking order gave me the advantage of being able to observe those who had gone before me, so that the actual receipt of the medal and scroll from the king of Sweden seemed quasi-normal by the time my turn had arrived.

The formal banquet in the Town Hall followed, and, here, my main impressions were those of admiration for the organizational detail. The precision with which some fifteen hundred persons were served a multicourse formal dinner could not have been anticipated. One representative from each of the Nobel disciplines was expected to contribute to the evening's entertainment by a brief postdinner talk. Several Swedish friends had repeatedly urged me to keep my remarks light and short, again, in part, because economics comes only at the end, and other scientists were expected to extend their remarks beyond those appropriate to the occasion. As a result of such advice, I tore up my earlier prepared statement, and I tried to ease up a bit with a very short comment that was intended to be humorous as well as gracious. I totally failed in the effort, and, as a result, only the very few intimate friends in my party and among the Swedes got the points. But, *c'est la vie*! I did not attend the follow-up and nightlong celebrations at the Stockholm School, where there was much more drink, much more food, much more dancing, and, yes, many more skits. My decision to act my age proved to be the right one.

For the day following the awards ceremony and banquet there remained the formal dinner hosted by the king and queen at the Royal Palace. This regal affair was attended by some one hundred and twenty guests, including the nobility, high society, the diplomatic corps, and, of course, the Nobel laureates as honorees. High living indeed.

The early morning of December 13 is reserved to allow the Nobel laureates to enjoy the experience of an age-old Swedish tradition. Maidens dressed in flowing white with lighted candles in their hair are supposed to wake us from our slumbers by singing "Santa Lucia." Unfortunately, for me, things did not quite work out as they were supposed to because of my built-in waking and working habits. By the time the maidens arrived, I had long since been up, dressed, and ready for breakfast.

The final two days in Sweden were spent, one each, at the two ancient Swedish universities, Uppsala and Lund, with lectures and related events at each. A notable feature of the Lund visit was the unexpected opportunity to meet and talk with Liv Wicksell Nordqvist, Knut Wicksell's granddaughter, a refined and cultured lady who had recently published a biography of her grandmother, Anna Bugge Wicksell. Talking to someone who recalled Knut Wicksell in person seemed somehow to bring me closer to a man who had long been one of my genuine heroes.

V. *Two Years of High Demand: 1987, 1988*

George Stigler, the Nobel laureate in economic science in 1982, told me shortly after my own award was announced that the event would disrupt my life for six months, but, after such an interim, things would return more or less to normalcy. With me, the period was two years, rather than six months, and I am not yet sure that normalcy will return at all. The years 1987 and 1988 were the "busiest" of my life, if "busyness" is measured by external lectures, talks, seminars, conferences, and miles traveled. And the costs must be measured in the papers and chapters in books that did not get written and, more seriously, in the ideas that may have emerged but now may never reach my consciousness.

The economist in me recognized that the post-Nobel increase in demand for my services need not have increased my amount supplied, and that fully rational choice behavior on my part should have enabled me to control my own schedule more adequately than I did. But why does an individual's supply schedule slope upward? Why did I accept more lecture commitments as the honoraria and fees moved substantially upward after the Nobel notoriety? Surely, I did not "need" the added income. I have no children to ruin by passing on a larger personal fortune; I do not get my kicks from larger personal payments to the Internal Revenue Service.

Did I, subconsciously, recognize that my normative message had become, due to the Nobel-induced attention, more respectable, and hence that I could, at least indirectly, now exert more ultimate influence on public opinion? In this case the higher fees would have been noncausal in my behavior. But I have long classified myself as lacking the didactic urge. I have, with reasonable consistency, eschewed the role of either preacher or prophet. Was I deceiving myself? Did I really seek to save the world after all?

I do not think I have been trapped in such self-deception. I think, instead, that my personal supply schedule slopes upward for the standard pecuniary reasons. As Lord Bauer suggested to me when we talked about this point in late 1988, "One can never escape from one's own shadow." Past experience describes who I am, and through almost all of my experience income, as such, did matter. And an ingrained pattern of supply response did not suddenly vanish due to the modified pecuniary circumstances that the Nobel Prize insured. In a very real sense the two years measure the time it took for me to begin to respond rationally to demands in my modified environmental setting. Perhaps George Stigler was simply a more rapid learner, or perhaps he was burdened less by an impecunious past.

But let me be honest with myself. There is another aspect of my behavior on the lecture circuit that does carry positive value in my preference function, over and beyond either pecuniary emolument or ultimate ideological purpose. I enjoy the "performance" itself, within limits, and given the appropriate setting. I enjoy the sense of command over and upon the attention of others; the actor that is deep inside all professors-teachers emerges to make me "feel good," to charge me up. And, so far as I can sense it, this positive feedback is largely unconnected with the subject matter of the argument and with the fee that I am being paid. It is this utility value that, at least in some part, determines the direction of my response to varying forms of invitation. I know the type of audience that works best for me, and I tend to be more receptive to the predicted audience and to the environmental setting for presentation than I am to the fee or to any anticipated ultimate influence on opinion.

The direction of response here is related to the "social distance" aspect of my Nobel award that I noted earlier. I am perceived, and widely so, as the only Nobel Prize representative of the "great un-washed" in American academia, those thousands of faculty members and students who spend their lives in the public and private colleges and universities of our land without the prestige of intellectual-scientific, and social, ranking. I am of the nonelite, from which it follows, more or less as a matter of course, that I get my warmest and surely my most wholesome reception during those visits to the academical villages, south, north, east, or west, that rarely see a Nobel Prize winner, and whose members hold potential "Nobelity" to be beyond their aspiration levels.

In these settings what I actually say in my lectures, seminars, postmeal talks, and informal discussions is much less important than the fact that I am there, as a Nobel Prize winner. But, as noted, to these particular audiences, I am a larger-than-life Nobel laureate because I have emerged successfully from an academic background and environment that members recognize to be analogous to their own. The very deep populist elements in my psyche are stirred by the direct feedback from my appearances in these settings. Thus, when I do a summary reckoning, perhaps the utility accounts are not so askew as they may seem when first examined. But two years was, for me, a sufficient time to enjoy the onetime plaudits of my genuine "fans." This part of "my show" surely ended with 1988.

VI. *Aftermath*

The beginning of 1989 marked a shift into a different role for me, and one that I can discuss only in prospect. The record has not been written as I write here, and I can only speculate about resolutions and intent. I shall, of course, return to my self-assigned duties as a constitutional political economist, and I shall pursue activities normal to such a role. But I must also reckon on the continued notoriety that the Nobel status imposes on me, a notoriety that I cannot walk away from, even if I seek to do so.

I have never been tempted to make pronouncements on this or that policy issue. Hence the fact that any statements on my part will, post-Nobel, necessarily, be more worthy of public notice need exert no feedback influence on my behavior. The "responsibility of Nobelity" in any direct sense of the term is surely among the least of my concerns. But there is an aspect of such responsibility that does raise issues of personal morality. I suggested that I have never felt an urge to save the world or, indeed, to treat myself to be more responsible in a civic sense than any other person. On the other hand I also recognize that unless someone, somewhere, takes the lead in promulgating constitutionalist ideas that are inherently "public," we could scarcely expect such ideas to enter into public consciousness. We shall not secure the social order that is within the realm of the possible if each of us sits by and waits for the process of social evolution to work its will. There is, for me, a categorical distinction to be made between the presumptive arrogance of anyone, Nobel laureate or anyone else, who takes it on himself or herself to tell others what they should do, and the attitude of someone who actively enters as a participant in a discussion of social change with all persons treated as reciprocating contributors.

The second of these roles does not, and cannot, be motivated directly by simple self-interest. There is little or no personally identifiable interest to be furthered in attempts to persuade other persons to agree to multiperson political "trades" that involve changing the rules by which we live together in a polity. Some ethic of constitutional responsibility is required here, some interest that extends beyond that which is of measured utility value directly to me, and which is, at the same time, something other than the single-minded pursuit of "truth" which describes the idealized ethical norm for the natural scientist. At least some of the players in the inclusive social game must attend to the rules that define the game; the constitution of order and such attention do not emerge from private self-interest, at least directly, or from "scientific discovery," as such. Within limits, we make our own rules for living together. And this central presupposition of the constitutionalist carries with it the implied ethical principle that dictates attention to the workings of the social order.

How does acceptance of this presupposition and this principle affect my own behavior in the aftermath of short-term "Nobelity?" Precisely because I am the only constitutional political economist that has achieved or seems likely to achieve Nobel Prize status, do I not carry on my shoulders the particular "burden" for all would-be constitutionalists? In a sense I surely must do so. And the acknowledgment of this fact alone offers me the incentive to put off the obscenity of retirement as long as it proves to be physically possible. Recognition of my uniqueness along this constitutionalist dimension of interest shapes the direction and content of my projected efforts in the 1990s.

My aims are limited. My tools are words that enter arguments presented in books, essays, and lectures, arguments that develop quasi-abstract ideas which challenge the minds of those who are members of the academies. I shall, now as before, eschew all temptation to reduce my arguments to surface journalism. My own experience, both pre- and post-Nobel, tells me that ideas do have consequences. But far too many of my peers in the social sciences and philosophy concern themselves too much with normatively defined consequences while neglecting the task of reinforcing, maintaining, and sometimes originating the ideas without which consequences lose all moorings.

Perhaps these final comments are little more than noble rhetorical flourishes in an autobiographical essay on "Nobelity." I like to think that more is involved, that the counters in my game that are necessary to keep the game itself interesting enough for me to play are themselves real and that they exist beyond the ranges of my own imagination.

12

Threescore Years and Ten

The days of our years are threescore years and ten; and if by reason of
strength they be fourscore years, yet is their strength labour and sorrow;
for it is soon cut off, and we fly away.

Psalm 90:10

ALBEIT BEGRUDGINGLY, I acknowledge the appropriateness
of the celebration of threescore years and ten (October
1989), an occasion to be placed alongside birth, one-and-
twenty, and death as markers of the time space joined to a name. I
propose to seize this occasion to offer a reflective comparison between the temporal life-cycle of all those who are roughly my generational peers and those of others who have lived both before and
after us in historical sequence.

My thesis is a simple one. Ours is an extended generation that
has enjoyed fortune's smile. We have got "more" than we were psychologically programmed to expect, and we have been granted time
to enjoy it. I have often remarked that, retrospectively considered, I
am indeed an optimist. I leave open the possible extension to
prospect.

I support my thesis by extended generational comparison, and
let me first consider that set of lives commenced within, roughly, a
decade of the century's turn. For them, childhood was spent during
waning years of a totally misunderstood age of civil order, during
which the passions of nationalism, statism, and socialism were

stirred in a post-Hegelian romance with unreality. Early youth was deflowered, notably in Europe, by the least holy of all wars, which involved a mutuality of slaughter that we still cannot locate in mental reconstruction. It is not surprising that, for all those who survived, their remaining youth should have been burned away in the false prosperity of the 1920s, consumed in the sometimes crossing fires of baptism and bootleg gin. These years did little more than prepare for the wastage of the 1930s, the decade during which my father's generation lived out its physical apogee. The scourges of hunger and joblessness and the European rumblings of war's renewal—these could not have been times of personal triumph, strength, or joy.

The war indeed did follow, and that generation watched its sons march off and waited on their return. And return they did, or most of them, those of us and Eisenhower's 1950s had arrived, only to reveal that those fathers were now old men, to be increasingly displaced by us, who claimed our share as earned. Is it to be wondered that my father's generation felt its time ill spent, and that the body politic, in its compassion, should have inaugurated institutional correctives that were as praiseworthy in motive as they were blameworthy in execution? Those who dated their names near to the century's turn watched in total bewilderment as their grandsons and daughters fouled their nesting places in the 1960s. How could these have celebrated their threescore years and ten in simple silent witness to the loss of glory that had been used to justify their own long-remembered wars?

Let us leapfrog over ourselves in my comparative enterprise here and now consider the extended generation that finds its name date astride the middle of the century. War, depression, war—these were sensed only through the tales on family nights and the accepted fiction of the old movies. The job, the house, the car, the electric things—these described no miracles. Instead, to you, these were among the ordered elements of a natural existence. And you recall the childhood query. Why is my dad so smug when he goes off whistling to his work which must surely be a second-best usage of a day?

Dr. Spock had offered the license of suburbia, and consciousness was edged by a near absence of deprivation. The best of times were the worst of times, since only now existed. And the tinsel prance and prattle of those who came along and called themselves the brightest and the best obscured the raw injustice of a purchased presidency. Crudely tautened and untested nerves were shattered in the abyss of assassination, and teenhood exploded in a world so suddenly estranged. The substantive injustices of race and an elitist draft became the excuses for escapes into substances.

This middle-century's generation backed into its adulthood in the 1970s both bewildered and distressed. Lost was the media-stimulated romance; what was left but to seize that which seemed available in the here and now? There were no passions to be spent. Came the 1980s, and Reagan's shining city on a hill, so real to their fathers and mothers, seemed fitting only for an ancient actor turned president.

Perhaps, just perhaps, my attempt at temporal displacement works less effectively in application to the life-cycle of those whose extended generation follows my own. Perhaps mine is the simple envy of the aging for all those whose promised years are longer. But accept my challenge. Think of the threescore-years-and-ten celebration to be staged in the second decade of the next century. Can that then remembered life and time hold candles to my own?

I must defend my thesis by completing the comparison. I must fill in the sandwich. Why do I suggest that ours, the extended generation whose members just now have, or will soon, celebrate threescore years and ten, was the one upon which fortune smiled? What was so special about us, and could not a critic from some displaced time date find us, too, unlucky by his standards?

I wonder.

Recall just where we have been placed on time's arrow of history. The prosperity of predepression did not enter directly into our consciousness. We grew to teenhood in the imagined and observed reality that made jobs, houses, cars the stuff of dreams. For me, in the late 1930s, a professorship at a teachers college, with a salary of $3,600, and a small house in a town—this was something to be marveled at, not attained. Our rational expectations were limited, indeed so much so that most of us did become rich beyond all inside measure.

But there is more to it than can be told in economics. Even that which offered little seemed worthy of defense when threatened by external enemies. And we marched off, most of us quasi-enthusiastically, to the country's call. It was no small thing to be lined abreast and told that one of three would not return. We, too, heightened our discount rates as we dated the girls of San Francisco, but our military "now" was always acted out within the limits of patrol.

Most of us survived, and the one-in-three promise was not kept. And for some of us, the war was both easy and informative. We learned much about ourselves through enforced encounters with generational peers from totally divergent cultures of our land. We learned that even the unwashed rednecks of Appalachia could stand to measure with the scions of Newport. We became national in a newfound sense, and we returned to stand together in pride of accomplishment to be appreciated by those whom we loved and respected. And precisely because we had some confidence in comparison with our inclusive set of peers, we worked hard to do what we now knew we could, whether it was further schooling through the GI Bill of Rights, the launching of new ventures, or the simple dedication to the jobs we seized.

The world that was Eisenhower's 1950s was indeed miraculous to us, and we rushed to work always with a shoulder's glance lest all come tumbling down again. Can either of my compared extended generations point to a decade of such realization so far beyond all rationally grounded hope? And, often, when we wax nostalgic and talk of days that were, it is of the 1950s that we speak.

The Cold War's reality and rhetoric spawned ideological dispute, especially as those who had earlier seen the truth in socialism began to glimpse the collapse of the romance. The envy-engendered hatred for those whose romance with the state had never blossomed spilled over into the academies, and some of us would suffer from the crude attempts at thought control; yes, even in America. And the near-thing electoral emplacement of a nonideological rich boy became the opening that the putative establishment intellectuals sought and imagined they had found.

For many of us, my extended generational peers, those were trying times. Never before had we sensed alienation from the America we lived. Things seemed all asunder, and passion burned within. The sometime stable, sometime trusted world of Eisenhower's

1950s seemed to have vanished in a Harvard wind of change, and to us there was the cold left only to outsiders.

We were befuddled, bewildered, and shocked by assassination, but, in a sense, relieved. And we had a natural sympathy for Lyndon Johnson, who seemed, again, to be of us rather than of them. We understood his dilemma in carrying on Kennedy's war, and we sensed his tragedy in the trap between the false rhetoric of a martyr's promise and the harshness of that beyond the words. We also understood that Johnson could do no other than seize the opportunity to do civil right, even while insuring the creation of a mythology that would put the wrong names to deeds.

What I am saying here is that we, my generational peers, had made our peace with Lyndon Johnson and the Great Society. We were beginning to feel that we had been invited inside once again, and that we did, in fact, requalify as citizens, this after our short-term sentence in that imagined Siberia of the New Frontier. Total negation did not describe our attitude in 1965. We understood a bit of why things were as they were, and we supported, in strategy if not in tactics, those whose responsibility it was to lead.

This somewhat distempered calm was shattered by the noisy obscenities that emerged on the grounds of the academies. And, quite frankly we were pissed off, royally so, by the ravings of those pampered youngsters who played around at protest against injustice. But we reserved our true contempt for those elders of academia, many of them our own pusillanimous peers, who climbed into beds, literally and figuratively, with those whose nappies they had laundered, all in some pretended parody of compassion. For some of us, our world seemed near to ruin, and we did, indeed, take on the role of doomsayers.

Again, however, our rational expectations were not realized, and in the same direction as before. The becalmed waters of the 1970s surprised us, and we stood bemused at the pitiful efforts to make of Watergate a moral issue of historical import. We recovered some of the balance we had lost, but with an added dose of cynicism as we watched our leaders bring America to shame. We were not burned by Vietnam, however, because we understood its origins along with the tragedy of its narrative.

We had lost our emotional faith in the politics of democracy with the purchase of the presidency in 1960, and we were strengthened in this loss by a developing intellectual understanding of the processes of governance. We understood both Lyndon Johnson and Richard Nixon; we shared with them an appreciation of the difficulties of choice, while at the same time we had learned to distrust any who would purport to govern in the public's interest.

By my generation's reckoning the 1970s made for a tolerable decade with improvement noted over the 1960s, but negatively distanced from the 1950s. We had little differentially positive hope for the 1980s. But, and for the third time, we were to be favorably surprised. We watched, and shared in wonderment, Ronald Reagan's emergence into serious contention for national office. Here seemed to be a man who carried in his gut those visions of America that so closely matched our own.

Could it be that our earlier disillusionments with the politics of democracy had been premature? Ronald Reagan's vision of a shining city on a hill did, indeed, inspire us. And we lost some of our cynicism, along with a bit of our solid sense, in some recovered cloak of shared community. How could this simple man have done so much? We could honestly raise such a question until the purchase with the terrorists revealed that Ronald Reagan was of our own construction. He was the one we sought to see, as Jack Kennedy was for others, and we had been duped by our longing for that which was never there.

Nonetheless, and despite our reluctant return to reality, there had been joy in the passing exhilaration of the Reagan times. And this domesticated thrust in our emotions was joined to the sounder base offered to us by the surprising, shocking, and unanticipated collapse of socialism, both in idea and in institution. Many of my peers are, themselves, too crusty to take in the sweeping changes we observe. But, for those of us whose intellectual and emotional arteriosclerosis has remained within limits of the tolerable, can there have been an imagined better dating for our threescore years and ten? Let us by all means drink deeply from the draught of vindication.

We have not been ill used by history. As earlier noted, I shall not be held to judge prospectively, and there may be reckonings ahead. But these will be past our time of celebration here, and, as doom-

sters, we have been severally upended. So let us rest on the record
that has been, and not on that that will yet be written.

I recognize that, in this summation, I have used the events of my
personal history, along with my now-remembered reactions to
them, to describe the evaluated life-cycle of others who are at, near,
or just past the threescore-years-and-ten occasion for celebration.
Scientifically, such generalization is illegitimate. But I defend it here
in my long-held supposition that I am not much, if at all, different
from others who have shared my times and places.

I also offer my apologies, if these be needed, for the rhetorical
flourish that has described this record of a generation's journey. But
all of us who write for fame or fortune must venture to try the purple
now and then, and if there is one who can suggest an occasion more
appropriate than threescore years and ten, let him speak!

The Blacksburg Story

I. *Introduction*

IN SEVERAL PLACES, including parts of chapter 7, I have offered my personal and remembered perspective on the origins, operational successes, and ultimate failure of the enterprise that was "Virginia political economy" and especially at its University of Virginia location in Charlottesville over the relevant decade, 1957–67. I have not, in this book or elsewhere, offered a comparable narrative account of "the Blacksburg story:" the fourteen years, 1969–83, during which the Public Choice Center, as an institution, and public choice, as a widely recognized subdiscipline or research program emerged and matured.[1]

As suggested in chapter 7, the "Blacksburg story" has its origins in Charlottesville, and the events to be described in this chapter would never have occurred had the program at the University of Virginia successfully survived the ideological onslaught of its academic enemies within the university. In many respects, of course, the Blacksburg program that emerged was a continuation of Virginia political economy, primarily described by relocation to an alternative university setting still within Virginia. Such a simplistic interpretation would, however, be grossly misleading.

---

1. A partial exception is my short note "Heraclitian Vespers," written for presentation at a 2001 conference.

Virginia Polytechnic Institute (VPI or Virginia Tech) in Blacksburg, Virginia, was never in play as a backup or default option in the considerations of those of us who moved "from" Charlottesville, rather than "to" alternative institutions. We, too, had taken on some of the arrogant veneer that permeates "Mr. Jefferson's university," and we looked with disdain on the state's "cow college," with its military and athletic emphases. Little did we recognize that "Virginia" would again soon emerge as our geographic base, and with a more narrowly focused, but ultimately more distinct, research program.

II. *The Academic Entrepreneurs*

How was the shift accomplished, from the essentially destroyed program in political economy in Charlottesville to a reconstituted program in public choice in Blacksburg—all within the space of two or three short years? Clearly, entrepreneurship was involved here; such institutional events do not simply "happen," as if in some naturally evolving course of change. And those who filled this role deserve to be singled out and commended, even at this lag of almost four full decades.

First of all, a disclaimer: I did not, personally, carry out any part of the entrepreneurial role here. I do claim credit, such as there is, for co-entrepreneurial efforts with Warren Nutter, in establishing the Thomas Jefferson Center for Political Economy in Charlottesville in 1957; and with Gordon Tullock, in organizing the initial group in 1963 that later became the Public Choice Society, with its subsequent components. But I was not privy to the early ideas that caused the Blacksburg program to come into being.

A bit of history becomes relevant here. As a state, Virginia was quite late in enacting a sales tax, which generated substantial revenues, especially in the 1960s. And the revenues came in before the competing claims on such revenues could be fully organized. This revenue potential, along with burgeoning enrollment pressures, made budgetary expansions in higher educational institutions more or less predictable. Couple this setting with academic-institutional leadership that was dynamic and daring as well as politically adept, and the stage was set for takeoffs to occur. In sum, the whole academic atmosphere at Virginia Tech in the 1960s was entrepreneurial. Under Marshall Hahn's banner, the change was made from a military, male, agriculture-engineering structure to a full-fledged university, which soon eclipsed its in-state competitors in size, as measured both in enrollments and in budgets.

This change was not made easily, and the accumulated academic underbrush had to be cleared away, sometimes ruthlessly. Hahn was aided in this necessary task by a strong provost, Warren Brandt, who had both the conviction and the courage to make the hard choices and to act as these dictated.

But how and why did economics come to be selected for support? Where was the gleam in someone's eye that marked the beginnings of larger things to come? My personal reconstruction involves several persons, with varying degrees of properly assigned credit. Wilson Schmidt had assumed the headship of the department in the mid-1960s, coming to Virginia Tech from George Washington University and with an appreciation for what might be required to build up a viable unit. Early in his tenure, he succeeded in getting Eugene Boyle, Vic Bonomo, and Charles Schotta, all of whom were respected research economists, to join the faculty. Schmidt also attracted Charles Goetz, who had been on the faculty at Illinois. Goetz was, in my view, the critical addition. He had been my very best graduate student at Virginia in the early 1960s, and, in retrospect, my sense is that Goetz was the first to recognize the prospect of getting both Gordon Tullock and me to return to Virginia under new institutional auspices.

It was Charles Goetz who sensed that Gordon Tullock did not really feel "at home" at Rice University, and who saw an opportunity to lure Gordon back. Wilson Schmidt was, I am sure, enthusiastic about this prospect. Once this initial appointment was locked up, Schmidt, encouraged by Goetz, and possibly also by Tullock, began to make overtures to me, even though I had scarcely touched base at UCLA.

Again some clarification is in order. I had left Charlottesville and the University of Virginia for UCLA in the fall of 1968 with every intention of making a permanent and long-term move. The prospect of a temporary move to UCLA as a way station toward a return east to Virginia Tech was never even remotely in my sights. Considerations of such a cross-continent return came into play neither from my own intentions nor from the Blacksburg sources, but were, instead, almost exclusively dictated by events at UCLA itself during the fall of 1968, and within a few months of my arrival on the scene.

Academically, I was pleased to join the economics faculty at UCLA.

Who would not have been, with colleagues like Armen Alchian, Jack Hirschleifer, Axel Leijonhufved, and Earl Thompson? Furthermore, Bill Allen, as departmental chairman, was enthusiastic about my coming on board. Logistically, I situated myself quite well with a house within short walking distance of the campus. And, to my surprise, Los Angeles itself proved both attractive and manageable.

But the university administration, led by Charles Young, was something else again. I could scarcely believe what I saw happen, which could only be described as overt cowardice in the face of terrorist threats. And when I observed that this stance was supported by the overwhelming majority of the general university faculty, I felt myself to be surrounded by alien beings who had somehow lost the elemental qualities that define humanity. For me, it was time to seek cover. What had I got myself into?

Meanwhile, back in the Virginia mountains, Wilson Schmidt, no doubt pushed forward by both Goetz and Tullock, sensed my rapidly increasing unease with UCLA and commenced seriously to put together a package deal that would make Virginia Tech a viable alternative for me. A key part of this package included the simultaneous recruitment of Betty Tillman from Charlottesville, who had been the secretary-administrator of the Thomas Jefferson Center at the University of Virginia during its mature years. With Betty Tillman in place as administrative coordinator, and with Goetz, Tullock, and myself on board, a genuine research center seemed to come within the realm of the possible. Hence, when Schmidt convinced Bill Mitchell, who was Dean of the College of Business, and who in turn convinced Warren Brandt and Marshall Hahn, that the whole enterprise was worth the outlay, I found myself, to my great surprise, ready to make a shift back to Virginia—this time to the mountains, and within a few short months of having migrated to Lotus Land for what I had thought would be a settled shift.

As I noted, the academic entrepreneurs in this enterprise—Goetz, Schmidt, Tullock, Mitchell, Brandt, and Hahn—warrant some commendation, even if belatedly.

III. *Beginnings and Some Relevant Geography*

While I welcomed the opportunity to escape from the academic absurdities that I observed firsthand at UCLA, I did not personally anticipate development of a major research program in Blacksburg. For me, the shift back to Virginia seemed more of a retreat to sanity than the launching of a platform for an expanded research enterprise. In a paper written for a 2001 conference, Richard McKenzie referred to the early years in Blacksburg as analogous to "circling the wagons" in the classic western films. I do not think that this is a good analogy at all. The fit is much better for the last Charlottesville years, where our socialist-inspired enemies were dedicated to driving us from the temple. There was never such an enemy, inside or outside, for the public choice enterprise in Blacksburg. The appropriate analogy would be a retreat to a safe haven protected by a firewall, behind which we might be able to carry on our own work unaffected by the almost literal burning of the academies of the land.

The beginnings in Blacksburg were not auspicious. To be sure, we were established as the Center for Study of Public Choice, with our own stationery, and with a secretariat independent of the Economics Department. But, initially, we were lodged in a very small house near the duck pond on the Virginia Tech campus, with no room for expansion and no space for visitors, seminars, or graduate assistants. After a few months of such existence, however, a significantly fortuitous circumstance arose. The university president, Marshall Hahn, moved out of the large house overlooking the campus into an off-campus residential area of the town, motivated in part by the concern about raising small children in such proximity to the increasing rowdiness of students in those revolting 1960s.

Gordon Tullock deserves full credit for proposing that, since the president's house on campus was to become vacant, this facility offered the ideal location for the Center for Study of Public Choice. Lo and behold, with the aid of Schmidt and Mitchell, Tullock's proposal became reality, and thenceforth, the Center secured for itself a geographical identity that was critical for the whole program over the ensuing years.

As noted, the setting was near ideal for a research institution of the size and scope of the Public Choice Center. Physically, it was separated from the main academic buildings, where classes were convened, but still within short walking distance. Also the house (see photo in this book) was situated on a hill amidst fine trees: aesthetically magnificent indeed. The rooms were spacious and in sufficient number to provide for both resident faculty and graduate students as well as academic visitors, who soon became numerous. The nonacademic atmosphere of the place was conducive to informal discourse, and there were ample spaces for small seminars. Those of us directly involved could not have scripted a more favorably situated location for the whole public choice enterprise in Blacksburg.

IV. *The Early 1970s, Winston Bush, and Anarchy*

As noted earlier, when I came to Blacksburg in 1969, the institutions of order everywhere seemed to be in disarray, and notably those of academia. Geographically, I sought refuge in the Virginia mountains, and intellectually there seemed to be challenge in analyzing anarchy itself—a task commenced in my cathartic book *Academia in Anarchy* (Buchanan and Devletoglou, 1970). In Blacksburg, only two years later, this project took on personal form through Winston Bush, whose influence was briefly discussed earlier in chapter 7. Bush came through Blacksburg and the public choice program like a storm, stirred up the fires, and then was gone. His story itself is worth a bit of telling.

Bush was a genuine redneck, from the pine woods and swamps of southeastern Georgia. He did not finish high school, and his first jobs were cutting pulpwood and running moonshine. Married in his teens, he moved to Jacksonville and got a job in the post office. He finished a correspondence course and applied to Florida State University. Within six years, he had received not only his BA degree, but also a Ph.D. from Washington University in St. Louis, where he was well trained by two good mathematical economists, Ted Bergstrom and Trout Rader.

Almost as soon as he arrived to join our faculty, Bush took up the challenge of analyzing anarchy. And, before we knew what was happening, he had all of us working on a genuinely joint project, in the most exciting continuing seminar with which I was ever associated. From papers prepared for this seminar, two small volumes, *Explorations into the Theory of Anarchy* (1972) and *Further Explorations into the Theory of Anarchy* (1974) emerged, both under Gordon Tullock's editorship. Also, stimulated directly by these discussions, Gordon Tullock wrote *The Social Dilemma* (1974), and I wrote my own book, *The Limits of Liberty* (1975). And then, tragically, as quickly as he had come, Bush was gone, killed at thirty-three in an accident on the way to his mistress after a student party. It remains impossible for me to imagine what Winston Bush might have done over a normal life span.

V. *The Research Program in Operation*

I was, personally, surprised by the early and continuing success of the whole research program in public choice in its new Blacksburg location. Again we were fortunate in being able to secure limited foundation support that allowed for minimal supplementation by university funding. This support, along with strong internal encouragement, allowed us to bring to Blacksburg a series of postdoctoral fellows, along with new appointments, all of whom focused their research emphases on public choice, as variously interpreted. More than a mere partial listing of names is not needed: Dennis Mueller, Nic Tideman, Bob Staaf, Roger Faith, Geoffrey Brennan, Loren Lomasky—these came as postdoctoral fellows, and Tideman, Staaf, Faith, and Brennan returned as regular faculty members. Dick Wagner joined us from Tulane and Bob Tollison from Clemson. And, as other faculty members, we added Mark Crain, Joe Reid, Tom Borcherding, Dwight Lee, Mel Hinich, Art Denzau, Bob Mackay, and David Friedman. To this still partial listing could be added a long string of international visitors who came for short or long academic visits, extending from a week to two years. Names here include—again, as a partial listing only—Bruno Frey, Fritz Schneider, Bob Sugden, and Alan Hamlin. Blacksburg, and the Center, became a mecca of sorts for scholars interested in the public choice research program.

The record suggests that Blacksburg and Virginia Tech were not so far out in the boondocks as my earlier Charlottesville biases had suggested. And therein lies a lesson: Given requisite institutional and financial support, viable research programs can be developed almost anywhere in the vast academic domain. The walls need be neither storied nor ivy; military gothic will indeed suffice. But with one proviso: The research program must itself be sufficiently differentiated from orthodoxy, and its direct participants must jealously guard against sometimes devious efforts to force emphasis back toward the familiar.

In its subject matter focus, the program surged ahead during the 1970s and 1980s, even after the initial excitement about the analysis of anarchy. Richard Wagner joined forces with me in producing *Democracy in Deficit* (1978), which is summarized as a rather straightforward application of public choice methodology to the whole policy thrust of Keynesian macroeconomics. A full decade before, Gordon Tullock (1967) had written his seminal paper on rent seeking which was brought into focus by Anne Krueger (1974) and Richard Posner (1975) in the early 1970s. Thomas Borcherding was both the primary contributor and organizer of a volume containing efforts to explain the observed explosive growth of government (Borcherding, 1977). Geoffrey Brennan joined me in two books (1980, 1985) which examined the question: How might government, even if its revenue-maximizing potential be acknowledged, be constitutionally constrained?

VI. *Disquietude*

In more than one sense, the research program in public choice in Blacksburg from 1969 to1983 was unique. Its internal momentum could not have been expected to be long sustained. The growing pains at the outset were replaced by the aches and pains of maturity, as the excitement necessarily waned over time. Charles Goetz, an early prime mover, was attracted by the newer program in law and economics, and moved on to a different setting. Wilson Schmidt, as the departmental head who had seen the program born and nurtured, was smitten by a severe attack of Potomac fever, especially after his extended leave of absence for a high position in the Treasury Department during the early Nixon years. Upon his return to departmental leadership, his interest in matters academic was no longer there. And, by more or less general agreement, decisions were made to change the administrative structure, to search for a new department head.

At this point in my narrative, I am obligated to acknowledge a character flaw of my own, one that has negatively impacted my career on more than one occasion. My initial reaction, when a group decision is to be made, is to opt out, to stay out of the loop, to let others do it. When I do this, however, and the decision does not work out well, I react strongly—and too late. I should have tried, but did not, to assume a leadership role in the selection of Schmidt's replacement as the Economics Department head. I sought to justify my inaction by claims of international commitments and did not attend to the necessary details of organizing coalitions, which seemed to me piddling and pedestrian activities. With naive arrogance, I simply assumed that, if I kept to my last by writing papers and books and keeping commitments with the world outside, internal administrative matters would come right.

When the relevant committee, after the search process, came up with the name of Dan Orr, I acquiesced in the appointment, without expressing either positive endorsement or negative reaction. I recognized Orr to be a well-trained and well-respected economist, whose general ideological attitudes were clearly within the limits of acceptability. I simply assumed, without conscious thought, that Orr would seek to build on the strengths of the existing faculty and program, which featured public choice as its most prominent component. Not within my wildest imagination did I think that Orr would do what seemed to me totally irrational, namely, to make a conscious effort to build up a competing pole of interest, and thereby to offset and reduce the effective distance between Virginia Tech economics and the conventional structures.

Dan Orr thought that the Virginia Tech program in economics, with its heavy public choice-political economy emphasis, was simply too far out of the mainstream, and he took it as his primary task to put things right. He failed to sense the positive elements involved in being able to put out a differentiated product and to recognize that, for a geographical and institutional location like that in Blacksburg, his own ideal accomplishment might be a fourth-rate imitation of MIT. As he assumed administrative leadership of the economics program at Virginia Tech, it soon became clear that Dan Orr lacked the self-confidence critically necessary to confront orthodoxy in the discipline along any dimension. Orr did not necessarily oppose the research program in public choice, as such. To him, it seemed misguided. Accordingly, he withheld support, since our research, by his lights, had not yet become integral to conventional practice as observed in those settings he wished to emulate.

As these comments suggest, the bases for the conflicts that emerged in Blacksburg were strictly in-house, so to speak: that is, within the ranks of the economics faculty itself, rather than between our faculty and outside enemies. In this respect, the problems we faced were categorically different from those faced in Charlottesville almost two decades earlier. Further, and as suggested, there were few, if any, ideological elements that entered into the Blacksburg arguments, quite by contrast to the Charlottesville scene where these elements were paramount.

The tension between Dan Orr, in his effort to shape the future of the economics program, and those of us in public choice who sought to exploit our differentiation from the mainstream, surfaced as Orr sought to make faculty appointments more or less explicitly aimed at making Virginia Tech more like comparable peer institutions—appointments that did not seem to be, in our judgment, warranted. The issue was joined; was Dan Orr to be allowed to shape the future of the inclusive economics program, or was public choice, through the Center and under my own leadership, to maintain its position as the dominant research emphasis?

It was at this point that I made a serious misjudgment. The ultimate choice rested with the Dean of the College of Business, William Mitchell, with whom I had established a decades-long personal friendship and mutuality of respect. Again, perhaps with naive arrogance, I presumed that the combination of personal understanding and the professional-scientific dominance of my side of the issue would leave no doubt as to the outcome. I was totally wrong; Mitchell came down squarely in support of Orr's authority, leaving me and my colleagues at the Center hanging out to dry, so to speak. Never in my whole experience, either inside or outside the academy, did I so misjudge a person, so much so that the whole affair remains mysterious to me, even after more than two decades.

I should re-emphasize here as I tell "the Blacksburg story" that there was nothing remotely comparable to the earlier Charlottesville failure. We were not driven "from" Virginia Tech. Indeed, quite the opposite; efforts were made, throughout the administrative hierarchy, to appease us, and me in particular, to secure our peaceful acquiescence in the loss of ultimate authority to shape the inclusive program in economics at the university. And, were it not for the entrepreneurship to be discussed in the next section, the Center for Study of Public Choice would have remained at Virginia Tech in Blacksburg, with almost all of its operation little damaged.

VII: *The New Entrepreneurs*

Those of us directly involved in the in-house conflict in Blacksburg made no special effort to conceal our disaffection from the external academy. More than one university made overtures concerning the possibility of a shift of the whole Center, with its faculty and program, to an alternate location beyond Virginia. None of these reached the level of serious discussion. But a shift, again within Virginia, came into play reasonably early, specifically in late 1981 and early 1982, instigated not from within our own ranks, but, instead, by the new entrepreneurs at George Mason University in Fairfax. These new entrepreneurs can be readily identified:

Karen Vaughn, Wade Gilley, and George Johnson. Both the setting at George Mason University in the early 1980s and the roles played by these leaders warrant some discussion.

George Mason was a new university, having secured its independence as a part of the Virginia state system of higher education only in 1972, when it split off from its filial relationship with the University of Virginia. The growth of the university was assured by its location in the burgeoning Washington suburbs; population alone guaranteed increasing political clout. But an academic institution does not grow in any pre-programmed pattern; choices must be made, and those on the ground who seize the day, so to speak, secure early advantage.

Karen Vaughn was chair of the Department of Economics, and, interestingly, she and her colleagues had already secured approval from the Virginia state council for a new Ph.D. program in economics. Karen was attempting to build up a faculty to go along with the Austrian research emphasis already in place. She learned about the disaffection of those of us in public choice at Virginia Tech, and she moved to cement relationships with key people involved. Karen Vaughn became a familiar figure in her several trips to Blacksburg.

Wade Gilley held the post of Executive Vice President and was well acquainted with the ins and outs of the state bureaucracy because of his stint as Secretary of Education under an earlier governor. George Johnson was president of the university, and both he and Gilley were openly receptive to initiatives that would allow particular programs to leap the threshold between community or branch college status to that of genuine, university-level research.

Even given the potentially receptive setting, it remains an achievement of major proportions when a whole research center, with several tenure positions, along with one staff member and a small, private endowment, is shifted from one university to another within a state's higher educational structure. The new entrepreneurs, Vaughn, Gilley, and Johnson, deserve credit. Contrary to much gossip, the shift was strictly a parallel one in terms of academic salaries and perquisites. George Mason University did not offer pecuniary advantages. In a sense, however, the program did move "to" Fairfax, over and beyond moving "from" Blacksburg. The opportunity to construct a new graduate program, with its potential for good graduate students, was indeed of major importance.

VIII. *End of Story*

I have entitled this chapter "The Blacksburg Story," but my narrative account may misleadingly suggest that Blacksburg was only a way station between Charlottesville and Fairfax. "Virginia political economy" was indeed brought to life in Charlottesville, and its productive decade at the University of Virginia has become a part of academic history. "Public choice," as a self-standing research program, and despite its origins in Virginia political economy, came alive only in Blacksburg, during the 1970s. The program could not have emerged without the supporting environment offered by VPI through its administrative leadership and its faculty.

The location may also have been more important than we realized. The relative isolation in the Virginia mountains may have conveyed to visitors and to prospective research students at all levels some sense of protection against the pressures for lock-step marching with the scientific orthodoxy. We could, in Blacksburg, "dare to be different," something we could not have done as easily in a more open and cosmopolitan setting.

The research program in public choice, in its maturity, was carried forward at George Mason University in Fairfax, but, again, the imprint of the Blacksburg years cannot be erased. These years are surely deserving of special recognition, particularly in any summation of my own personal academic record.

References

Borcherding, Thomas, ed. *Budgets and Bureaucrats: The Sources of Government Growth* (Durham, Duke University Press, 1977).

Brennan, Geoffrey and James M. Buchanan. *The Power to Tax: Analytical Foundations of a Fiscal Constitution* (New York: Cambridge University Press, 1980).

_____. *The Reason of Rules: Constitutional Political Economy* (Cambridge: Cambridge University Press, 1985).

Buchanan, James M. *The Limits of Liberty: Between Anarchy and Leviathan* (Chicago: University of Chicago Press, 1975).

_____. "Heraclitian Vespers," in *The Production and Diffusion of Public Choice Political Economy: Reflections on the VPI Center*, eds. Joseph C. Pitt, Djavad Salehi-Isfahani, and Douglas W. Eckel (Oxford: Blackwell, 2004), 263–71.

Buchanan, James M. and Nicos Devletoglou. *Academia in Anarchy: An Economic Diagnosis* (Basic Books,1970).

Buchanan, James M. and Richard E. Wagner. *Democracy in Deficit: The Political Legacy of Lord Keynes* (New York: Academic Press, 1977).

Krueger, Anne O. "The Political Economy of the Rent-Seeking Society," *American Economic Review* 64 (June 1974): 291–303.

Posner, Richard A. "The Social Cost of Monopoly and Regulation," *Journal of Political Economy* (August 1975): 807–27.

Tullock, Gordon. "The Welfare Costs of Tariffs, Monopolies and Theft," *Western Economic Journal* (June 1967): 224–32.

Tullock, Gordon, ed. *Explorations in the Theory of Anarchy* (Blacksburg, Va.: Center for Study of Public Choice, 1972).

_____. *Further Explorations in the Theory of Anarchy* (Blacksburg, Va.: Center for Study of Public Choice, 1974).

_____. *The Social Dilemma: The Economics of War and Revolution* (Blacksburg, Va.: University Publications, 1974).

Wagner, Richard E. "Public Choice as an Academic Enterprise: Charlottesville, Blacksburg, and Fairfax Retrospectively Viewed," in *The Production and Diffusion of Public Choice Political Economy: Reflections on the VPI Center*, eds. Joseph C. Pitt, Djavad Salehi-Isfahani, and Douglas W. Eckel (Oxford: Blackwell, 2004), 55–74.

14

No Regrets

I. *Introduction*

THE OVERARCHING THEME of this book, both in its initial and extended form, is a celebration of life in the academy, especially over the second half of the last century, especially as contrasted with the hard times my parents endured in the rural poverty of middle Tennessee during the first half of that century. My life has, indeed, been "Better than Plowing," if attention is confined to the simplistic intergenerational and interoccupational comparison. Further, as suggested in chapter 4, my only seriously considered alternative to life in the academy was continuing my successful military service beyond the end of World War II. But once I made the hard but happy decision to enter the University of Chicago and earn a Ph.D., the die was cast. I was never tempted to use the formal training as an economist as an entry point for nonacademic employment, either in the private or public sector. The few opportunities that might have come my way were summarily dismissed.

I was bound for the academy. But the academy is itself a very broad and inclusive territory, and there are many decision nodes confronted, many forks in the road. At each of these, a critical choice must be made. This chapter is about two such critical choices, both of which were made in the early 1950s—choices that have not entered at all into the preceding chapters. Both were "pre-Virginia" choices, but both were influential in shaping my career, at least as I now evaluate it. And because they were so important, they deserve treatment in this book.

In both cases, the road not taken, the other alternative considered but rejected, the "might have been," would have been damaging to me, perhaps in the extreme. *Maud Muller* is a poem about regrets and states that the "might have beens" are the saddest words of tongue or pen. In this chapter, and indeed in this book, I am turning the tables. I emphasize that, for me, in the settings described, the "might have beens" would surely have been much worse than those options that were realized. From this perspective, having avoided the relevant "might have beens" is a part of the measure of a happy life.

II. *From Tennessee to Tallahassee*

I faced no financial worries during my graduate student years, 1946–48, at the University of Chicago; I was supported by my wife's employment, by the GI Bill, and by a handsome fellowship awarded by the Southern Regional Training Program in Public Administration. The single constraint was that, for this fellowship, I had agreed to return to the South after completion of my studies. And, although my options were slightly limited, I felt no sense of constraint when I accepted a position at the University of Tennessee, where, as noted in an earlier chapter, I had spent one year of graduate work prior to military service. Further, I was offered a fully competitive salary, along with the rank of associate professor. Among my peers, it soon became known that I was somewhat unique in never having gone through the assistant professor ranks.

I spent three full academic years, 1948–51, in Knoxville. In retrospect, these years seem pleasant enough. I taught my assigned courses—many of them, since the teaching load was heavy—I enjoyed the social status of an accepted member of the academic faculty; I purchased and improved my first home, proudly and enthusiastically. I shared a large office with three other faculty members, only one of whom made any pretense of research. I enjoyed the relationship with Charles P. White, whom I had come to admire in my earlier tenure, largely for his strong work ethic.

There was no sense of going anywhere with my life of the mind. I was indeed "pulling my load" by comparison with my university colleagues. But to what ultimate purpose? I had not yet come to the realization that the rewards of academia come from engagement with ideas, and that the instructional elements were, and should be, treated only as by-products. During this Knoxville period of my career, I had not escaped from the delusion that my tenure as a student was finished. I failed to sense that only by remaining a genuine student can the academician-scientist realize the promised utility gains from the whole enterprise—only then is life in the academy "better than plowing."

In part, this failure stemmed from my own naiveté. I had not been long enough associated with others who conveyed the excitement of ideas. But in large part, my failure in Knoxville is attributable to the absence of any idea-driven enterprise among my faculty peers. The University of Tennessee, then and now, has not met and does not meet the standards of quality that my home state deserves. There was then, a half-century ago, and remains today an academic-scientific "deadness" about the whole Knoxville institution. These are harsh words, but they sincerely express my personal assessment. Surely, the dominance of quasi-professional athletics has, for this university at any rate, been damaging.

I was shocked from my slumber in 1951 when, to my surprise, an attractive offer for a position at Florida State University arrived. I was not personally associated with anyone involved, but, as it turned out, Earl J. Hamilton, whom I discussed briefly in Chapter 5, was largely responsible for the offer. Hamilton had been on the faculty at Duke University, and while there he was a colleague of Clark Allen, who had subsequently taken over the chairmanship of the Department of Economics in Tallahassee, where the whole university was in a rapid growth phase. Hamilton had strongly encouraged Allen to recruit me to the faculty.

As I reflect, more than a half-century later, on my decision process, I remain surprised at my reaction. I did not know the Florida State faculty in economics or in anything else. I did not know about the university, and I had never visited Florida, north or south. Admittedly, I was pleased by the offer, this time for a full professorship and a salary differential over my Knoxville stipend. But, as I soon learned, Tennessee immediately met Florida State's terms. And importantly, I was not considering moving "from" Tennessee. My situation in Knoxville was tranquil, if not exciting.

Despite this environment, I did accept the new position, and in August 1951, we made the shift from Knoxville to Tallahassee. Physically, the change was not portentous. The economics faculty was initially housed in an old military barracks a few miles from the main campus, with no air conditioning, despite the heat and humidity of north Florida. Matters were only slightly improved when, soon after my arrival, we shifted to a small house near the campus, still with no physical amenities to warrant notice. The whole university was experiencing serious growing pains, which affected all elements of its operation.

This setting, however, made for part of the excitement. Florida State had within a few years emerged from its status as the women's college of the state into full-fledged university status, nominally coequal with the formerly male counterpart in Gainesville. Enrollments, both male and female, were burgeoning, and facilitating budgets allowed rapid and general faculty expansions. The whole place was alive, and there was little or no encrusted bureaucratic opposition to change. Aside from the top of the hierarchy, the administrative officials were newly appointed and were, necessarily, relatively young by comparison with their peers in other institutions. Department heads and chairs were brought on board, almost all of whom were external to the Florida system, and who were, without exception, "young Turks"—quite willing to challenge established routines, which were, themselves, scarcely existent.

The university that was Florida State in those heady years of my tenure there, 1951–55, had spirit, and I must have somehow sensed its presence when I accepted the offer and left for Tallahassee. For me, however, much more than the general university setting was involved in my choice to make the move several hundred miles farther south. I could not possibly have recognized or predicted the impact of this shift of location on my own attitudes, outlook, and understanding of myself as a member of the academy. There was, indeed, a "Tallahassee transformation," but the sources remain mysterious. There was no remembered epiphany, no surge of self-confidence traceable to a particular happening. But somehow, in some way, I achieved an awareness of the excitement of ideas that I had not previously possessed, despite my earlier exposure to Frank Knight.

The persons among my peers most directly responsible for my transformation were Clark Allen and Marshall Colberg, both solid price theorists. Working alongside these two colleagues, and especially in the writing of an elementary textbook (Allen, Buchanan, and Colberg, 1954), I commenced to sense the vulnerability of so much of the conventional wisdom in economics. With the aid of their critical yet supportive comments, I moved further beyond the role of applied public-finance economist in my generalized attack (Buchanan, 1954a) on the whole discussion prompted by Kenneth Arrow's impossibility theorem—a discussion that dominated the professional journals during my Tallahassee years. Almost by the intellectual back door I found, to my surprise, that almost no attention had been paid to the analysis of individual choice behavior in the voting process, or in politics generally. My 1954 article (Buchanan, 1954b) comparing individual choice behavior in the stylized market and voting processes was the first step in filling what now seems to have been an awesome gap in political economy.

I make reference to these works, all written during my tenure at Florida State, not to summarize their content or to argue for their significance, but instead to express my near-certain conviction that these works would never have been produced had I remained in Knoxville. There was no direct influence on the ideas, as such, that can be traced to my Tallahassee colleagues, either Allen, Colberg, or anyone else. But the spirit of Florida State University in the early 1950s, as conveyed and translated through the economics program expressed for me through Clark Allen and Marshall Colberg, must have, in some way, provided me with the self-confidence I needed to challenge the analytical authorities of the science.

One "road not taken" could be represented by a decision in 1951 to remain at the University of Tennessee. What might my career have been like had I chosen this path? No one can know, since, as George Shackle taught us all, rejected alternatives can never be realized. But some highly subjective speculations may yet be proffered. In Knoxville, I should have remained a pedestrian, applied public-finance economist, and I would have been productive within the limits of criteria relevant to that narrowly defined academic environment. My intellectual life would have, perhaps, been interesting but scarcely challenging. I should not, however, have realized the limits of my horizons, since rejected superior alternatives cannot be known any better than their opposites.

III. *Saying No to Chicago*

Shortly after my decision to move from Tennessee to Tallahassee, I was faced with a second choice that was critically important for the direction of my subsequent career. And, similarly to the first case discussed, I avoided making what I would now consider to have been a major misstep.

Almost without exception, those who go through graduate training at the University of Chicago, then and now, take on the aura of the place. There is, quite simply, no other setting in the world that is quite so intellectually stimulating as Chicago. I say this with some conviction, and I suggest that this feeling is one that is shared by a very large proportion of those who have passed through the experience. This attitude about, and admiration for, the university almost guarantees that a subsequent invitation to return to Chicago as a member of the academic faculty remains among the top rank of personal objectives.

In this respect, I was no different from anyone else. Hence, I was both excited and flattered by the inquiry about my interest in a position on the Chicago faculty, and especially within only a few short years after leaving the institution. As was the case with my decision to make the shift to Florida from Tennessee, I do not quite know how I made the choice. But I did not take long to reject the provisional offer. In part, perhaps, I reacted against the part-time commitment to the economics of education that the position contained, but this element was surely not itself determining. Also, a second move after the shift to Florida might have seemed too disruptive. But to turn down the opportunity to return to the Chicago faculty—this was behavior that would seem, both in prospect and retrospect, to have been bizarre.

Perhaps the gods were with me, because I think that acceptance of the offer and a return to Chicago in the early 1950s would have been disastrous for me, at least by comparison with the success that did come my way along the path that I did choose.

Consider the comparisons and the contrast. In Tallahassee, I was the rising "star" in a growing department within a dynamic university setting, though admittedly still in a second ranking. The "big frog in the little pond" metaphor fits. A return to Chicago would have put me in the position of junior faculty member in a department with senior professors whom I respected, admired, and held in awe. The "pond" was the world's best, that I fully acknowledged, but how would the "small frog" make the adjustment?

I did not lack self-confidence, and there was no conscious fear that tenure might not be achieved. My concern, which can now be interpreted more accurately than it was sensed at the time, was centered on my fear that I might not be able to maintain my intellectual independence in relationships with colleagues who were my acknowledged superiors in understanding, in facility with technical tools, and in argument. I faced the prospect of being cowed into acquiescence by the likes of Milton Friedman and George Stigler.

And I was right. Had I returned to Chicago in the early 1950s, I am sure that I should have been successful in carving out a niche for my own research, modifying here and there the received wisdom on relatively minor points of analysis. And always looking over my shoulder, as it were, fearful of the criticisms that might come my way. What I could not and would not have done is to take the larger and more comprehensive perspective, as reflected in my critical assessment of the Arrow discussion—a perspective that was possible in the less pressurized intellectual climate of Tallahassee. The Chicago atmosphere, at least in economics, was, or would have been for me, supercharged with the assumption that the grand design had been set and that the task for underlings remained that of embroidery around the edges.

The research program that later came to be known as public choice would surely have emerged, sooner or later, at Chicago or elsewhere. The gap in the analysis of political behavior was simply too large for this whole subject matter to have remained long neglected. But my own role in the development of this program, as it did in fact emerge and grow, would have been totally different, and, possibly, nonexistent. A return to Chicago was, for me, a well-avoided road not taken.

IV. *Other "Might Have Beens"*

As I have noted, there are, of course, many decision nodes confronted over a long career, in academia or elsewhere. I have isolated only two of these for discussion in the preceding sections because they seem, in retrospect, to have been critically important for me and, further, because they were not at all emphasized in the narrative accounts in earlier chapters. Several of the events that were treated in these chapters could have been discussed in the dichotomy of seized opportunity versus no regrets. For example, a failure to initiate and to go through the Fulbright research year in Italy, 1955–56, would have modified my whole outlook on man's relation to the state.

One additional "might have been" warrants mention, although it seems less critical than those already examined. The positive choice to spend three extended leaves of absence at LSE in London during the

1960s yielded returns that would not have emerged had I remained in Charlottesville. I became acquainted with the academic atmosphere in economics at LSE, and I developed important personal and professional relationships with colleagues, notably with Peter Bauer and Jack Wiseman. These London visits gave me a sense of "belonging" to the world of economic discourse beyond Virginia; they allowed me to "come inside" the international discussion while remaining an "outsider" to the American setting. Further, the London environment may have been in itself critical in influencing me to carry forward my work on cost, which was, in one sense, an extension of work done at LSE by others (see Buchanan, 1969; Buchanan and Thirlby, eds., 1973).

The same sense of "no regrets" cannot be applied to the Fulbright year at Cambridge, 1961–62. I sought out the Oxbridge experience, but I was disappointed in almost all aspects of the long visit. The work that I did that year was, in fact, completed within the confines of my rooms at Sidney Sussex College, with no stimulation from Cambridge colleagues. I could just as well have done the work in Virginia. And, aside from the graciousness of James Meade and Dennis Robertson, there was nothing of personal or professional relevance to have missed had the visit never occurred. For me, the Cambridge academic year was essentially a wash.

It would be relatively easy for me to identify less significant decision nodes for which, from the vantage of the new century, I might assign positive, neutral, or negative values to the choices actually made. When separately confronted, these choices may have seemed important "in the small," while cumulatively adding up to the sequence that describes the whole career path. But the spillover effects seem in almost all cases to have been constrained. For me, there have been no plunges into disaster, and, aside from the critical choices already discussed, no major dangers avoided. Literally, I have no regrets.

References

Allen, C. L., James M. Buchanan, and M. R. Colberg. *Prices, Income, and Public Policy* (New York: McGraw Hill, 1954).

Buchanan, James M. "Social Choice, Democracy, and Free Markets," *Journal of Political Economy* 62 (April 1954a): 114–23.

_____. "Individual Choice in Voting and the Market," *Journal of Political Economy* 62 (August 1954b): 334–43.

_____. *Cost and Choice: An Inquiry in Economic Theory* (Chicago: Markham Publishing, October 1969).

Buchanan, James M. and G. F. Thirlby, eds. *LSE Essays on Cost* (London: London School of Economics, 1973).

Whittier, John Greenleaf. "Maud Miller," *Complete Poetical Works* (Classic Textbooks, 1895).

Influences on My Academic Life
and Thought

I. *Introduction*

IN LATE 2002, I received a letter from Professor Ole Wæver who is editor-in-chief of a Danish journal, *Politologiske Studier* (renamed *Tidsskriftet Politik*). The letter invited me to contribute to a projected special issue of the journal, with the separate contributions expected to satisfy specific constraints. Each author was requested to select ten sources that had exerted the greatest impact on his or her academic life and thought, with each source to be identified by a name and a specific representative work. One-page reviews for each of the ten sources were to be written, making for a ten-page contribution. The initial plan was to invite ten such contributions, making for an issue of one hundred pages in total. However, the project proved more demanding than originally thought, with the result that publication was delayed until late 2004.

I found this invitation to be an interesting challenge, and especially within the narrow constraints imposed, both as to the number of sources of influence and as to the length of the separate reviews allowed. This chapter is a somewhat revised version of the material that was submitted in response to the invitation.

How should I choose the ten works that "have had the greatest impact on (my) academic life and thought"? What criteria may be used?

These questions can best be approached by noting at the outset (1) that I have, from early exposure to the teachings of Frank Knight, adopted the philosophical stance of classical liberalism, (2) that I was trained professionally as an economist at the University of Chicago, before the mathematization and scientification of the discipline had fully developed, and (3) that my own volition led me to use what tools I had in application to problems of political order. My interests have been more philosophical, less technical, and less "scientistic" than those of my peers. And, although my analytical efforts have been value-free in any explicit sense, they have been driven by an underlying normative purpose—that of understanding more fully the necessary elements of the institutional structures of a society in which persons are at liberty.

I should also note that my contributions are perhaps properly classified as "American provincial." I have come increasingly to the view that even our most dispassionate "window on the world" of social and political interaction is affected by our own private history and culture, and that there are identifiable differences between the American and the European heritages—differences that show up in research emphases as well as general attitudes. My own concentration on the necessary distinction between the rules of the ongoing political game and the operation of ordinary politics within these rules stems more or less directly from the American understanding of and veneration for "the constitution."

There is a paradox, of sorts, in the broader acceptance of my work in Europe than in America. Despite the provincialism noted, my work has perhaps been more fully appreciated in Europe than in my own country. A distinguished German philosopher once paid me the compliment of saying that I was the most German of American economists, by which he meant that my interests were on more general issues than those of my economist peers. Translators have told me that my work is difficult to translate, despite the fact that I rarely use technical jargon. But the structure of my argument is often logically abstract, reflecting my interest in the basic ideas discussed as opposed to practical application.

These elements of my work are, to an extent, reflected in the ten works that I have selected for review. The works chosen vary somewhat in the directness and the manner of their influences on my own efforts. The separate reviews will be helpful in these respects.

With the partial exception of Adam Smith, I have listed the ten works more or less in the temporal order of their impact on my research program.

II. *Frank H. Knight*

Frank Knight's *The Ethics of Competititon* (1997) is representative of the whole corpus of his work. Other books might have been listed here, but Knight's influence on my development was not primarily through his writings. As many who know my own outlook recognize, Frank Knight is the most important figure to be included among any listing of my mentors. It is difficult for me even to imagine whom I might have been and what I might have written, if anything, without Knight, who became my role model in so many ways.

Interestingly, perhaps, Knight's influence was not effected through any transference of identifiable ideas. It was, instead, the conversion to an attitude, a stance toward the world that each of us must personally face, whether this world be described as scientific, philosophical, aesthetic, or personal. How can I possibly convey what it meant to me, an academic neophyte from the boondocks, to encounter someone who, quite simply, held no authority in awe, who stood ready to question critically anyone or anything, who had confidence is his own ability to identify confusion where he found it, and to challenge even the gods of his epoch?

It was exhilarating to share in Knight's toppling of the absolutist idols, but also to be pulled up short from any threatened plunge into nihilist oblivion. Knight recognized the partial validity of many claims to knowledge in the realms of economics, ethics, and politics. He stressed the plurality of insights, and he held out the prospect of simultaneous visions of the same phenomena.

Importantly, Knight was willing to order such claims through his usage of the term "relatively absolute absolutes," a concept that I have, personally, found to be indispensable in many applications. At one level of critical inquiry, nothing is held to be sacrosanct. But at other, more mundane examinations, work proceeds best "as if" the framework precepts are not open to challenge. This stance allows us to reject any and all claims for absolute validity without, at the same time, shifting to the other pole of unbounded relativism. This concept, or principle, has motivated much of my work in constitutional politics where we can make the distinction between constitutional rules—which are relatively absolute in one sense while at the same time being subject to critical examination in another—and ordinary politics, which does take place within the rules, as fixed.

Frank Knight would have rejected as simplistic many of the over-extended explanatory applications of the *Homo economicus* models of behavior that have been made during the decades after his major works. Indeed, the modern behavioral economists who are reacting to this body of work as if they are discovering new scientific territory could learn much from the essays in this volume. Knight recognized that the *Homo economicus* model was explanatory, but only of some elements of human behavior, and that economically quantifiable motivations exist along with several other forces, some of which may be dominant in some settings. Given this attitude, Knight would surely have been highly critical, despite the sophistication of measurement techniques, of the many efforts to interpret economics as an empirical science. (See chapter 3 for further discussion of the Knightean influence.)

III. *Knut Wicksell*

External readers would almost surely identify Knut Wicksell's *Finanztheoretische Untersuchungen* (1896) as the most important precursor of my work. I did, of course, translate this work in the literal sense (1958), but, also, much of my analytical effort might be interpreted as a generalized translation of Wicksellian ideas into the scientific postwar environment.[1] It remains surprising that these ideas were basically neglected for a full half-century, even in Wicksell's native country, as illustrated by the fact that the work, written in German, was only translated into Swedish after I called it to wider attention in my 1986 Nobel lecture, "The Constitution of Economic Policy."

In the broadest sense, Wicksell was the outstanding contributor in a European effort to extend the analytical tools of neoclassical economics to the collective or public sector, both in a positive and normative application. He sought to remove all vestiges of a residual idealism from the analysis of collective-political action. His first, and emphatic, admonition to fellow economists was to the effect that they should cease and desist from presuming their role to be that of proffering advice to a benevolent government ready and willing to listen. As Wicksell stressed, legislators are interested in furthering the objectives desired by their constituents, rather than in promoting some mystical "public interest."

---

1. Relevant portion translated by James M. Buchanan as "A New Principle of Just Taxation."

To secure better political outcomes, Wicksell stated that reform in the rules should be considered. First, he suggested imposing the simple requirement that any proposed item of spending be matched by a corresponding proposal to raise revenue in support. Second, and more controversially, he suggested replacing majority-voting rules in legislative assemblies by qualified supermajority rules, with the rule of unanimity serving as the benchmark guarantor for efficiency. The logical identity between Wicksell's unanimity norm and the more formal, and more familiar, Pareto criterion emerges if preferences, as revealed through agreement in collective choices, are taken to be the only indications of welfare-enhancing change.

Substantial parts of my research have been aimed at employing these Wicksellian insights in application to the institutional structures of modern politics, and notably in the American setting. This setting is somewhat more conducive to consideration of Wicksellian ideas because of the "implicit" constitutionalism that describes American political attitudes. Wicksell did not explicitly make the categorical separation between the constitution, defined as the rules within which ordinary politics operates, and ordinary politics itself. But he can surely, and without ambiguity, be classified as a genuine "constitutional political economist."

IV. *Kenneth J. Arrow*

The scientific community in social science was stirred up by Kenneth J. Arrow's small book *Social Choice and Individual Values* (1951). Arrow's central argument, which involved rigorous logical proof of the "impossibility theorem," stimulated an extensive discussion in economics, political science, and related disciplines. This theorem seemed to suggest that democracy, interpreted as collective action through majority-voting institutions, was inherently unstable. Even if the preference orderings over collective alternatives for all members of the polity exhibit properties of rationality, there is no way that such preferences could be aggregated into a social or collective ordering that satisfied reasonable conditions. Political equilibrium need not exist, and voting outcomes may cycle endlessly among alternatives presented for choices. Along with Duncan Black, who had simultaneously discovered (or rediscovered) the majoritarian cycle, Arrow seemed to have driven a major hole in the whole normative case for liberal society.

Almost all of the criticisms involved efforts to get around the Arrow result by variously restricting the domain over which individual preferences might range, or by modifying the set of conditions that the "social welfare function" sought for should meet.

This whole body of work, Arrow's book along with its critics, provided me with a standing challenge. Something seemed amiss, and in constructing a response, my own conception of collective action was more rigorously formulated. My criticism was more basic than that mounted by other critics. I challenged the whole enterprise that aimed at constructing a "social welfare function." My simple query was: Why should anyone expect that separate individual preferences could be aggregated into a consistent social ordering? Further, if these preferences should, perchance, be such as to generate the majoritarian cycle, would this not be precisely the result desired? What was the justification for the sacrosanct status accorded to majority voting? Where was there, in the whole construction, any normative concern for the potential exploitation of minorities in those settings where social orderings are consistent?

I also challenged Arrow's extension of his logic to apply to market as well as collective choice mechanisms. Properly understood, market solutions emerge from the interdependent choices made by separated traders who do not act on any ordering of "social states." Indeed, such an ordering must be irrelevant since "social states," as such, cannot be within the choice set of any participant in the market nexus.

As noted, Arrow's work, along with that of his critics, stimulated me negatively in the sense that I was forced into constructing a generalized criticism of the whole research program that involves usage of a "social welfare function." In so doing, however, my own methodological position itself became more coherent.

V. *Antonio de Viti de Marco*

First Principles of Public Finance, by Antonio de Viti de Marco (1936) exerted both a specific and a more general influence on my own research program. As the single English translation from a whole Italian tradition in the *scienza delle finanze*—a tradition that extended over most of a century—this book alone must have inspired me to examine this body of work more fully. As a result, I learned Italian, spent a full research year in Italy (1955–56), and absorbed critical elements of the Italian perspective on politics. In a more general sense, this book, and de Viti de Marco, was only one representative of the research tradition that had its origins in the works of Ferrara and includes Puviani, Montemartini, Barone, Fasiani, Einaudi, Griziotti, Cosciani, and others.

The influence of this body of Italian work on my own scholarship was indirect, although, in retrospect, it is readily identifiable. The English-language tradition in public finance and public economics was and had been almost exclusively utilitarian in its normative aspects, as well as idealist in its political presuppositions. Despite the large and increasing share of value allocated through collective rather than market institutions, almost no attention had been paid, at mid-century, to efforts at explaining, either analytically or empirically, how collective allocative processes work.

In this critical respect, the Italians were dramatically different. The literature was informed by the recognition that some theory or model of the state must be incorporated in any critical inquiry into public finance issues and, further, that the behavior of agents of the collectivity is directly relevant for any such theory or model. De Viti de Marco, in the book listed here, developed this whole analysis through parallel treatment of the monopolistic state, on the one hand, and the cooperative state, on the other.

My chosen exposure to this body of work reinforced my own interest in and emphasis on the extensions of the economist's models to the realm of politics. And, perhaps even more importantly, the "hard-nosed," indeed cynical, attitudes toward politics and politicians employed descriptively by the Italians allowed me to develop the self-confidence that was required to challenge the then-prevailing orthodoxy that presumed that political agents are benevolently immune from ordinary incentives. (See chapter 6 for further discussion.)

VI. *Rutledge Vining*

Economics in the United States of America (1956) presents Rutledge Vining's critical interpretation of the state of play in economics at mid-century. The monograph, as such, did not influence me at all, but the thrust of Vining's criticism did indeed exert a major impact on my thinking. For an extended period of some six years (1956–61), when we were departmental colleagues at the University of Virginia, Vining and

I spent literally hundreds of hours in informal discussions that ranged from tastes in whiskey to the deepest of philosophical issues.

I was, from the outset, sympathetic to Vining's approach. We shared an appreciation for the ideas of Frank Knight, with whom we had both studied, a decade apart, at the University of Chicago. Knight stressed the importance of rules in the functioning of social order, and he made frequent use of the game metaphor, which facilitates the analytical separation between rules and play within rules. Further, Knight emphasized that the appropriate ethics for the free society is that of sportsmanship.

Vining accepted these Knightean precepts but he moved beyond our mentor in more specific application to the political economy. He also reinforced my earlier criticisms of Arrow's efforts to derive a social welfare function. Vining stressed the elementary but essential point that we can only choose among rules for social interaction, that specific outcomes are not within the choice set of any chooser. Instead, outcomes emerge from interdependent choices separately made.

From this perspective, it follows that, for any given set of rules or constraints, an outcome space is delineated. It becomes important, therefore, to know something about the stochastic pattern of outcomes that given rules might generate. The relevance of theoretical statistics to Vining's methodology becomes evident. He wanted, first of all, for his fellow economists, in their advice to policy makers, to understand how much of the observed variations in outcomes can be explained by stochastic patterns. Unfortunately, Vining did not have available the modern computer technology that allows simulation at relatively low cost.

Vining's basic criticism of the work of economists did not exert the impact that might have been expected. Compared to the others who are listed as having influenced my work, Vining is, relatively, the most neglected. Through his emphasis on rules, Vining was a rather direct precursor to my development of "constitutional political economy," which has become a research program in its own right.

VII. *Gordon Tullock*

The Politics of Bureaucracy (1965) was the first book written by Gordon Tullock, although its date of publication is later than others. Early drafts of this book contained a mixture of hardheaded analysis supported by anecdotal evidence based on Tullock's several years of personal experience in the United States governmental bureaucracy. The double strands of discourse made publication of the early drafts difficult, and only after I, personally, made the considerable effort to copyedit the manuscript, did ultimate publication become feasible. This necessary chore work, which did indeed involve much cutting and pasting (before the time of word processors), along with coauthorship of *The Calculus of Consent* (1962) almost guaranteed that Gordon Tullock would exert a major influence on my own scientific development.

To summarize this influence, I can return to an earlier reference to Gordon Tullock as a "natural economist," despite the absence of formal training in the discipline. *Homo economicus*, somewhat narrowly defined, inhabits the world of social interaction that Tullock thinks he observes, so much so that those who personally encounter Gordon are often surprised to find that he is, in fact, "a kind man." Tullock seems, however, genuinely to think that the basic economic model of behavior is much more than one among several explanatory models, that it is essential to the construction of our understanding of political activity at all levels.

The Politics of Bureaucracy involves the direct application of this central behavioral model to the behavior of bureaucratic agents at all levels. At the start of the new century, the simple point that bureaucrats respond to incentives like everyone else and that, therefore, incentive structures do matter, seems elementary as well as obvious. Such was not the case, however, in mid-century, when Tullock called upon his personal experience in support of these propositions which, at the time, were revolutionary. We are not at all surprised to learn that Tullock was not a roaring bureaucratic success, given the way he looked at his fellow agents, who claimed to act always in "the public interest."

From my effort at getting the early manuscript into shape for publication, my own thinking was substantially clarified. As I indicated in my "Foreword" (1965) to the book, there is a categorical separation between the market and the political relationship between and among interacting persons. In the stylized limit, that of fully competitive markets for both inputs and outputs, the individual faces no costs of exit from any relationship. The individual is maximally free from the power of others. In dramatic contrast, the individual in a political relationship is necessarily subject to the exercise of some power or authority by another. In the stylized limit, this power is absolute; no exit is possible, regardless of cost.

Tullock's book enabled me to secure a better understanding of the differences between market and political relationships—an understanding that had, for me, both positive and normative implications. My analysis of individual behavior within institutional structures was sharpened, and my classical liberal presuppositions in support of market arrangements were reinforced.

VIII. *John von Neumann and Oskar Morgenstern*

Theory of Games and Economic Behavior by John von Neumann and Oskar Morgenstern (1944) has exerted a major influence on the work of any social scientist whose active career covered the second half of the last century. My own case has perhaps been typical of the way this influence has operated. I was not initially attracted to the applications made by economists to the theory of games, which involved, for the most part, analyses of strategies for firms in noncompetitive settings. However, as discussion shifted to solution concepts in more general terms, and as the derivative elaborations and extensions, some of which were in themselves major contributions, were developed, the usefulness of the basic theory for my own work became apparent.

Under the early influence of the ideas of both Knight and Wicksell, my research concentration was on the choices among rules, especially in collective settings, as opposed to the choices among allocative outcomes. And it soon was obvious that the metaphor of games clarified the analysis. Any attempt to model a game requires that a categorical separation be made between the rules, which describe the game itself, and the play within rules. Despite the failure of early game theorists to pay much attention to the choices among rules while concentrating on the strategic choices within rules, it was evident that there are direct analogs with the distinction in democratic politics between constitutional choices and the workings of ordinary politics within constitutional constraints.

As the formal game-theory constructions shifted more toward analyses of cooperative, or positive-sum, games and away from noncooperative, zero- or negative-sum, games, applications for political institutions took on more meaningful content. The "game of politics" contains elements of both conflict and cooperation among the players, and players would not long voluntarily accept sets of rules that generate negative payoffs.

Acceptable rules for politics, described as the constitution in being, must, when considered over a whole sequence of periods (rounds of play), yield positively valued returns to all participants. As indicated, the game-theoretic approach was helpful to me quite early in my research career as I tried to analyze constitutional structures.

A second and distinctly different influence of game theory in my own work was much more gradual in making itself felt. From my initial criticism of the Arrow enterprise in the early 1950s, I had come increasingly to reject the economists' conventional emphases on maximization, with the implication that, given the maximand, there is a single allocative solution that is optimal. In market interactions, solutions emerge as participants make their own maximizing choices within the constraints separately faced. The solution finally generated is not itself within the choice set of any participant.

I came quite late to the realization that the best way to illustrate this simple point is through elementary game theory. Players choose among strategies; the interdependence among these strategic choices generates an outcome that no player chooses or could choose. It is as simple as that, and, even now, economic theory could be made more coherent by wider understanding of this quite elementary fact.

IX. F. A. Hayek

The work of F. A. Hayek was not seminal for my own early development. In my course of graduate study and during the years immediately following, I do not recall having read any of Hayek's books. I knew, of course, that *The Road to Serfdom* (1944) had stirred up much discussion, pro and con, in the quasi-public argumentation about the viability of socialism.

Hayek's influence on my own work came later. It was only during the 1960s, when I tried to articulate my methodological position and particularly to reconcile my analysis of public debt burden with neoclassical orthodoxy, that I effectively discovered Hayek, and fellow Austrians, notably Mises. The influence for me was, therefore, by way of providing independent and indirect support for sometimes inchoate ideas that had come to inform my own efforts.

More specifically, the Hayekian emphasis, best expressed in his classic article "Economics and Knowledge" (1937), that the ultimate data for economic theory can only be subjective allowed me to understand my own logic more fully. I was able to grapple with and to respond more clearly to those critics who had seemed to inhabit a realm of ideas quite foreign to what had seemed natural territory to me. Hayek, his fellow Austrians, and a whole tradition at the London School of Economics, itself influenced by Hayek's presence, offered a framework upon which I could ground a general treatment of opportunity cost (*Cost and Choice*, 1969), as well as extensions to several applications, including collective action.

Relatively late in my work, Hayek's conception of a "moral order," as distinct from the genetically derived "moral community," was important for my own efforts to describe differing societies in terms of the relative moral attitudes in social interaction.[2] Further inquiry into the ethics minimally required to insure viability of the Hayekian moral order remains on my research agenda.

A much different influence was exerted by Hayek's entrepreneurial role in constructing the organizational structure within which the philosophical ideas of classical liberalism were preserved and advanced, especially during the mid-century decades when the contrasting socialist ideology dominated the world's academies. Early membership in the Mt. Pelerin Society, almost exclusively Hayek's creation, gave psychological legitimacy to my own burgeoning interest in political philosophy, reinforcing earlier and more direct influence from Frank Knight.

I found Hayek's faith in the power of basic ideas congenial, and I shared his criticism of much modern social science to the effect that the philosophical foundations of the liberal social order were being sorely neglected. I admired Hayek personally, as a scholar who remained tolerant to the ideas of others even while he was treated with intolerance by those who were in the spell of "the fatal conceit" of the socialist century.

X. *John Rawls*

The academic career of John Rawls was roughly contemporaneous with my own. And, in a sense, I considered his work always to be parallel to rather than influential for or influenced by my efforts. I recognized that we were "plowing different fields" of inquiry, so to speak, but that there were relevant intersections between our endeavors, both of which were

---

2. F. A. Hayek, *Individualism and Economic Order* (Chicago: University of Chicago Press, 1948).

informed by a commonly shared set of values. Unlike so many of my peers in economics in particular, I was never motivated to mount a criticism of the Rawlsian enterprise. Indeed, the opposite; I was motivated, when pressed, to defend Rawls, despite the possible differences between my own interpretation and his own understandings.

Why, then, have I included Rawls in my listing of major influences on my own contributions? I have done so because Rawls did, almost single-handedly, change the whole research agenda in political philosophy—an agenda that must provide the basis upon which any constructive undertaking in constitutional inquiry is grounded.[3] Rawls sought to formulate "principles of justice," which are prior to any formulation of constitutional precepts. Efforts aimed at the second of these objectives are necessarily derivative from something akin to the Rawlsian foundations.

I have summarized the Rawlsian corpus as "justice among natural equals." But persons differ, one from another, along many dimensions. How, then, can any presumption of natural equality be introduced? Rawls accomplished this feat by shifting the stage of discourse; he placed persons behind a "veil of ignorance" where identification is impossible and where persons necessarily confront one another as equals. This step in the argument allowed an escape from the distinction between narrow self-interest, as identified, and something that might be called "public interest," without calling upon altruistic motivations.

The Rawlsian method here was parallel to that presented in *The Calculus of Consent*, which I wrote jointly with Gordon Tullock, where we used what has since been called a "veil of uncertainty" to analyze the choice of constitutional rules expected to remain in place over a sequence of periods. The affinity between our work and that of Rawls is clear.

My differences with Rawls stem almost exclusively from the questions concerning how far we can go beyond precepts for procedural justice (or constitutional rules) derivative from our commonly shared methodology and formulate specific substantive principles, as instanced by the Rawlsian requirement of equal liberty, and, lexicographically attached, that of "maximin" access to primary goods. Limitation of the analysis to the derivation of procedural norms would have made for a more defensible structure of argument, but this limitation would, at the same time, prob-

3. John Rawls. *A Theory of Justice* (Cambridge: Harvard University Press, 1971).

ably have prevented the work from exerting the major impact that it did have. Hence, even if somewhat wrongly understood by many readers both in the academy and beyond, the Rawlsian edifice has exerted a beneficial effect on Western liberal thought.

XI. *Adam Smith*

Any economist can properly list Adam Smith as an influence since, after all, the discipline might never have come into being without the analytical foundations offered in *The Wealth of Nations* (1776). Adam Smith and this book have been and remain an integral part of the culture of economics. For this assignment, however, something more specific should be required for any claim of direct impact on a research career. I do make such a claim, based on three separate, but related, strands of argument-analysis in the 1776 *magnum opus*.

Through the instruction of Frank Knight and Henry Simons, my Chicago teachers, I was forced to absorb fully the simple principles of market allocation, as best illustrated by Adam Smith's fable of the deer and the beaver. What conditions must be presumed to be present if the Smithean results are to hold? (As George Stigler enjoyed reminding us, with Adam Smith it is always best to presume that he was correct.) If persons are at liberty to shift among specializations (between deer and beaver hunting), and if outputs are produced at constant returns beyond specialization thresholds, the relative costs of production, measured in units of the single homogeneous input, must set relative prices in some natural equilibrium. Once this simplest of Smithean models is mastered, a genuine understanding of how markets work becomes relatively straightforward.

Implicit in this simple analysis is a second element that Smith stresses more fully in other parts of his treatise. Despite the book's title, which is in this sense unfortunate, Adam Smith's purpose in the whole exercise was to demonstrate that if allowed their natural liberty within a structure of established "laws and institutions," persons would generate results that would be satisfactory to all participants. His emphasis on the justice of natural liberty tends to be overlooked by undue concentration, in post-Smithean economics, on the production of aggregate value. This oversight, in turn, has caused economists to miss a primary implication of Smith's argument that reduces dramatically the necessary scope for collective-political action. If, within the proper institutional framework, persons acting through their own initiatives within markets can generate a beneficent order, the sometimes-intrusive imposition of politicized control is not required at all.

A third element in Adam Smith's work, and which is also implicit in the simple deer-beaver parable, was very late in its direct impact on my own conception of the economic process. Yet, from an inclusive perspective, this element was the most basic in Smith's whole vision despite its relative neglect in neoclassical economics. Adam Smith explained the mutuality of benefits from trade or exchange by the advantages of specialization, even in a setting of natural equality among potential traders. Again refer to the deer and beaver hunters, each of whom can readily shift between these occupations. By rather simple extension here, once beyond the rude state of society, growth (and the wealth of nations) emerges as specialization proceeds, limited only by the extent of the market or trading nexus. The economy as a whole must, therefore, operate under generalized increasing returns.

The argument in support of open and free markets is straightforward. Any arbitrary closing off of entry or exit from exchange reduces the level of value realized. Note in particular that, in this elementary Smithean logic, there is no need at all to bring in Ricardian comparative advantage to explain the mutual benefits from exchange. And there is no basis for distinguishing between domestic and foreign trade. Persons do, of course, differ in their productive capacities, and the market does allow for specialization based, in part, on comparative advantage. But this logic must be secondary in any basic explanation of the efficacy of free exchange. As economic theory developed, however, the Ricardian logic was allowed to take precedence over the more basic Smithean understandings. The classical emphases on the wellsprings of economic growth, which were central for Adam Smith, came to be replaced by the neoclassical emphases on maximizing value from fixed resources, requiring a constant returns presumption for which the Ricardian apparatus seemed more convenient.

Only in the last decades of the twentieth century did economists begin to return, albeit begrudgingly, to the Smithean sources for explanations of economic growth. And, importantly, this basic element in Adam Smith's teaching has not yet found its way into the elementary principles of the discipline.

XII. *Further Thoughts*

As noted, part of the challenge in the Danish invitation was that of being required to work within the constraints imposed, both in the number of influences and in the lengths of reviews. For me, a more natural number would have been twelve, since I find it relatively easy to list two other sources of my work that have necessarily been left out. The two leading lights in economics who belong to the generation immediately preceding my own, Milton Friedman and Paul Samuelson, would have rounded out a more defensible package. Milton Friedman, both as my mentor in price theory and, more importantly, as the conduit for Popperian scientific method, exerted direct influence on several of my early papers. And Paul Samuelson, with his short but seminal paper on public expenditure theory, clarified much of what remained murky for me as I tried to promulgate the basic Wicksellian insights.

Extension beyond an even dozen would have been more difficult for me and would have required that I look for sources in the wider cultural environment that the different parts of this book describe.

References

Arrow, Kenneth J. *Social Choice and Individual Values* (New York: Wiley, 1951).

Buchanan, James M. "The Constitution of Economic Policy," *American Economic Review* 77 (June 1987): 243–50.

_____. *Cost and Choice: An Inquiry in Economic Theory* (Chicago: Markham, 1969).

_____. "Foreword," *The Politics of Bureaucracy*, Gordon Tullock (Washington, D.C.: Public Affairs Press, 1965), 1–9.

_____, trans. "A New Principle of Just Taxation," in *Classics in the Theory of Public Finance*, ed. R. A. Musgrave and A. T. Peacock (London: Macmillan, 1958), 72–118.

_____. *10 x 10*, Special Issue, *Tidsskriftet Politik* 4 (no. 7, 2004).

Buchanan, James M. and Gordon Tullock, *The Calculus of Consent: Logical Foundations of Constitutional Democracy* (Ann Arbor: University of Michigan Press, 1962).

de Viti de Marco, Antonio. *First Principles of Public Finance*, trans. E. P. Marget (London: Harcourt Brace, 1936).

Hayek, F.A. "Economics and Knowledge," *Economica* 4 (1937): 33–54.

_____. *Individualism and Economic Order* (Chicago: University of Chicago Press, 1948).

_____. *The Road to Serfdom* (Chicago: University of Chicago Press, 1944).

Knight, Frank H. *The Ethics of Competition* (New Brunswick: Transactions Publishers, 1997).

Rawls, John. *A Theory of Justice* (Cambridge: Harvard University Press, 1971).

Smith, Adam. *An Inquiry into the Nature and Causes of The Wealth of Nations* [1776] (New York: Random House, Modern Library Edition, 1937).

Tullock, Gordon. *The Politics of Bureaucracy* (Washington, D. C.: Public Affairs Press, 1965).

Vining, Rutledge. *Economics in the United States of America: A Review and Interpretation of Research* (Paris: UNESCO, 1956).

von Neumann, John and Oskar Morgenstern. *Theory of Games and Economic Behavior* (Princeton: Princeton University Press, 1944).

Wicksell, Knut. *Finanztheoretische Untersuchungen* (Jena: Gustav Fischer, 1896).

CHAPTER 16

Out to Pasture

I. Introduction

IT IS INAPPROPRIATE TO INCLUDE two separate "final" chapters in a book of autobiographical essays, and I am quite willing to allow Chapter 12, above, to stand as a summary perspective on a life's experience, despite the temporal extension that has given me the opportunity to write the additional essays. I entitle this chapter "Out to Pasture" to convey the notion that for most of the period since completion of the essays in the earlier edition, Chapters 1–12, I have been "beyond" the academy, at least in any formal sense.

The first point to note is that the metaphor "out to pasture" is not nearly so applicable to the career of an academic scientist or philosopher as it might be to that of the ordinary septuagenarian or octogenarian whose career involved "work" in the commonly understood sense of the word. In a very real sense, to be discussed further below in section II, the academician remains always "out to pasture" in that no tangible product or service is directly transferred to others in any observable process.

Being "beyond" the academy also implies, as section III emphasizes, the presence of an evaluative distance between the activities in question, whatever these may be, and the assessment of the worth of these activities. Age does have its rewards—in this instance, the necessary increase in the objective elements of judgment. The insider, as judge and jury, gradually gives way to the outsider, who stands apart from particularized commitment. For the autobiographer, a depersonalization of sorts becomes possible; a decoupling occurs. Age itself allows for the construction of a type of bridge between identifiable and separable interest, on the one hand, and more general criteria, on the other.

In section IV, I explore the nature of retirement for the academician. And, in section V, I look at the road ahead, even as I avoid looking back. Section VI offers a summary assessment.

II. *What Is the Quid Pro Quo?*

A former colleague, the late Bob Staaf, could never escape from the feeling that the academic life is fraudulent, that all of us are engaged in a gigantic shell game aimed at the exploitation of the general public. Staaf had, as a teenager, worked in his father's bicycle repair shop in Pittsburgh, and he felt, quite strongly, that such work was the only genuinely productive activity he had ever done. In this shop, he was, demonstrably, creating value; he fixed bicycles. There seemed to be no comparable creation of value, no quid pro quo in the "exchange" between work in the academy and some measurable final product.

What value is created as the scholar-scientist carries on his work? What is the academic equivalent of the bicycle-as-repaired? Note that, as I have put the question here, concern is focused on the activity of the scholar-scientist who engages with ideas rather than on the teacher or instructor who passes along discovered knowledge to others. These two roles are often confused, both philosophically and institutionally, as later discussion will indicate. But, for now, I concentrate on the first, in part because that has always been my own self-imagined stance. I have never thought of myself as "supplying," either directly or indirectly, educational services to students who, having the embodied wisdom transmitted to them by my activities, become more productive members of society. For me, a career described as "teacher," in any remotely pure sense, would not have been at all stimulating, and certainly no more personally rewarding than several of the other "might have beens," whether military or civilian. In terms of the inclusive metaphor of the book's title, a career devoted primarily to "teaching," as such, would indeed be a version of "plowing."

One possible response to the question as posed is an acknowledgment that there is no quid pro quo between the pure scientist-scholar and those who seem to "purchase" his services. There is no value product created for which the public is willing to pay. Instead, the scientist-scholar engages with ideas only as a by-product of his professional role as teacher-instructor, the value of which is recognized. This response must be rejected out of hand because its acceptance requires the presumption that the whole institutional structure in which the two roles, the scientist-scholar and the teacher, are intertwined in a complex set of relationships is somehow grossly inefficient from the perspective of public or collective purpose. If, indeed, there is no recognizable value created by the endeavor of the scientist-scholar-philosopher, as such, apart from the by-product value of teaching, surely we should have expected the evolutionary success of the pure teaching institutions to have been more in evidence.

Clearly, something of value is created, and is deemed to be created, by the scientist-scholar as he engages with ideas. But it is equally clear that this "something" is quite different from the ordinary quid pro quo of the marketplace. Nor is the discovery metaphor helpful here. It is not as if someone says "thar's gold in them thar hills, go and find it, and, of course, share it with me." The quo is not even probabilistically defined, as this metaphor might suggest. The scientist-scholar is not expected to create anything so tangible. His role in the very complex division of labor is one of engaging with ideas, activity that, in the process, may or may not yield returns that may or may not be measurable on any concrete scale. The academician, thus stylized, is a specialist in thinking, in speculating about what is and what might be.

A distinguishing feature of the very indirect exchange between the scientist-scholar and those who provide succor and support is the necessary absence of any sense of sale or purchase. The academician, so defined, cannot and must not think of himself as "performing" a service for those who finance his activity. His "exchange," if such word be appropriately used at all, is with ideas that challenge, not with those supporters who observe from afar, who are beyond the consciousness of the one who thinks. Here the useful metaphor is with the operating theater in the classical medical school depiction. The surgeon, bent over the patient, concentrates exclusively on his task, operating on the patient, quite oblivious of the observers who stand above and outside.

The situation is, of course, one of joint supply, in which the production or generation of one "good" necessarily involves the simultaneous production of another "good." As with the surgeon in the operating theater, however, the second good, the spillover by-product, is entirely gratuitous and the basic canon of science is surely violated if the scientist's motivation, even in part, is concerned with the value of the by-product. The scientist, or the surgeon in this illustration, cannot consciously be affected in his behavior by the knowledge that others, in this case, students, may be learning from their observations of his activities. The scientist's "exchange," if such a term is at all appropriate, is not with those who might benefit from the use of the by-product, even in some indirect sense. The speculative activity of engaging with ideas cannot be considered, even in small part, as "performance."

There are many parallels outside the academy. The player, whether amateur or professional, in organized games is not and cannot be simultaneously a competitor, fully engaged with the opponent, and a performer who aims his actions toward the plaudits of the observing spectator. The difference between the Harlem Globe Trotters and the Los Angeles Lakers is precisely along the dimension accentuated here. Even the actor who is taking on the personification of a fictional character in a drama cannot consciously "perform" for the audience, as such, in violation of the script's implied relationship to the other characters. The concert pianist must engage with the score; to the extent that he modifies his activities to please the audience, he becomes Liberace.

In a very real sense, the whole quid pro quo for the stylized academician is contained within his own psyche. He gives up alternative pursuits and engages with ideas in exchange for the intrinsic rewards that such activity offers. The fact that others, society at large, are willing to provide sustenance is irrelevant in this context. It is, almost literally, as if "the others" throw coins over the ivy wall without conscious recognition by those who remain cloistered inside. Such language is suggestive and the modern scientist-philosopher becomes the successor to the medieval monk whose labor for the glory of God was rewarded only by the inner satisfaction of the penitent.

In post-Enlightenment liberalism, truth replaced God, and those who specialize in truth-seeking, here variously called academicians, scientists, scholars, or philosophers, carry on the tradition without any meaningful quid pro quo between their own activity, their "work," and its direct effect on "others" beyond the walled gardens.

III. *What Is the Net Product?*

In the absence of such a quid pro quo, however, why have the "others," acting through the institutions of society at large, remained ever-willing to subsidize the activity of the isolated and independent truth seekers, the specialists in speculative thinking?

One familiar response cannot be readily extended beyond applicability to the natural or physical sciences. The pursuit of truth in pure science may be subsidized because of a faith that the findings of the endeavor will ultimately be handsomely rewarded in application, in the achievement and control over the physical environment that will increase the size of the bundle of valued final-products. And over the last two centuries, this faith has been justified. We are enabled to live "better" lives, under almost any criterion for betterment, because of scientific advances.

It is difficult, however, to stretch this response beyond pure science, as such. The activity of the philosopher who speculates on good and evil, who seeks the beautiful as well as the true, can scarcely be brought within the economists' utility scalar, even in some remote relationship. And it may be highly misleading even to force the activities of the natural scientist under the utilitarian umbrella. Even if we could know, in advance, that there would never be any practical applications of the scientific endeavor, we might still want to insure that the activity of science and scientists goes forward. The "need to know" is deep within our nature as humans, and there is a measure of satisfaction with every pushing back of the constraints imposed by the realm of "unknowledge."

This natural curiosity, this need to know more than we do know, explains in part the collective willingness to subsidize those who specialize in pushing back the frontiers. But only in part. Human beings do indeed want to "know more"; but they also want to "be better" than they are. As Frank Knight was fond of emphasizing, persons aim, not so much at satisfying existing wants more fully, but at trying to create better wants. And they expect the "thinking classes," the scientists-philosophers, to assist them in this quest. Even if they, themselves, cannot attain the realms of discourse imagined to occupy the minds of the speculative thinkers, persons hold up such idealized activity as potential achievement to be admired from afar. There is a general recognition that there are first-hand starters behind the second-hand dealers in ideas that they directly encounter.

IV. *Retirement from What?*

I am aware that in the two preceding sections I have shifted from the autobiographical mode that has described the essays in this book. I find myself offering normative justification of the academician generally, rather than myself. As noted earlier, there is perhaps legitimacy of sorts the move away from personalized identification offered by the lengthened age perspective. In further defense of the seeming detour, however, let me suggest that my purpose has been explanatory rather than justificatory. I find it necessary to examine the quid pro quo between the academician, generally, and the public that supports his activities in order to explain and to understand my own position as it exists well beyond formal association with the institutions of academia.

Only by appreciating that there is no ordinary quid pro quo between the academician and the institution, organization, or person for whom he nominally "works," and who pays his salary, can I begin to understand and to explain why I did not undergo a psychological shift of some sort when I was officially taken off a university payroll. I sensed no relief from some continuing obligation to provide services. There was no feeling that constraints on my behavior had been slackened or removed.

"Retirement" for me, therefore, was not a threshold—a shift in the basic dimension of life itself. Any flows of value product associated with my efforts, if such there were and are, did not cease with truncation of my formal "employment." I am as obligated now, several years into formal post-retirement, as I ever was to engage with the ideas that attract my interest. As noted earlier, the exchange metaphor does not fit well here, but, if applied at all, it is best treated as if any exchange lies within the psyche of the academician-scientist-philosopher, who contains within himself both parties to trade. In this context, "retirement" could only mean some deliberate shedding off of half of life itself. For me at any rate, any such "retirement" would seem obscene.

I recognize of course that I have, personally, been twice blest by the relative absence of binding constraints on my liberties of choice and action during the course of my formal academic employment, and especially during the final decades. I was allowed to do more or less as I pleased, in terms of both organization and substantive content of instructional and research agenda. The fact that my interests were always well within the boundaries of academic propriety gave me the sense of openness required for energized effort. (Only the partial exception represented by the ideological prejudices encountered during the Charlottesville years [chapter 7] warrants mention in this connection.)

What could I possibly retire "from"? For me, it would have been inconceivable to drive the nation's highways in an RV displaying the obscenity "Retired" plastered on the rear window. To have allowed the withdrawal of a formal salary to modify, even slightly, my pattern of activities would have amounted to internal subversion of sorts. I should have felt that I would be "letting the side down" by any such behavior. And I have not done so, in these several years beyond the threescore and ten. Nor is any such behavioral change contemplated. In this meaningful interpretation, I shall never "retire," until physical limits intervene.

V. *A Sea of Challenges*

Adam Smith told us that the task of the philosopher is to observe everything, but he did not follow up and tell us that the ultimate purpose is to understand that which we observe. To achieve such understanding, however, requires specialization. The scientist-philosopher must choose from among a whole sea of observations. He must, for almost all of that which he observes, accept his sensory perceptions along with the conventional or received knowledge available. He must accept the world as it seems and is known, in a "relatively absolute absolute sense." The scientist-philosopher selects as the object of his critical inquiry some small subset of this apparent reality that he confronts. And for the elements in this subset, he seeks to unravel its mysteries, to understand its inner workings more fully than that which describes the conventional wisdom.

I shall make no effort here, aside from the references in earlier chapters, to explain why and how the ideas with which I have personally engaged attracted my attention. The processes of selection are perhaps mysterious, even to those who must make the choices. My point of emphasis here is rather to suggest that the challenges are and must remain open-ended. It is not as if there pre-existed a row of ideas waiting to be challenged by my particular set of capacities, which, being toppled one by one, marked a sort of progress toward completion. No such relief is in store, and I should indeed be saddened if there seemed to be an end-point to my explorations. Hence, the metaphor used for the title of this section: "a sea of challenges." The ideas that will attract my attention remain, for me, in the realm of the "unknowables." But, let me assure myself that there will always be some such ideas over the horizon.

VI. Summation

Life during the several years "out to pasture" has not been the rocking-chair tale of song and story. I have enjoyed the company of my dogs much less than I might have imagined. The pull of the ideas waiting to be clarified has simply been too strong to allow diversion into what seem always simple pleasures.

The tools with which I work become increasingly outmoded, and my sometimes-wobbly efforts at communicating with those whose primary emphasis seems to be on the tools rather than on the ideas themselves often fall flat. But the clarification sought for is as much for me as for any others. I have never, as noted earlier, been motivated by some arrogant faith in an ability to change the world. The academy will move forward, both by evolution and by constructive (and destructive) reforms. My piddling contribution to the dialogues will be in the mix so long as books remain in print.

What else is there?

INDEX

Kaufmann, Walter, 140–41, 143
Kedourie, Elie, 141
Kelliher, Thomas, 58
Kennedy, John Fitzgerald, 179
Keynesian economics: 103–4, 187;
    and public debt, 8, 83
Knight, Frank H., 1, 4–6, 13, 43,
    68–81, 95, 96, 99, 110–11, 129,
    134, 138, 140, 148, 152–53,
    197, 204, 205–206, 210, 212,
    214, 216, 219, 225
Krick, Harold, 61
Krueger, Anne O., 188, 193

Land, Edwin, 131
land, ownership, 110, 117–18. *See
    also* property rights
laws and institutions, 217–18
Layton, E. T., 52
Lee, Dwight, 187
Leland, Simeon, 70
legislation, Gramm-Rudman-Hol-
    lings, 104
Leijonhufved, Axel, 184
Leoni, Bruno, 89–90, 95
Letwin, Shirley Robin, 143
leviathan, model of state, 12
liberalism: classical, 204, 214; post-
    Enlightenment, 223; and respon-
    sibility, 148. *See also* Knight
Libertarian socialist, 72
liberty: equal, 216; limits of, 12; per-
    sonal, 156
The Limits of Liberty, 186, 192
logic: Ricardian, 217; Smithean, 217
Lomasky, Loren, 187
London School of Economics (LSE),
    200–201, 214

MacArthur, Douglas, 57
Mackay, Robert, 187

macroeconomics, 155
Madison, James, 9, 98, 106
Madisonian vision, 113
majoritarianism, 207, 208
market: extent of, 217; free, 217; and
    independence, 124–26
market behavior, 198
market failure, and public choice, 99
market order, and politics, 72
markets, 216
Marshall, Alfred, 83
Martelli, Paolo, xii, 82
Marxian economics, 70
masters and slaves. *See* social
    ordering
Maud Muller, 195. *See also* choice,
    personal (Buchanan)
"maximin," 216
Maxwell, Grover, 41
Mazzola, Ugo, 87
McKenzie, Richard, 106, 185
McKeon, Richard, 139
McMorris, C., 59
Meade, James, 201
Mebane, W., 44
Middle Tennessee State Teachers
    College, 2, 35–47, 69, 74
Middle Tennessee State University, xi
Midway, Battle of, 54–56
military service, 48–67
Mises, Ludwig von, 213
Mitchell, William, 184, 185, 190
model: Crusoe, 17; general behav-
    ioral, viii, 211; cooperative, of
    state, 209; monopoly, of state, 7,
    209; public interest, 11. *See also*
    leviathan
Modigliani, Franco, 161
monopoly state. *See* model
Mt. Pelerin Society, 214
Montemartini, Giovanni, 87, 209

moral order, and moral community,
214. *See also* Hayek
Morgenstern, Oskar, 84, 212–13
Mueller, Dennis, 187
Muller, H. J., 133
Murdoch, Iris, 143
Musgrave, Richard A., 6, 91

Natural economics. *See* economics
natural economist. *See* Tullock
natural equals, justice among, 215.
    See also Rawls
natural equilibrium, 216
natural liberty, 216–17; justice of,
    217
Naval War College, 50
New Deal, 31, 69
Nietzsche, Friedrich Wilhelm, 129,
    132, 137, 140, 143, 144
Nimitz, Chester W., 3, 48, 51, 58–60,
    75,
Nixon, Richard M., administration,
    188
Nobel prize (Alfred Nobel Memorial
    Prize in Economic Sciences), xi,
    xii, 29, 35, 154, 158–73
Nobel lecture, 206, 217. *See also*
    Wicksell
Nordqvist, Liv Wicksell, 169
Nozick, Robert, 102
Nutter, G. Warren, 16, 92, 94, 97,
    99, 182

Ohlin, Bertil, 95
opportunity cost, 8–9
order, civil. *See* civil order
order, market. *See* market order
order, moral. *See* moral order
ordering, social. *See* social ordering
Ordway, Ann, 42–43
Orr, Dan, 189–90

Ortega y Gasset, José, 137
Orton, W. A., 135
Orwell, George, 141–42
ownership. *See* land

Pantaleoni, Maffeo, 87
Papi, G. Ugo, 86
paradigm, exchange. *See* exchange
    paradigm
Pareto, Vilfredo, 207
Parravicini, Giannino, 84, 86, 89–90
Peacock, Alan T., 6, 91
Peltzman, Sam, 103
philosophy, private and public, 147
Phipps, Cecil G., 78
Piaget, Jean, 139
Pigou, Arthur C., 10, 81, 83
Plato, 140–41
Polanyi, John C., 166
Polanyi, Michael, 95, 129, 166
policy: editorial, 77; fiscal, and public
    choice, 104; Keynesian fiscal, 104
political economy: contractarian,
    106; normative and positive,
    152–54, 204, 206–7, 211; as
    order, viii, 111; and public choice,
    99–100, 189; *raison d'être*, vii–
    viii; research in, 198, 204; struc-
    tures, institutional, 204. *See also*
    constitutional political economy;
    Virginia political economy
political philosophy, 214, 215–16
political theory, and economic theory,
    213
politics: and market, 72; ordinary,
    206. *See also* idealism, rules
The Politics of Bureaucracy, 211, 219
*Politologiske Studier. See Tidsskriftet
    Politik*
Pope, Lewis S., 31
Popper, Karl R., 138–39, 218

populism, 1
Posner, Richard A., 188, 193
Potter, E. D., 48
power, taxing. *See* taxing power
price theory, 197, 218
property rights, 81
public choice: and catallaxy, 73–74;
    and deficits, 11, 104; and fiscal
    policy, 104; and mainstream eco-
    nomics, 189; and market failure,
    99; methodology, 187; origins,
    9–10; and political economy,
    99–100; and political failure, 99–
    100; research program, 82, 181,
    182, 186, 187, 188–90, 192,
    200; and social choice, 73–74
Public Choice, the journal, 100
Public Choice Society, 10, 113, 182
public debt, 8–9; burden of, 83, 213.
    See also Keynesian economics
public expenditure theory, 218
public finance, Italian tradition,
    208–9
public finance economist, applied,
    197, 198
public goods, 10
public interest, 206–207, 211, 215
public interest model. *See* model
Puviani, Amilcare, 87, 209

Rader, Trout, 186
Rawls, John, 14, 102, 214–16, 219
Reagan, Ronald, 179
Reid, Joe, 187
relatively absolute absolute(s), 78–
    79, 205–206, 226
religion, and early life, 34
rent seeking, 187–88
Rescher, N., 130
resources, fixed, 217
responsibility, individual, 148

retirement, 225–26
returns: constant, 216; increasing,
    generalized, 217
Reynolds, Tommie, 43
Ricardo, David, 217–18
Ricca-Salerno, Giuseppe, 87
Rice University, 183
The Road to Serfdom, 213, 219
Roberts, Moira, 142
Robertson, Dennis, 201
Rockefeller, William, 49
Röpke, Wilhelm, 136
Ross, R. G., 134
Rowley, Charles, 40
rules: choices, 13; constitutional,
    206, 215; and order, 210; po-
    litical, 213; reason of, 15, 105;
    supermajority, 207; and voting,
    207; of unanimity, 14, 207

Samuelson, Paul, 218
Schneider, Fritz, 187
scholarship, Fulbright. *See* Fulbright
    scholarship
Schönberg, A. 145–46
Schultz, Theodore W. 70, 77
Schumpeter, Joseph A., 103
Schutz, A., 131
science: and discovery, 151; empiri-
    cal, 206; of economics, 17. *See
    also* economics, social science
scientific method, Popperian, 218
Schmidt, Wilson, 183, 184, 185,
    188
Schotta, Charles, 183
scientist-scholar-philosopher, role of,
    221–23, 224, 226–27
service, military. *See* military service
Shackle, G. L. S., 130, 198
Sidney Sussex College, 201
Simons, Henry, 216

Simpson, Roy, 44
Sims, Carleton C., 40, 45–46, 70
Smith, Adam, vii, 108, 110, 122,
137, 205, 216–18, 219, 226
Snell, Mary Frances, 29, 42
social choice, 207–208; and public
choice, 73–74
Social Choice and Individual Values,
207, 218
social contract, 12–14
social cost, 81
The Social Dilemma, 186, 193
social interaction, vii
social ordering, viii, 6
social science, 149–50
social welfare function, 208, 210
socialism, viability of, 213
Soden, Carl, 48, 61
Solow, Robert M., 163
Southern Regional Training Program
in Public Administration, 195
southerners, 49, 126
specialization, 216, 217
Spencer, Herbert, 129
Spencer, Roger W., xi, xii
Spruance, Raymond A., 53, 55,
59–60
Staaf, Robert, 187, 221
statistics, theoretical, 210
Steve, Sergio, 84, 86
Stevenson, Robert Louis, 137
Stigler, George J., 103, 169–70, 200,
216
stochastic pattern, 210
Stockholm School of Economics, 167
Stone, Richard, 161
Stubblebine, W. Craig, 10
subjectivism, and economic theory,
214
success, and chance, 37
Sugden, Robert, 187

supply, in teaching, 221–234
Sutcliffe, T., 130
Szenberg, Michael, xiii

taxing power, 12
Taylor, Overton H., 95
teaching, 44–45; product value of,
221–23, 224
theorists, price. *See* price theorists
theory: of autobiography, 80; of
clubs, 10; of states, 209. *See also*
game theory, incidence theory,
political theory, price theory, pub-
lic expenditure theory
*Theory of Games and Economic Behav-
ior*, 212, 219
A Theory of Justice, 215, 219
Thirlby, G. F., 201, 202
Thomas Jefferson Center for Political
Economy, 182, 184
Thompson, Earl, 184
Thucydides, 132
Tideman, Nicolaus, 187
Tidsskriftet Politik, 203
Tillman, Angela, 167
Tillman, Betty, xiii, 162, 184
Tollison, Robert D., 10, 80, 103, 187
truth, and truth-seeking, 223
Tulane University, 187
Tullock, Gordon, 9–10, 13, 14, 16,
40, 94, 97–101, 103, 112–13,
115–17, 153, 182, 183, 184,
185, 186, 187, 193, 211–12,
215, 218, 219

unanimity norm, 207
University of California–Los Angeles
(UCLA), 183–84
University of Chicago, 68–81, 194,
195, 198–200, 204, 210, 216
University of Tennessee, 195–96, 198